Praise for Matthew W. Hoffman
and
Krista Hoffman, L.C.P.C

"Hattie's Advocate details the art of foster parenting. Many caveats wrapped into this easy-to-read storyline. An excellent resource for parents and professionals. Bravo!

-Rajendra Lowtan, M.D., Director of Committed to Change

"A beautiful story and firsthand account of the trials and tribulations of foster care and adoption. It is an inspirational read told with humor and heart. A must read... especially for anyone considering foster care or adoption."

- Harlee B. Levy, Attorney at Law

"This book is a good read and an outstanding guide for new and veteran foster parents. It is also an excellent resource book for understanding the multifaceted world of foster care."

- Wanda Soares Nottingham, UMBC Africana Studies Support Staff, Foster and Adoptive Parent

Demarche Publishing LLC
P.O. Box 36
Mohegan Lake NY 10547
http://www.demarchepublishing.com

Hattie's Advocate: Adopting a Family Through Foster Care

PRINTING HISTORY
Demarche Publishing LLC/ March 2011

For purchase information contact:
Demarche Publishing LLC
P.O. Box 36
Mohegan Lake NY 10547

Library of Congress Control Number: 2010936793
ISBN-13 **978-0-9823077-4-8**   ISBN-10: **0-9823077-4-8**
Printed in the United States of America

Hattie's Advocate

Adopting a Family Through Foster Care

Matthew W. Hoffman
and
Krista Hoffman, L.C.P.C.

Demarche
PUBLISHING

In memory of

****

Evelyn Marie Grahl
&
Myrtle Watson

They taught us an unforgettable brand of
no-nonsense love

****

Hedwig Elisabeth Hoffman

Thanks for the "Going Away" Party

****

Grandy Lewandowski

Thanks for the foster furniture

****

Finally, I dedicate this work to my entire family,

and to every child experiencing foster care

Hattie's Advocate

Adopting a Family Through Foster Care

Matthew W. Hoffman
and
Krista Hoffman, L.C.P.C.

Disclaimer

This book describes the author's experience with the American foster care system. It is an autobiographical work of fiction, and with the exception of the author's immediate family members, only fictitious characters fill roles throughout the story. The characters do not portray any particular person in real life, living or dead. Additionally, aliases protect the privacy of the author's immediate family as well as the privacy of anyone associated with the author's immediate family.

About the Authors

Matthew and Krista Hoffman were licensed foster parents in the Baltimore/Washington area who specialized in therapeutic care for nearly a decade.

Matthew graduated with a B.A. in Sociology from the University of Maryland, Baltimore County (UMBC) and spent time working in special education classrooms and healthcare.

Krista graduated with a M.A. in Clinical Psychology from Loyola University, is a Licensed Clinical Professional Counselor, LCPC, and a Parenting Coordinator for the Howard County Circuit Court. Krista began her career in psychology at University of Maryland Medical Center's Division of Child & Adolescent Psychiatry, and now works in private practice. She has mentored children through The Choice program at UMBC and has taught English and Psychology at Mount De Sales Academy.

Together Matthew and Krista have achieved their greatest accomplishment, nurturing several foster children in a therapeutic and loving environment.

Contents

Preface

From The Authors - Sharing Good Fortune

In one form or another, foster care has been around since the beginning of humanity, and is a function of society that touches the lives of countless individuals. Over the years, my wife and I have had the opportunity to foster parent a number of abandoned children in the Baltimore/Washington area. Through fate, we have learned the intricacies of the foster care process, which includes parental licensing, child transitioning, and aging out.

Foster care contains a complete lifecycle of advocacy that is a unique experience for each child and family involved. The foster children themselves, the birth children of foster families, and the extended families, all play important roles in the foster care process. Politicians, lawyers, social workers, teachers, and medical providers are involved in the process as well. As foster children experience our governmental system of regulated childcare, every member of society finds themselves directly or indirectly affected.

I, as well as those who know me, never imagined the unlikely chain of events that would lead me to an involvement with foster care. After fumbling through adolescence, I wound up subconsciously drawn towards sociology. Later, I found myself married to a psychologist and eventually became the impromptu father to numerous foster children. Ten years later, I ended up writing this book. My unintentional connection with foster care has become a part of my identity. Now foster care has become my true area of expertise.

– **Matt**

The children we have encountered have suffered from every form of misfortune and their stories have inspired our family. They are often subject to the results of luck, fate, and coincidence. Many unexplained moments occur throughout life and foster children have experienced their fair share. Sometimes these chance happenings are good and sometimes they are not. Creating good luck, facilitating a timely coincidence, or being the pivotal moment of redirection became our joint vocation. It is our hope that by sharing our foster care experience, others may find the motivation to assist these discarded children.

– **Matt & Krista**

Acknowledgements

Without the experiences I absorbed from the individuality of my children, this book would not exist. I would like to thank each one of my kids for inspiring this piece of work. My family and friends stepped up to support my writing efforts with words of encouragement and with editing help.

I offer a special thanks to my wife Krista, my mother Beverly, and my friend Bob Ferraraccio for proofreading and feedback. Thanks to Demarche Publishing for taking an interest in Hattie's Advocate and thanks to my father for his insight into patience.

The schools, the medical professionals, the social workers, and our non-profit foster care agency played a pivotal role in my family experience. I send a sincere thanks to the teachers and faculty members of Howard and Baltimore County Schools; the pediatricians, therapists, and psychiatrists; especially the devoted and overworked social service staffs of our non-profit foster care agency, Baltimore County Department of Social Services, Baltimore City Department of Social Services, and Child Protective Services. Individuals in these organizations make decisions that affect the abandoned, neglected, and abused children of Baltimore. They carry the stories of success and failure for the rest of their lives.

I would like to thank the collective grandmothers of Baltimore City, and beyond. As foster parents, kinship parents, and as concerned neighbors, you care for the lost children. You are an example to society that one person can adopt the responsibilities of another and make a difference.

Thanks to all of the kindhearted and hardworking parents of foster care... may each child in your home find peace under your dedicated guidance.

Finally, thank you Grandma Hattie, for who knows what you truly endured.

Part I – Getting To Know The System

Chapter 1

Once An Orphan

Hans called back over his shoulder, "Come on Hattie... hurry up!" then pushed forward through the moving herd of passengers. He and his wife Becky gripped hands tightly as they finagled their way onto the loading plank of a large grey ship. Bold black lettering on the side of the hull read, *S.S. George Washington.* "Keep up with us girl!" Hans called back again.

Following behind was a young lady named Hattie who had been placed under his care for the duration of their journey. Hattie could barely hear the calls of her temporary guardian over the clamoring sounds of the busy shipping port.

Today was nothing like the usual weekday back in Hattie's quiet Munich orphanage. Cautiously, she replied, "Coming." Before today, she had never boarded such a gigantic vessel. Previously, her only time spent on water had been a short boat ride along the Isar River with her father. Now the memories of past family outings seemed like dreams from long ago.

Even the smell of the river seemed foreign. Unlike the Isar River in Munich, the winds blowing on the Weser River emitted an odor of salt mixed with exhaust. The dreams from long ago were vanishing, displaced by a nightmare.

Hattie, the onetime child of a wealthy family, found herself sold down the Weser River. A day earlier, her father retrieved her from the local orphanage and placed her on a train, headed for Bremen. Without her knowledge, he decided her future over dinner the prior night and she was now bound for some place called Cincinnati, Ohio. The fourteen-year-old, now placed in the custody of two strangers, was traveling to a new world.

With only the clothes on her back and a black satchel of extras, she hustled onto the deck of the ship. She was functioning in a state of shock and felt numb to the commotion around her. Hans called out again, "Just keep up with us and don't lose track!"

He and Becky continued across the deck and moved towards the rear of the ship. Hattie kept shuffling along with the sea of immigrants that poured onto the surface of the vessel like bees buzzing through a hive. She kept sight of her travel companions as they veered left and headed down into a stairwell. Trying to keep up, she held firmly to the railing of the stairs and worked her thin, short frame through the masses.

The couple ahead reached the second level, two floors down, and moved forward along a grey corridor. They eventually turned right, into an available cabin along the hall. Shortly thereafter, Hattie reached the cabin and lumbered in with a family of travelers. Hans took Hattie's small black bag and stored it above the seats alongside his own luggage.

Hans spoke up, "Now that we have our spot reserved let's head to the main platform and say goodbye to the homeland."

"Yes dear," replied Becky.

Hans continued, "Hattie, are you going to join us?"

Nervously, she replied in a soft voice, "Yes sir." The girl was overwhelmed with all that was happening around her. Forlorn and confused, she followed closely.

Hans exclaimed, "Cheer up girl. We are heading to America… and on the German built ship that once delivered President Wilson to the shores of France. You should feel privileged." Hattie did not think she had much to feel privileged about… or much pride in her country. She felt abandoned by her father, orphaned by her country, and now, was being sent to work as an indentured servant in a foreign land. Hans led the trio with Hattie following the couple up the stairs and into a corridor towards the deck of the ship. Meanwhile, other passengers were settling into every available space along the dim hallway.

The three worked their way through the travelers and onto the outside deck until they found a tight spot along a small section of railing. Although Hattie stood surrounded by what should have been the warmth of the pressing crowd, she never felt colder or more alone. Just like the last six years of her life, she wanted to forget the dark skies of the Bremen docks. Like a tattered orphanage dress, she felt neglected, discarded, and simply donated.

A young man of seventeen stood next to Hattie, making room for her as she settled in along the railing of the ship. The lad was wearing a faded overcoat and a beaten driver's cap. He turned to her and passionately exclaimed, "I can't wait to get to America!" Hattie offered a hollow smile.

She was not as excited about embarking upon this ten-day journey across the Atlantic Ocean. Her future was uncertain and she did not know what to expect upon arrival. The young man glanced over towards the young couple standing beyond Hattie and continued, "I'm Julius Rieter from Berlin. Are those your parents?"

Guarded, the frail girl stiffened, "No, I no longer have parents… and people call me Hattie."

"Well Hattie, what are your plans for America?"

Solemnly she replied, "I'm traveling with a couple on my way to Cincinnati… to work as a servant."

"What a coincidence! I am heading for Cincinnati to be a servant as well. What are the chances?" He smiled with the confidence of a young man embarking on a great adventure, "Perhaps we'll meet up in the city once we're both residents? I have family in Cincinnati, and since I have lost my family here, I have decided to search for my relatives in America. Are you another orphan?"

The shame of her father's abandonment brought tears to her eyes as she stared at the stains on her dress. "My father still lives in Munich… but he is starting a new family… and… it wasn't my place to remain."

"Sorry to hear that, but don't you worry, you aren't the only one in that situation. I have already met a few others in the same boat. No pun intended. Well, once we get moving and the decks clear I will introduce you to some of them including Johann, Rosa, Katharina, and Peter. This ship is full of similar stories."

The bellowing shouts of dockworkers drowned out the last of the young man's comments. As she turned to respond, the ship lurched left nudging away from the dock. The *S.S. George Washington*, free now from its moorings, moved towards the vastness of the Weser River. With nothing more than a small bag of clothing, Hattie was about to transition to her next placement in Ellis Island, New York.

In 1909, a little girl named Hedwig "Hattie" Elisabeth Weiss was born in the outskirts of Munich, Germany. Her young mother cared for her along with two other siblings, a brother and a sister. Their father Phillip worked long days as a furrier processing the pelts of animals that were delivered for manufacturing from varying outposts. Hard work and long hours were necessary to support a healthy lifestyle and family of five. Their mother helped with the business and taught the children proper etiquette along with the lessons of an occasional read. It was a good life for a young girl in the early 1900's. Life revolved around learning and growing while the family patriarch operated the family business. Life would not remain as simple and as carefree.

In the summer of 1914, a Serbian Nationalist assassinated the heir apparent to the Austria-Hungary throne and the German leader Kaiser William

II declared unmitigated support for Austria. Several countries declared war against one another, eventually taking sides. This ignited the first Great War. At the age of five, the little girl named Hattie watched as troops wearing silver helmets amassed and marched through the city of Munich, but the soldiers of WWI were only one fragment of her impending nightmare. After three years of war, a more ominous agent of death had penetrated the safely protected borders of southern Germany. Death overtook the Western and Eastern fronts of war in the form of the Spanish Flu It attacked the innocent and warmonger alike. This new plague would alter Hattie's destiny forever.

In 1918, Hattie watched as her mother, brother, and sister fell ill to the devastating pandemic crippling the world. With little she could do to help her dying family, she stood at their bedside. At the age of eight, she saw her siblings and mother pass into the dark shadow of death. Her father Phillip fell into a deep depression but continued his work as a furrier to support himself and his daughter.

After the end of the war and another year of mourning, Phillip met a woman and remarried. Ready to forget his past and start anew, he placed his only surviving daughter into an orphanage at the request of his new bride. Hattie would never forgive him. The young girl, not orphaned by negligence or abuse, was abandoned due to her father's weakness and the will of her new stepmother. Hattie spent the start of her teenage years within the confines of an overcrowded orphanage.

This orphanage in the main town of Munich was a better alternative than living on the streets of post World War I Europe, but it did not compare to the comforts of her youth. Fortunately, the orphan school and boarding house, supported by the Protestant Church, received mandated contributions through government taxation. The orphanage secured the welfare funding provided by a collective society so that children would receive clothing, food, and shelter. It operated like a village school with basic education and the functions of boarding. At the time, many children in Europe were dying of starvation and an orphanage was often the best option. Their state and church run facilities were the predecessors to our modern day Department of Social Services.

Still, Hattie's father searched to find a better option for his teenage daughter. Phillip managed to contact a sister named Ida who had immigrated to an American city called Cincinnati. The two designed a plan. As an indentured servant, Hattie would live and work for Aunt Ida. In a modern context, Aunt Ida was the designated kinship parent in exchange for promissory servitude. At the age of fourteen, Hattie transitioned from the Munich orphanage and began her journey to America. Phillip arranged for Hattie to travel to America with a local couple named Becky and Hans Olengarthy. They would oversee Hattie to New York. After the day Phillip placed his only daughter on a train for the port city of Bremen, they never spoke again.

On August 31, 1924, Hattie arrived at Ellis Island and logged into immigration as Elisabeth Weiss. Released from immigration on September 28,

1924, she was ready to begin her new life in America, free from abandonment and the orphanages of Munich. On the day of her release from quarantine, she informed the records clerk that the date of her birthday was the same day that she arrived in America. After several train rides to Cincinnati, she began her new life working as an indentured servant for her aunt. Eventually she found herself caught up with a wry sailor named William F. Hoffman, where her story continued until her death in 1988.

Hattie's story is my history.

I… as are so many others… am the American descendant of an orphan.

Chapter 2

I Can See Daniel Waving Goodbye

It was spring 2001 and she caught me in a good mood. The trees were blossoming with thick green leaves and the chill of winter had departed. I was almost thirty and overly optimistic. In other words, I was ripe for the picking. Krista appeared through the doors of the hospital lobby, walked over, and climbed into my car. She strapped on her seatbelt and turned down the volume of my radio. Immediately I thought, *What did I do now?* She looked over, sat up in her seat, and prepared herself to ask a question. Then she turned and spoke, "Do you remember my friend Desmond from work?"

I had met a number of her co-workers at a recent work party over the holidays, and I did remember Desmond. He was a likable fellow, friendly, tall, and burly. The guy reminded me of a football lineman that never played ball on account of his oversensitivity. He is the kind of man even Mr. T would just want to hug. I paused for a moment to think, *As long as neither Desmond, nor Mr. T wanted a hug from me, this conversation was going in a safe direction.*

"Sure I remember him. Nice guy."

"He has a second job working for a foster care agency. He thinks I would be a great candidate for foster parenting."

Once again, I paused for a moment... then asked, "What did he *think* about me?"

"He didn't mention you."

I would not have expected him to. My new wife Krista had recently begun working in a child psych unit at The University of Maryland Hospital. I had met her co-worker Desmond only once. He had worked alongside my wife while she accumulated the hours needed for a license in psychology. Their job included clinically treating children identified by the Department of Social Services as "in need of psychological services." In my mind, all children were in need of psychological services.

Many of the children on the hospital unit were foster kids gathered from the streets of Baltimore City. They had stories involving every form of abuse, neglect, and treachery possible. I had heard many of the stories more frequently than I would have liked. One particular boy named Daniel stood apart from the rest. In Krista's mind, he had reached a pedestal worthy of an angel. She regularly updated me on Daniel, the boy referred to as "the sweetest kid on the unit." All of the nurses and attending staff adored this kid as well.

I first noticed my wife's interest in the boy as the song *Daniel* continually played on the stereo of my car. The old song by Elton John was good, but not that good. Lately, whenever it was Krista's turn to select the music, she chose *Daniel*. The good news was that Elton John's *Greatest Hits* demoted her usual playlist of torturous Broadway musicals. I was thankful for that. Daniel had saved me from the musical rifts of *Les Miserables* and *Miss Saigon* so I owed the kid a favor.

"What do you think?" she continued.

I turned off the CD; then answered, "I think I'm tired of listening to that song." I knew where this conversation was going, and knew that it would end with my Terms of Surrender, so I nonchalantly replied, "Sure … . Why not? Can I change the music now?" I was overdue for some mind numbing techno sounds and needed a thumping vibe to wash away the sandy grains of this conversation.

She repeated my comment with a look of confusion, "Sure why not?"

I continued, "Yea… sure. Why not? You are talking about foster parenting… right? That *is* what you are suggesting? Well… what does it entail?"

She stared at me in a state of shock. My simple and non-combative reply threw her off balance. My wife had climbed into the car prepared for a good old-fashioned verbal beat down, and rightfully so. The fact is I would argue for hours over simple things like hanging curtains in the living room, but this time I gave no resistance to the idea of inviting a stranger into our house.

My Y chromosome had taken complete control of my thought process. Having the ability to make quick decisions is the best thing about having "The Y." Amazingly, this single strand of protein molecules can completely stump a female in an argument. Decisions, big or small, usually come easily due to the Y.

Lacking the Y chromosome, my wife uses an entirely different decision making process than I do. Hers, based upon a double X chromosome configuration, often requires lengthy discussions using the word "feelings." I avoid these things called feelings, meant to weigh the pros and cons of every conceivable scenario for every possible decision.

Logically speaking, the decision to become a foster parent was simple in comparison to hanging curtains. First, I knew that I could not tolerate curtains. They block light, cost money, etcetera… but I also knew that I liked kids. What harm could they do? For me the decision to foster parent was like a decision to buy Girl Scout cookies. There really was no decision to make. Cookies taste good and purchasing them helps a good cause, and more importantly, cookies taste good. In comparison, kids are pleasant and fun… and taking in a couple of kids helps a good cause, and more importantly… kids are pleasant and fun. Obviously, I had never been a parent.

To quote my wife quoting me, I declare the following: "*I am smarter than you will ever know.*" That is the wonderful thing about having a Y chromosome. It gives me that male chauvinistic, lack of reality trait that emits, "I know *everything* and I don't have to ask 'Why?'" Y is hardcoded into my DNA so why waste time thinking about why. I will use my brain cells for better things like video games and six-packs of light beer. In fact, before I had kids I do not think I ever thought too much about anything. I pictured my part in foster parenting similar to my role in our wedding. I would show up, smile a bit, and get it over.

As if referring to an upcoming church picnic, I turned to my wife and said, "Just find out the details and get back to me."

She cautiously replied, "Uhhh, okay." I reached down, ejected the CD, and handed *Daniel* over to my wife. I did not realize that choosing the next CD was actually the beginning of my parenting experience and ten years of wrestling with bureaucracy. Mindlessly, I had agreed to enter into the world of Baltimore City Foster Care. *Foster parenting… that sounds like a piece of cake.* As some coins vibrated in the ashtray of my car, my mind drifted off towards some other random topic. That was the last thought I had pertaining to whatever my wife was saying. Little did I know that thanks to some guy named Desmond, our life was about to change direction… drastically. Blindly, we moved forward, not realizing that a hidden world of child abuse, neglect, corruption, and abandonment was just around the corner.

****

Desmond was right about one thing: My wife was a perfect candidate for foster care. She was a young psychologist already specializing in the needs of disadvantaged children, and she had always taken an interest in less fortunate kids. In college, she had volunteered for the Big Sister program as a role model and as mentor for the kids of Baltimore City. I remember meeting one family back when we were still dating. Krista and I took the kids out for a day at the park and then returned them to their home on the crime-ridden streets of northeast Baltimore. I did not even want to unlock the car as the children casually strolled from my vehicle back to their dilapidated row home. Many of the neighborhood houses did not appear inhabited and had windows covered with boards.

I soon realized that Krista also enjoyed volunteering my time to the people of the inner city. One time she selected me for the job description, downtown deliveryman. In order to assist the hospital food fundraiser, my job was to transport the contents of a Thanksgiving food collection to a designated family in need. The family was located somewhere on North Avenue, just beyond Martin Luther King Boulevard – otherwise known as the MLK.

What Krista did not understand is that I had already signed a contract with the devil, and the upcoming Thanksgiving Day mission was in clear violation of that agreement. Following through with this particular philanthropy was surely a conflict of interest, which would guarantee a lack of success. I knew better than to attempt any good deed on my own, but still I followed through with Krista's instructions and moved forward with the plan. That time the Under-Lord punished me with a broken down truck. New and in excellent condition, my Chevy Silverado decided to die alongside the MLK and a squashed sewer rat. The mechanic never did figure out what went wrong with the truck.

I remember the evening well. Standing there stranded with Camden Yards at my back, I stared up at the Bromo Seltzer tower and checked the time. It was time to phone a friend. After several attempts at phoning for help, I managed to reach my goodhearted cousin, Ronny. He lived just outside of the city and fortunately owned a truck. The forty-year-old biker's life centered on work, a Harley Davidson, and a two hundred pound rottweiler named Sheeba. He came to my rescue and thankfully left Sheeba behind. With Ronny's help, we moved the food from the back of my truck to the bed of his and we picked up Krista at the nearby hospital.

My wife led us towards a rundown section of North Avenue to deliver the bounty of food and Thanksgiving supplies. Deep in the alleyways of the inner city, we found the location of our family in need. An elderly grandmother slowly peeled back the door of a dimly lit row house and welcomed us into her home. The woman appeared to be in poor health and somewhere near the age of seventy. I thought to myself, *How does this woman take care of herself, much less a handful of kids?*

A little boy stood at her waist blocking the entranceway until the voice of a teenage girl prompted him to clear out, "Come on D. Get out of the way! These people have food to bring in." Then the little boy scampered off, disappearing into a collection of kids that had formed in the living room.

The teenage girl stepped outside without another word and helped us carry the groceries into the kitchen. It was obvious that she was no stranger to carrying heavy items as she moved with the grace of a parcel pickup boy turned ballerina. We worked together moving the bags into the kitchen until the job was completed. After everything had been unloaded, my cousin elected to stand outside and wait by his truck. I followed the ballerina into the house and stopped near Krista as she talked to the elderly grandmother now sitting in the living room. The woman offered us a seat on the couch, but we graciously declined. Just then, several more children came downstairs to join the woman on the sofa.

I looked around the room and noticed that there were clusters of roaches nestled comfortably on the wall. They sat a short distance from the sole source of heat, a table lamp resting at the end of the sofa. It was as if the roaches were at ease, relaxed, and waiting for grandma to put in a movie. I considered introducing myself. The bugs held tight to the wall, perched around the couch, seemingly oblivious to the fact they could potentially die from the blow of a swift shoe. They were fearless little buggers that clung to the shadows like bloodthirsty vampires. Heaven help us if the light should falter; they looked ready to pounce and attack.

It was winter and the house did not appear to have heat. Yet the cold temperature of the place had not been a deterrent to the roaches. After the grandmother apologized for the infestation I retorted, "What, those? If you think those are bad you should've seen my place before Krista moved in… now those were some big roaches." She did not realize I was referring to my old collection of roommates.

We stayed for a bit as she and my wife continued their chitchat. Krista gave the woman words of encouragement and bantered with the grandchildren as I kept my distance from the kids and roaches alike. As the children searched through the bags of groceries, we bid them farewell. This was my first exposure to life in foster care. Many of the grandmother's kids were there under the kinship placement designated by the Baltimore Foster Care system.

As we pulled away, I looked into the rearview mirror. The children stood watching our truck until we turned left at the corner. They wore expressions of joy, mixed with longing and uncertainty. For the first time in my life, I understood my wife's desire for philanthropy. For the first time in my life, I could see Daniel waving goodbye. As Ronnie reached for the dial of the radio, I asked him a question. "Hey, do you happen to have any Elton John?"

****

I did not have much knowledge on the subject of foster care and like many an endeavor, I was jumping in feet first with my eyes wide shut. A week after our conversation in the car, my wife brought home some information and a potential start date for our initial forty hours of training. I had recently switched to working nights and was just happy not to have to use all of my vacation on Krista's latest side project. I pictured this foster care adventure as lasting about as long as her last hobby, "The Juiceman."

The salesperson who successfully threw a pitch to my wife was an old man jumping around in an infomercial. A white-haired senior citizen wired on energy drinks convinced my wife that she should join him and his fluffy eyebrows on a quest to *juice!* A hundred dollars later Krista was juicing away as if she was in her own commercial. I walked into the door from work and she greeted me with a glass of her freshly squeezed juice. "Here, try this!" she exclaimed.

I took a sip and answered, "Ummm yummy." It was difficult to fight back the sarcasm in my tone. It tasted like she had just juiced my old shoe and the whole house smelled like rotten food. I could hear the dogs barking in the backyard. As I stepped in the kitchen to look for the remnants of my old Reeboks, I saw a pile of fruit pulp lying on the countertop.

Krista exclaimed, "This stuff is so good. I have never felt healthier, or had more energy! You've *got* to start juicing with me!" She spoke with the mania of an auctioneer.

If I did not know better, I would have thought the inside of the juicer came shipped coated with methamphetamine. In less than a month, she had already squeezed about half an orchard. The juice kept coming and the squished remnants of carrots, apples, and tomatoes piled up in my backyard. The dogs did not know what to think of it. She even tried feeding some of the pulp to them. "It will make their coats shine," she proclaimed. She continued to dump fresh pulp into the dog bowls, but our two Border Collies were not enthused about Krista's new endeavor and refused to partake of the fruit and vegetable leftovers.

My wife was on a juicing kick and pumped up like the old man on the television commercial. Then one day, it simply ended.

I came home from work and the juicer was sitting abandoned on the kitchen counter. A week later, I packed it up, and put it away. In just one month, the juicer fell silent, like the old man after his amphetamines wore off. I wondered, *Was I ever going to have to pack up a kid and store him above the microwave?*

Chapter 3

The Pursuit Of Maturity

It all started in January 2000, when the changes in my life were literally the changes of a new millennium. Feeling somewhat like a displaced foster child, I was an immature newlywed, still learning the ropes of marital sharing. My wife and I were married in the late fall of 1999 and our wedding ushered out my old roommates while ushering in my new matrimonial one. I had spent the previous six years living in the southwest suburbs of Baltimore County in a bachelor pad that I had furnished. Now, the pool hall atmosphere had vanished along with my past roommates and the smell of their musky colognes. Everything was different from what it was before. Although my house transformed from forest green to flowing pink, I was still green.

****

A year earlier, my father and I had performed maintenance throughout the interior of my home. Pre-marital changes included electrical, plumbing, and other physical upgrades to the structure that was once a former slave quarters. The building sat behind an original farmhouse that was once a part of Lord Baltimore's domain. My father could never have imagined the future changes for which he helped prepare. Unaware of what was to come we burned the midnight oil working to complete several construction projects on the home all at once.

My father appeared to enjoy the time we spent together; at least he relished the opportunity to convey his stockpile of knowledge. Interspersed with little home-improvement techniques, he often tossed snowballs of advice in my direction. Hidden within the opinionated snowballs were my father's rocks of wisdom like, *"Make sure you attach that electrical outlet to the ground wire, otherwise you might kill some little son-of-a-bitch!"* Much of what he said seemed to have a cold surface, leaving me to try to comprehend the nugget of advice hidden beneath the ice. His home improvement remark was meant to communicate something more like, "Matthew, I love you and your siblings very much, therefore I have incorporated safety precautions into every home improvement project." Sensitivity was not his forte.

My old man went by the nickname Grumpsy and he spoke using a short, matter-of-fact tone. Whether I was tearing down a wall or putting up a light fixture, I would keep working away while listening to a symphonic background hum of his oft spoken phrases. One of his favorite sayings was *"Patience Matthew... patience."* You could say those words haunt me to this day. I never digested all of the underlying wisdom that came with each of his Archie Bunker-sounding expressions, but I imagine each one held some sort of insight. I ended the work with my father not knowing that a future wife and mother-in-law would take over where we left off.

****

Y2K did not release Armageddon, but Krista and her mother Beverly did. The living room, now filled with new décor such as two pink rockers and a flowering sofa, had blossomed. A small decorative shelf once used to display sports paraphernalia was on a new assignment as a spice rack in the kitchen. The holidays had just passed and we had successfully navigated our way through our first Christmas as a married couple. All of our relatives came to see the nest that Krista and her mother had built.

Krista and Beverly had managed to transform my meager starter home into something much more advanced. There were now curtains and sash, oriental rugs, and flowering bedspreads all over the place. To paraphrase my own reaction I would say that I was... *having a difficult time adjusting.* Several temper tantrums gave my new mother-in-law a questionable impression of the creature that her daughter had chosen to marry. What did they expect... just add some floral patterns and poof... instant acceptance. After discarding half of my possessions, they took what was left of my pad and turned it into something from Martha Stewart's worst nightmare.

"Where did my German beer steins go?"

"My mother and I put them away."

"Away?"

"Yes. We put them into the storage room... with your sports stuff."

"What sports stuff? Do you mean my Brooks Robinson autograph and my Cal Ripken memorial baseball?"

"I guess. You know... all that old stuff that was on the shelf."

I turned and looked at the flowering display of furniture that had replaced my old brown sectional sofa. "What the heck is that thing?"

"That's called a coffee table."

"First of all, we don't drink coffee. And second, it's made out of *glass!*"

"So?"

"So, that thing's not going to survive two days around me."

"We'll see."

"Yea… we'll see."

To give Bev and Krista credit they did lower me gently into the boiling water. The furniture had come free from her grandmother, as did the console television. Many of the accessories were gifts from her mother as well. Even the new green throw rug was a freebie hand-me-down. My mother-in-law was generous in saintly proportions. All I had to do was fork up the money for paint and various supplies. I was content in the fact that our wedding money did not adorn the house with plastic flora and crystal table lamps. Krista was not very happy with my lack of enthusiasm, but I was doing my best. I do not *do* change well, and interior decorating as well as my new marital status were not the only changes knocking on the door.

We had fallen into an unexpectedly bad financial situation. At the beginning of my newlywed life, my fifteen years of steady income had come to an abrupt end. Only one month after our wedding, I tried to change jobs to try for a better salary. This change did not work out very well. The expectations of the new job far exceeded my expectation of new work. After three years in information technology support, I had upgraded to a company with better monetary benefits, but also unexpectedly long hours. Unfortunately, I can only tolerate forty hours per week in the army of the mundane and my new job demanded sixty. Just before Christmas, and on the verge of a nervous breakdown, I quit.

It was sudden, and it was the first time I ever terminated my employment without having another job already lined up. Fortunately, Krista at the time held a job as a Catholic schoolteacher, so I decided to search for a new career while Krista took care of the bills. It is one thing to depend on a church for potluck dinners, but our attempt to depend on the church to pay our bills was a different matter. Soon we would be digging through the food bank collection for the one golden can of ravioli hiding beneath the overflow of evaporated milk.

I was extremely nervous. My street-smart warning system was blinking with the neighborhood Christmas lights and I knew the road before me required a better paying, toll-free detour. Since leaving my childhood home, I had never before depended on any other person for financial support. Now Krista legitimately dictated my future, and our lives. For the first time in my life, I was riding in the passenger seat and I was not wearing a seatbelt. I was frightened with a new person in control of my life, someone other than me.

I did not have a lot of confidence in my wife's new role as provider. At this point in her life, she had never paid a bill or lived on her own. She was a book-smart perpetual college student who was financially independent from her parents for the first time in her life. Her personality was easy going and her grades were straight A's, but with our delicate financial situation, I did not know what to expect. Like a child that had lost everything, I felt insecure and longed for familiarity. Now I had to prepare for Krista's first order as commander-in-chief.

Usually, a married man gets one full year before he receives the primary persuasion proposal pertaining to pets. *(Try saying that five times!)* Krista is an ardent dog lover and had astutely prepared her proposal early. She would be thirty in less than two years and needed to accelerate the pet to child transitional process. Around Christmas, she had softened me on the subject of puppies in order to prepare me for the upcoming spring.

I was not ready for a new dog after losing my childhood companion five years earlier but Krista was determined to begin the parenting phase of our lives. My new wife was the one with the decent paycheck, and that little detail found its way into the conversation when she was ready for a dog. To compensate for my lack of income I had taken on a part-time job substitute teaching. Even so, my new pittance did not legitimize any perception that I was King of the Universe.

As Krista sat flipping through the back of the local newspaper, she called out to me, "Matt! I've found a litter of puppies that are ready to go!"

"So?"

"So, I want a puppy."

"I want a four wheeler."

"Come on, you love dogs. We should go out next weekend and look at this litter. It can't hurt to look."

"Sure it can. It's hurting my wallet already."

"You mean *our* wallet." Whether I liked it or not a puppy was coming, and I had a better chance of becoming President than winning this argument.

"Oh, okay... one female... *maybe!*" I agreed to one female, hoping that our new pet would be as sweet as the dog of my youth.

****

As the cold winter passed, I enjoyed the experience working with kids as a substitute teacher while chasing a dream on my days off. I wanted three things: to travel, to help others travel, and to have fun doing it. My idea was to take tour groups on daytrips around the Baltimore/Washington area. Like jeep tours, snorkeling trips, and the booze cruises of vacation destinations, I was going to market short jaunts to "Little Mideast" vacation destinations.

To sell my services I walked streets of downtown Baltimore that even seasoned policemen fear. The locals stared at me as though I appeared mentally challenged. I was not complaining; it was my best form of defense. Occasionally I would sing out an odd sound effect like, *"Booogaloooga, Boogaloooga-Looga."* I was clearly in the wrong place if I were to attempt to use insanity as my only form of defense.

I trudged along the crumbling sidewalks and took solace in the fact that there were still kids playing outside in the streets. As I walked by a group of teens I wondered, *Why are all these kids outside playing on a weekday afternoon? It isn't summer.* I was in the Northern High School area of the city. *Perhaps school is closed for some obscure holiday? Maybe these teens are homeschooled?*

I walked through the city neighborhoods and spoke with representatives of various church groups, senior centers, and downtown Baltimore clubs. The social organizations were only interested in gambling trips and free buses were available to take them to Atlantic City. I could not convince one city club to go "downey ocean" or spend an afternoon in Amish Country. My new venture was simply, not meant to be. If nothing else, I learned a little something about life in the inner city. There are plenty of kids in the city missing school, but they are not missing school for my local excursions.

****

It was time for our first parenting experience to begin. An investigation of one particular litter of dogs produced an unexpected result. Before I could voice my opinion, two sister Border Collies became my wife's desire and Krista began to channel Sally Fields. It was like a scene out of the film, *Not Without My Daughter.* She blurted out, "We can't just take one sister and leave the other one behind!"

"Why can't we?" My wife had a hard case of sister envy and secretly wished that her only brother had been born with ovaries. Now she wanted to experience sisterhood vicariously through these two dogs.

The breeder spoke up, "Give you two for five-hundred."

"How much would I give you for one?"

"Three-hundred," the woman responded flatly.

Krista interjected, *"That's like half off!"* Krista never was very good at math. She looked at me waiting with hopeful anticipation.

I had no choice and replied, "Do you take checks?"

Five hundred dollars later, instead of going home with a new dog, we went home with two and we embarked upon our journey into canine parenthood.

Over the remaining weeks of spring, we transformed ourselves into the perfect pair of dog parents and we ended up with overly proficient pets. They could give a high-five, play dead, or catch a Frisbee. They could even speak on demand while at the same time drinking a glass of water. Any more lessons in dog behavior and they could have opened their own finishing school. Overall, dog parenting had gone well.

****

Krista decided to enroll in classes for a psychological therapy license and found a part-time job working for a psych unit at The University of Maryland Hospital. The job had nice benefits. One benefit was that she received a salary to obtain the required working hours she needed for a license in psychology. Tuition reimbursement would also help us pay for her courses.

As she worked towards her license, she encountered the abandoned children of Baltimore City. The program at the hospital cycled through twenty kids, in three-week sessions. Many of the kids were in foster care, or had been so at some point. Some were future wards of the state and some designated for therapy by the Department of Social Services or DSS. The DSS enrolled foster children into the program to receive a healthy combination of therapy along with three meals-a-day. My wife was touched – sometimes literally – by members of each cycle and absorbed their personal stories of hardship.

****

Autumn disappeared faster than the leaves that rest along the edge of Baltimore's Liberty Dam. We spent most of the seasonably cool days walking our Border Collies down the fire trails of Liberty Reservoir. Krista and the canine sisters even had a photo shoot taken along the waterfront. The photographer must have thought we were completely out of our minds but my wife wanted photos ready for Christmas. When the holidays arrived, we enjoyed our first Christmas with the pups.

Our combined parenting skills had worked out well for the dogs. They were spoiled to the core, but also healthy and well trained. The next illogical step would be to incorporate children into our lives, but I wanted more time to travel and live without the responsibility of parenthood.

Krista made another one of her suggestions, "Why don't we start trying for a baby?"

"We just got two dogs!"

"Oh come on. She'll love the new dogs."

"*She…* don't I have enough bitches around here already?"

"Funny," Krista replied, flatly. Oftentimes, she did not appreciate my attempt at humor.

"Sorry, but we're all out of checks. Besides, you cannot get babies half-off at a farm and they do not do very well if left at home by themselves. I've got travel plans for the next few years, and only *you* are invited."

I knew that dogs could stay with a neighbor, but a baby might put an end to my traveling endeavors. There would be no more carefree vacations with one of *those* creatures in tow. My wife was fond of babies, but I happen to believe they take the "social" and the "life" out of what I liked to call my social life. Good dogs or not, I was not ready for a crying, pooping, Mr. Potato Head.

Chapter 4

Y-Me

According to the Adoption and Foster Care Analysis and Reporting System (or AFCARS) report, on September 30, 2001, there were about 542,000 children in the U.S. foster care system, so what was I going to do about it? I had been lucky over the years not to create any foster kids of my own, or at least none as far as I knew.

When I was younger, my sexual revolution, stymied by the killer virus known as AIDS, was not much of a revolution. I do not think I even had a "sexual revelation," much less a revolution. The media as well as my mother successfully relayed the message that prophylactics were the "in" thing. Once, while folding laundry, my mother brought up the topic. "Matthew, I don't want you running around having sex."

"I hope I'm not running when it comes time for that."

"You know what I mean. Everybody is dying of the AIDS! So far, our family has been lucky. I don't know *how* your sisters managed to avoid it, but our family might be running out of luck." I noticed that she did not mention my brother in the AIDS scenario.

"Mom... I *really* don't want to talk about this."

"Do you know about protection?"

"Yes Mom! I *am* almost twenty."

"Okay then, just make sure you use protection."

"Don't worry Mom. I'm not going to get AIDS."

"Okay, just don't trust those Catholic girls. They could get the AIDS and then spread it around." On that note, I hustled off with my clean shirts... and what was left of my dignity.

The seventies were in the past and abstinence was the latest social trend. At that time, I was not Catholic so condoms were completely kosher, but then, I always found myself in relationship with a Catholic girl. Abstinence was more popular than I would have liked.

To get back on track, there were thousands of kids in the U.S. foster care system and none of them belonged to me, so why not do something about that? After haphazardly agreeing to be a foster parent, I decided to do a little soul searching on the subject. I began by mulling it over with my entourage of cave dwellers. Maybe they would have a few grunts of advice to share. Many of them were reluctant to even speak on the topic of parenting, much less foster parenting. It was as if the mere spoken word "child" might cast one of them into a parallel universe filled with unwanted responsibility.

"Krista and I are talking about doing foster care."

My fellow caveman replied, "Why the hell would you want to do that?"

"You know. Krista works with the kids and wants to do more."

"If she wants to do more, then tell her to go get another job."

"I don't think that is an option. So really, what do you think?"

"What do I think about foster care? I think you are crazy! Good luck with that."

Not one of my male friends advised me to move forward with my foster care endeavor. Each unshaved counterpart offered his own version of good advice. One even alluded to my current state of immaturity and the fact that I did not maintain a level of responsibility expected of a foster parent. I figured I would receive negative feedback from any woman I had dated, but not from my loyal group of beer-swigging chums. I had led them on adventure after adventure, and every one of them managed to come through in one piece. If these accident-prone drunks were still alive, why could I not take care of a few sober kids?

After all, my dogs had survived the idiosyncrasies of my parenting skills. Then again, dogs can revert to their natural instincts. If I took my dogs hiking along a steep overlook, they knew to stay away from the edge. A human child might not have the same internal warning system protecting him from my lack of parental expertise. Another fellow cave dweller chimed in with a grand bit of wisdom, "Maybe you can find a kid that can bring you beer... like that dog from the Stroh's commercials." It was the best bit of advice I had received yet.

To be fair they did remind me of other issues such as diapers, Disney films, and the loss of freedom that result from responsibility. A lack of freedom is what scared me the most. I did not want to "piss my youth into the wind," so I decided to think positive and take another approach towards parenting. I imagined that being a foster parent would not stymie the prime years of my life, but could actually enhance the immature aspects of my personality. Along with my original group of cavemen, I would now have a new, younger group of cave-children. I could live vicariously through them as they played in a creek bed or built a fort in the woods. With a positive attitude, I washed away the negativity and moved forward in my quest for consensus.

Next, I held a conference with my mother. Normally I avoid listening to her as she is a bit of an old-school financial worrywart and rarely debates past the cost of any endeavor. My mother is the richest poor person I have ever known, her views created by the original big downturn in the U.S. economy. She was around five years old when the Great Depression hit the United States and frugality was the cornerstone to her philosophy on life. Hence, my four siblings and I had experienced a budget version of the seventies and eighties while living under the financial guidance of a 1930's pack rat. I am surprised she had not turned all five of us into money-saving accountants like my eldest brother.

Consequently, the foster parenting advice my mother offered pertained to the dinner table, food bills, and the household budget. Starting with the cost of food, how much could it cost to feed one or two more mouths at the local TGI Fridays restaurant? Over the years, my mother had taught me how to store a lifetime supply of food in old Cool Whip containers, and I am sure that lesson would come into play. Additionally, my mother brought up some good points. Would I have to pay for other needs of a child such as health care, college, or even braces?

Then, like my tribe of cavemen, she chimed in about my level of personal responsibility, "Matthew, I don't think you are ready to handle children." Apparently, my own mother had little faith in my ability to raise a child. Did everyone think there should be a restraining order to keep me away from the youth of our society?

My mother continued advising me. "Matthew, most *men* are not usually interested in fathering another man's child." That really did not matter too much to me, and it had not even crossed my mind. I realized that foster care kids came from the loins of others, but I still liked the idea of foster care. I imagined that the phrase *"You're not my dad!"* echoed within the walls of the average foster home on more than one occasion. That did not matter to me. I relished the opportunity to respond to a rebelling youth with a witty reply such as, "No, but I've traveled back in time to warn you about Judgment Day," or "Luke... *I am* your father."

My wife and I discussed the impact upon our home life. How would a foster child, or foster children, affect our relationship? The first year of marriage had been tough. More married couples divorce in the first year of marriage than in any other. So far we had survived year one. Would we face similar challenges in our first year of foster parenting? A foster child might or might not help our newlywed relationship. Would the second year of marriage be twice as hard as the first, or had we actually worked out some of our marital kinks?

Actually, the conversation went more like this. "Hey Krista, when we're foster parents, we can still travel, right?"

"I think so. They have some sort of babysitting service."

"Cool. I'm just making sure we're on the same page."

"Don't worry Matt. You'll still get your trips to Cancun and Jamaica." Krista rolled her eyes.

"Okay. I'm just making sure."

They say the first two years of marriage are critical, and here we were ready to throw a loaded bomb into the equation. As a couple, we hoped to help some kids, but we did not want to destroy our marriage in the process. Adjusting to married life was tough enough, and there were many questions. What about having biological children? When would they come? Would they come? How, or would, they be affected? Frankly, I did not think much about any of these questions or the related concerns. Krista was the one investigating the real issues; she handled the thinking part of the process. I just said, "Okay" and showed up for the Monday morning foster parent training.

The only real concern I had pertained to my own ideas for raising a child. Was I my father? Would I become my father? Is that a good thing? I cannot say that I was too afraid of becoming my old man. He had a nice experience as a father. After working long hours as a government drone he spent his evenings relaxing in a reclining chair. He would arrive home to his castle and enjoy a home-cooked meal while taking in several hours of uninterrupted television programming. I knew better than to cause any disturbance other than during a commercial.

What kind of father would I be? In college I was voted most likely to bleed, not succeed. People thought I was crazy, and maybe I was. What other reason would I have for signing up as a foster parent? Except for Krista, my family and friends were telling me that I was crazy for even considering it.

My parenting environment was going to be much different in comparison to my father's parenting environment. For starters, I chose a wife that could not, or would not, even cook a frozen dinner. I had not factored in food preparation when it came time to select my significant other. I married my wife for her tennis skills, charming smile, and ability to tolerate my toilet humor. She was also a great companion for my favorite activity, traveling. I married the opposite of my mother.

So much for an easy chair and home-cooked meal lifestyle while the wife handled the kids. If I wanted a home-cooked meal, I was going to have to make it myself. If I wanted kids, I was going to have to get off my ass and help. I rationalized that foster parenting could not be that difficult. Maybe it was just like regular parenting. That seemed easy enough for my old man.

Unfortunately, times have changed; being a Dad today is nothing like the days when my father filled the role. The testicularity of men has moved from the yard and the den to the kitchen and the nursery. My father would be appalled.

I realized that if we became foster parents I would have to be the Mom/Dad or MAD. My wife would have to play the part of Dad/Mom or DAM. I would need to perform a MAD dash to work, do forty MAD hours of insanity, and then keep up with the MAD amount of freaking bills. Groceries and dinner would somehow fall into place. Krista would have to perform her DAM job, as well as get the DAM kids off to school and then help them complete their DAM homework once they got off the DAM bus. Then there would be the MAD carpools to the DAM activities. Parenting was starting to sound like a DAM MAD world. No wonder more and more young adults were choosing to avoid parenthood.

Perhaps I needed to take another approach to examining parenthood and look at it from a childhood or teenage perspective. After all, I do not remember my parents being involved in too many personal growth experiences, and I am happy about that. What I do remember is that I reached adulthood relatively on my own. Thankfully, my parents were not in attendance the day I learned about the birds and the bees. They were not sitting with me in my first school detention. Nor were they alongside of me the day I took a state-guided tour of a penitentiary as a guest of the Scared Straight program.

These events were the turning points in my life that helped me grow. They had nothing to do with the advice of my parents. Maybe this is what I could offer a foster child. Perhaps I could share the things I learned from my own youthful mistakes. I found most of the answers to life's questions through my own experiences, and even though my parents had been unable to deliver the magical ingredients of maturity to me, perhaps I could share my own knowledge with a troubled youth. After all, I was nearly thirty and I must have something to share with society.

The lessons of my youth were worth their weight in gold. My big sister taught me that the zipper of my pants should always face front, especially after a neighborhood game of doctor. My fourth grade teacher taught me that erasing a woman's panties from a newspaper ad is inappropriate, especially when sharing with the entire class. An inmate named Bubba taught me that crime, shoplifting included, really does not pay, especially considering his offer to perform a unique brand of "room service."

Maybe I could help a kid before he or she learned things the hard way. After all, learning things the hard way had become my subject of expertise. A swarm of bees taught me never to use a baseball bat to screw with Mother Nature. A sprained ankle taught me not to consume alcohol and run around a parking lot. I had so many important lessons to share, preferably with a young man similar to myself.

Slightly more than half of U.S. foster children were male. This is a surprisingly low number considering the fact that most of the children treated on my wife's unit were male. Perhaps boys require more psychological services than girls require. And I always thought women were the crazy ones. Krista would be happy to retort, *"Wrong again,"* or she might agree with me. I never knew what to expect.

Becoming a foster parent required working with three groups: unusual birth families, an array of social workers, and kids that I had never met. I had some sort of connection with all three groups and there was the fact that I, like most of the kids in Baltimore foster care, was a male. Somehow, my unlikely calling as a foster parent was beginning to make sense.

For starters, I was born to, and found myself around... unusual families. The members of my own family could fill a *Ripley's Believe It or Not* exhibit with their odd displays of actions and personality. There was always some sort of drama going on in the family lives of my siblings. If a particular sibling was not directly involved in some current controversy, you could count on some event being in play pertaining to a spouse, in-laws, or child of the sibling.

My mother would call me regularly with updates, "Matthew, I'm so upset I don't even know what to think."

"What is it Mom?"

"This time it's your nephew Jonathan. He has begun imprinting himself with tattoos."

I would bite, "What kind of tattoo did he get?"

"A cross with the message *Only God Can Jude Me.*"

"What? It says *Jude Me?*"

"Yes yes. Next week he's having it corrected to say *Judge Me*, but that's not the problem."

"Then what's the problem?"

"The problem is that he doesn't even go to church!"

Family updates were as exciting as any episode of Oprah. My mother was always preoccupied with the pending crisis. Amazingly, only one sibling has ended up divorced, and no one is either dead or in jail. The lot of us have managed to wrestle with own our individual dysfunction. It made sense for me to work with the dysfunctional members of birth families, because I had been doing it my entire life.

Secondly, social work was my accidental pastime. In college, I took sociology as a second major, simply for fun. I loved the eclectic gang of students attracted to the sociology major. Before I realized it, I had graduated with enough sociology credits to enter the field. I was not even aware I had an affinity for the subject. In fact, my bachelor degree reads Sociology when I actually have more credits in Information Technology. I must be the most technologically insensitive, sensitive man around. If someone had properly advised me, I might have ended up as a male therapist.

The sociological field has a great need for males to provide assistance to the lines of young men waiting for psychological services. Male therapists are in great demand. I would get a psychology license if it did not require more schooling, but I made a promise to myself and to the rest of America that I would never return to college. It would be far too dangerous for myself as well as for anyone else involved.

Finally, the third group, kids, was also one of my specialties. After all, I was hardly more than a big kid myself. I needed an excuse to buy more toys and I wanted to make new friends. Is there a better way to accomplish this than to incorporate foster kids into my life? I could have somebody to play with, somebody to appreciate my potty humor, and somebody of which I could relate.

Maybe I could get some sound advice from a kid! In fact, a kid might help me to rediscover mainstream society. Becoming the "old guy in the club" was no fun, and I was in no way prepared to be the "new father in the neighborhood." I needed to find an acceptable place for myself within the community. Watching my best friend break dance in bars was not going over as well as it did back in the nineties. I was finally realizing that spinning on your back is no place you want to be at age thirty.

The kid side of me needed someone to bring me up to speed, reconnect me, and teach me the meaning of today's freaky new lingo such as "schizzle-d-nizzle." It appeared as though colloquial English has taken a turn for the worse and slang was not even comprehensible anymore. What happened to the simple statement, "Word"? I would even settle for "Groovy."

Others my age had gone on the offensive in order to keep up with today's generation. One friend who went by the name Jack had created a modern lingo "cheat sheet" and posted it on the wall of his office cubicle.

"Hey Jack, what is that sheet hanging next to your phone?"

"Oh, that's my list of key words. You know, so I can culturally relate to the new generation."

I took a closer look at the list, "Shaka brah?"

"Yea, it's a Hawaiian greeting."

"Mate?"

"Australian greeting."

"Sup?"

"Compton greeting."

"*Douchebaguette?*"

"…Ex girlfriend."

He would refer to the hanging document for words like "bro, cat, or stoked" when connecting with members of the younger generation. I was not about to go that far and would rather let my youth slip silently into that good night before resorting to slang cheat sheets, so before hair starts growing in my ear, I was ready for the foster parent journey into vicarious living.

Chapter 5

Initial Requirements

Being a good foster child means making good decisions, but being a good foster parent also means a whole lot more. For one thing, it means forty hours of initial training, which opens a door to the long list of therapeutic foster parent requirements.

Hold on! How did the word "*therapeutic*" pop in there? I missed that one detail somewhere between entering the showroom floor and signing a contract for vehicle undercoating. My wife had asked me to become a foster parent, but I did not know that I had volunteered for something more. Therapeutic foster parenting was foster parenting at the graduate level.

Regular foster parents primarily support kids without diagnosed mental or physical disabilities, but therapeutic foster parents receive the whole kit and caboodle parental experience. Krista, bless her soul, volunteered us to parent a population of children that contain an array of concerns. The children selected for therapeutic foster homes have issues that range from physical disabilities to severe psychological impairment. Medically fragile children also fall under the category of therapeutic care. This means that a child might have multiple psychological disabilities such as a speech impediment combined with a learning disability. Take that into account, and then throw in another diagnosis such as bi-polar disorder and you have one tall order. A kid in that state might stomp through my living room the way Godzilla tears apart a small Japanese village.

I discovered a long list of categorized disorders that kids and teens fall under, such as: Attention Deficit Disorder, Attention Deficit Hyperactivity Disorder, Obsessive Compulsive Disorder, Reactive Attachment Disorder, Borderline Personality Disorder, Separation Anxiety Disorder, Conduct Disorder, Oppositional Defiant Disorder, Dissociative

Identity Disorder, Fetal Alcohol Syndrome and an entire collection of Pervasive Developmental Disorders. I thought I was offering my assistance to help Tiny Tim. Apparently, I was not. I continued to research and learned more about psychological lingo and acronyms: BPD-ADD-ADHD-OCD-RAD-BPD-SAD-CD-ODD-DID-PDD-FAS. RUNuts? YMI?

Krista and I were jumping ass-backward into this new and challenging world of foster care. After going through the alphabet soup of mental issues, I almost overlooked the other two categories pertaining to therapeutic foster care. Those are the medically fragile and the physically impaired. The lists of medical issues and physical disabilities are endless, but they do not sound nearly as bad as the symptoms and descriptions of the psychologically impaired. A kid hooked up to an intravenous tube, or one missing a limb, might not be as inclined to slash my throat while I slept in my bed.

To understand therapeutic foster parenting I investigated two common medical categories affecting foster children. First, I discovered that there are a lot of AIDS babies, or those born with H.I.V. This viral epidemic has claimed enough victims to become a category of its own. Sadly, a large number of Baltimore/Washington babies are born each year infected with H.I.V. and they often end up under the care of a foster parent.

The second category, the medically fragile, is not specific to one condition. This category includes numerous medical conditions that often have one specific antecedent: Drug-contaminated pregnancies. These compromised kids are often born with major deficiencies such as underdeveloped brains. Sometimes they also have underdeveloped hearts, lungs, or other health problems resulting from poor prenatal care. They spend time, up to months, in a Neonatal Intensive Care Unit (or NICU) until they are healthy enough to transition to a suitable therapeutic foster home.

Caring for someone with a physical disability seems like a piece of cake compared to the needs of the medically fragile. For example, a child born without a limb has technology options that can help him or her compensate for the physical disability. Nothing can compensate for the compromised immune system of an AIDS baby.

The blind, the deaf, the mentally disabled, and many others also fall under the category of physically disabled. I was sad to discover that many blind and deaf children ended up abandoned to the care of the state. Like others, such as the mentally retarded, they become the responsibility of society because their parents cannot, or will not, care for them. These kids are often left to fend for themselves, or are delivered to the front steps of the Department of Social Services. Survival of the fittest is sometimes the unspoken law of a neighborhood overrun with drugs and crime. Already born with a disadvantage, they are unable to survive without additional services provided by the state.

There is one other group to discuss that I have not yet mentioned. Many of the kids that require foster parents or social services fall under the diagnosis of Pervasive Development Disorders, or PDDs. This includes children diagnosed with Autism, Asperger's Syndrome, Rett Syndrome and Childhood Disintegrative Disorder. These children require a significant amount of services or specialized care that an undedicated, drug-addicted parent is unable to fulfill. In some cases, the cause of one of these disorders is either poor prenatal care, drug abuse by the mother, or simply a birth defect.

****

One day my mother's name appeared on the caller ID and I picked up to answer the phone. "Matthew, I'd like you to join me for a visit to your sister's house."

"Which sister are you talking about?"

"Jennifer."

"Why?"

"She's very upset about some treatment she is receiving."

"Then you should treat her better. I've been telling you that for years."

"*Matthew!* This is *no* time for jokes. Jennifer was accidentally stuck with a needle at work and now she has to go through the precautionary treatment for everything... including AIDS."

Being used to my mother's over dramatization, I replied with dramatic sarcasm, *"Jenny might have AIDS?"*

"Probably not, but she is very upset. It would be nice if we visited her."

As I noted before AIDS is in a league of its own, a scourge hiding within the underground drug society of Baltimore. My sister Jenny spent many years as a delivery nurse at St. Agnes Hospital. She witnessed the affects of AIDS on Baltimore's newborn babies and their mothers. Many of the babies she delivered were born with H.I.V. or born to a mother who had contracted H.I.V. The infected mothers and their babies receive treatments of antibiotics and autoimmune medication before, during, and after birth.

Jenny has only gone through the frightening experience of H.I.V. testing and treatment after being stuck with a dirty needle. Her patients have faced every AIDS scenario. Some of the infants were fortunate enough to avoid contracting the virus from their mothers while others were simply born malnourished from a lack of prenatal care. *Those* are the lucky ones. Unfortunately, many other children were born deformed or underdeveloped, and some were even stillborn. Many children never overcome the disadvantages of being born to a drug-addicted mother.

There are amazing people who have dedicated themselves to the adoption of medically fragile babies. Some foster parents specifically volunteer to deal with AIDS babies. I was not one of them. The precautionary details of caring for an AIDS baby fit my physical and emotional persona like a bull in a china shop. I cannot express enough admiration for the parents who dedicate their lives to receiving disadvantaged children. These parents raise the medically fragile from birth until death, even if it is only for a few weeks.

Those that care for the physically disabled are amazing as well. I am far from amazing and was in no way prepared for that type of parenting. Those kids needed someone special and I was not that special, so I expressed my reservations to my wife. As I reviewed the information pertaining to therapeutic foster care, I thought of facets I had not previously considered. On the drive to our first session of training I asked, "How does it work? Do we simply pick a kid from a list?"

Krista replied, "I don't know. I think they match us up with a child."

"So what kind of kid are you thinking? I'm not ready to handle H.I.V. or anything like that."

"I couldn't handle that either. I was thinking about a child with a psychological dual diagnosis. A lot of foster kids on my hospital unit have a dual diagnosis."

"What if we get a psycho kid, and he tries to kill us in our sleep?" I pictured a young version of Anthony Perkins placing my corpse in a dress and propping me up in a rocking chair.

"We'll lock our bedroom door," she replied. She had thought this through more thoroughly than I.

"Don't forget to lock the dogs in with us." The murdered dog scene from the movie *Cape Fear* has replayed itself in my mind many times since I first saw it in 1991. I could hear the voice of a six-year-old Robert De Niro calling out to me, "*Coun*-se-*loooor.*"

"Don't worry. I have seen kids like this before on my unit. Their rap sheets are a mile long but they are usually just *fine.*" She informed me that "rap sheet" is a slang term used for the history of a child. As I thought about her choice of words, I realized that "fine" was a very ambiguous description.

I mumbled to myself, "Fine! Fine with what? Starting fires?"

Chapter 6

Learned Me Something Good

The initial registration process began and it contained more requirements than just listening to speeches about "advocating" for a child. It included every procedural requirement possible short of a colonoscopy. I even learned how to give the Heimlich maneuver to a choking goat. What I mean is… learning about a goat's air path will probably be a new requirement next year. First, in addition to the primary forty hours of training there is enough initial paperwork to give Leo Tolstoy writer's cramp. We wrote away, page after page, until we completely rewrote *War and Peace* and the foster agency knew every possible thing about us.

The initial training itself was one week long, Monday through Friday. It started with a thick packet describing each governmental requirement for anyone wishing to be foster parent. A blue, three-inch binder included every detail of foster care, and the rules of the game. The first item that caught my attention was the requirement for every applicant to denounce their right to bear arms. I did not realize that the State of Maryland's foster parent regulations could supersede the U.S. Constitution. Since Krista was not Dirty Harry, and I prefer meat from the grocery store, I signed away. The only arms I bear are my left and my right ones. I do own a one-pump BB gun, but I was not going to put that down on the form. The only exception to the foster care anti-constitution requirement is that an active duty police officer may still own a weapon. Thank goodness for that!

As the training continued, we received more information about regulations. Foster agencies and foster parents must maintain client confidentiality on many matters pertaining to children. In other words, only certain information is permissible when talking with friends or neighbors about a foster child. Our job was to remember what could, or could not, be spoken during conversations at the bus stop. For example, medical information is a restricted topic with anyone other than the child's physician. As we signed away, our right of free speech became restricted to the limits of the state's foster care guidelines. I was beginning to wonder what other aspects of speech were managed. Are school grades, medical diagnoses, or family histories off limits too? What are you supposed to say when a neighbor asks about your foster kid's birth family? Do you say, "The stork brought him" or "I'd tell you… but then I'd have to kill you." Keeping my big mouth shut is not one of my strengths.

Next, I agreed to keep our household water temperature below one hundred and three degrees. This makes for a cold shower in about fifteen minutes. What happened to my right to bear hot water? I guess you never want to scald a foster child, and I needed someone to tell me this. The training course went into specific detail concerning this topic. I did note that even though the agency frowned upon boiling children, it was just fine to freeze their butts off. There was no legal stated minimum temperature for bath water, so again I signed away. Perhaps cold showers would be an incentive for me to save water. I turned to Krista, "You're going to have to cut back on those long hot showers."

"I don't think so."

"That's fine with me, but with this new hot water rule, you'll be cold in about ten minutes."

"That's *not* going to happen!"

"Don't worry. I imagine an agency inspector will come to our house for the inspection. Then, he or she will turn the hot water thermostat down to comply with the regulation. Then, a mysterious hot water fairy will creep in and turn the water temperature back to normal."

"Then you'd better give that hot water fairy a call."

"Oh, don't worry. I've got plenty of fairies on my speed dial."

The water temperature issue was simply one small facet of the complete home inspection. The list of requirements can be a bit alarming. Working smoke detectors must be present throughout the home including one smoke detector placed inside of each designated foster care bedroom. "Krista, check out the section on smoke alarms?"

"Where is that?"

"Page forty-three. How many of these kids have set fires in the past?" I hoped this rule arose from a concern for young smokers, and not from a situation like Drew Barrymore in the movie *Firestarter. Was I about to foster a future arsonist?*

The list went on. All cleaning chemicals needed to be in a locked cabinet and out of the reach of small children. It was time to take the guns out of the gun cabinet and replace them with Lemon Pledge. That stuff is flammable. You should probably install an extra smoke detector above the Pledge cabinet, just in case. The next item after cleaning chemicals in our foster parent "Welcome Packet" were the instructions for posting a fire escape plan. The plan came complete with the appropriate method for installing a rope escape ladder. *What am I getting myself into?* I realized that half of these requirements were probably just to address liability issues, but it was beginning to sound like these kids were recruits for Al Qaeda.

My wife and I learned about more regulations. There are specific rules pertaining to the setup and occupancy of each designated foster care bedroom. First, there cannot be any bunk beds. It does not matter how new or sturdy they happen to be. The state of Maryland is not going to take any risk of an accidental fall. Too many lawsuits and consequential payoffs are associated with the double-decker beds. I had a bunk bed for most of my youth and somehow I managed to survive. In fact, learning to climb up and drop down from a bunk bed is a probably a good skill to have. It might come in handy for a city kid if he needs to scale a fence to escape a pack of angry pit bulls.

The next set of rules pertained to sex and age. Only children of the same sex can share a bedroom, even when they are siblings, and they must be within three years of each other in age. This makes sense. It was a rule of my own. I do not need any late night games of doctor on my watch. I did not see as much logic with the age bracket rule, but I suppose it is in place to deter any form of abuse from one older child towards another. Either way, I did not have to worry. I had two separate bedrooms for the kids and each could have his or her own space. Therapeutic foster parents are limited to two children per home in the state of Maryland and I see that as a good guideline.

****

The two children per therapeutic foster home limit in the State of Maryland keeps its foster care system out of the local and national news. This rule effectively prevents foster parents from cashing in on the provided funding.

Stories of tragedy and inhumanity haunt the U.S. foster care system. In 2005, a couple in Norwalk, Ohio received two years in jail for keeping eleven special needs children in wire and wood cages. In court, they argued their good intentions. They did not want the kids to hurt one another. Perhaps if they had been limited to two kids, they would not have resorted to the use of cages. Better yet, if each kid had had his or her own room, they would not have needed a human chicken coop. Fancy that!

In the fall of 2009, ten former foster care children filed a lawsuit against the City of New York Welfare Administration. They did not appreciate the twenty years of torture they had experienced that included the use of restraints, handcuffs, and locked cages. Their foster mom managed to adopt a whopping twenty-two children. In 2005, a forty-nine pound *teenager* wearing a diaper lived with an adoptive mother who was not attending to the needs of her three foster children. Evidently, even three kids were too much for her to handle. How do these people get a license? How are they able to torture kids for decades? The two special needs children per household limit is one of the best rules enforced by the State of Maryland. It limits abuse, and deters those big-hearted honest folks who probably should not attempt to care for more than two kids.

Maryland foster care is not perfect either. In September of 2008, Calvert County authorities discovered the bodies of two foster children encased in ice. The kids were ages nine and eleven, found dead in the freezer of their forty-three-year-old adoptive foster mother, Renee Bowman. One other sister who survived the adoptive placement transitioned to a new home, and Bowman is now spending time in jail. It is hard to imagine that this killer used to spend her days planning how to spend the two thousand, four hundred dollars a month she received for the two innocent children she murdered.

****

Why do people do horrendous things to children in foster care? With the exception of cases rooted in dark, twisted, mental disorders, the reason people do these horrible things comes back to *money*. The state budget pays government-funded stipends to foster parents to cover the cost of clothing, housing, and feeding foster children. Therapeutic foster parents usually receive higher stipends depending upon the needs of the child. Standard foster parents usually receive a lower stipend amount. Adoptive parents receive even less, or sometimes none at all. Most of the time, bio family parents, or "kinship" parents, receive almost nothing. Interestingly, birth parents have actually informed me that they did, or could, receive monetary stipends in exchange for housing their own biological child. Now that is what I call a child tax credit.

It was interesting to hear that money from government-funded foster stipends might be available to birth parents. This type of welfare goes hand-in-hand with other programs like the government funded Woman, Infants, and Children program otherwise known as WIC. Sometimes it is complimentary to government-funded food stamps, known in Maryland as the "Independence Card."

If I am using the Independence Card, then what am I independent from… working? Could the program use a more accurate title such as the "*D*ependence" Card? I embrace helping people who need assistance, but why should the name of the program misrepresent what it actually is? Where is the motivation to stop using forms of welfare?

They did not name the foster care program, The Child Independence Program. They did not call the bread lines of the Great Depression, "The Lines of Independence." If they did, I might be standing in that line today, seeking independence in the footsteps of my grandmother Hattie. Fortunately, she got out of line to make her own bread.

In college, a professor confronted me about my views on the welfare system. Evidently, my point of view was not the same as his so he kindly advised me to drop the class. My professor had his panties in a bunch because I had written a paper titled "The Lobster Card," which was an honest, first-hand depiction of the improper uses of the government-funded food stamp card.

The fact is some welfare recipients use the government-funded Independence Card inappropriately. In some places, this type of funding is available for psychics or for gambling in casinos. In Maryland, some abusers use it to exchange seafood for drugs. During my five years working as a grocery store cashier, I had been an accomplice to the crime more times than I could remember. A man named Jax, among others, would use his food stamp card to buy "uncooked" lobsters. Then he took the live crustaceans out the front door and traded them for drugs. The exchanges occurred right in front of the store window. It gave new meaning to the term, "Crack Pot," and at age sixteen I did not know what to think of it.

Consequently, I received an "F" on my college paper. After a bit of debate, I dropped the class, still graduated, and posted this particular writing on my refrigerator for all to see. I am not a huge fan of welfare abuse, but I am a big fan of welfare reform. Think twice every time you hear someone touting the benefits of the government-funded Independence Card. Who thinks these things up? Is there a special government-funded committee on disillusionment?

****

Back in foster parent training, the instructor reviewed many of the additional rules and regulations of foster care. Pools must have a fence and hot tub covers must be locked shut when not in use. Stair railings have height requirements, and banisters have minimum dowel spatial standards. Of course, my dowel space was an inch too wide. I threw in another row to meet the correct spatial criterion. Fortunately, my custom-made spiral staircase did not throw a wrench into our inspection process. However, one key problem was my dryer vent: It required firm reattachment to my wall.

One other problem pertained to my fire extinguisher. It was far too small, but that was the story of my life. I turned to Krista with a smirk, "I'll need to run out and get a bigger fire extinguisher."

Krista laughed, "I could have told you that."

A short trip to Home Depot and everything would be fine. Our home, located in Violetville, Maryland was now ready to go. But like any government agency, program, or department, there was more red tape retarding progress. More paperwork, more requirements, and more bureaucracy were on the forefront of our docket. Considering the stories from Florida, Ohio, and New York, I guess too many safeguards are better than not enough.

Before starting our foster parent training, Krista and I had to submit our fingerprints for a background check. While we sat through training classes, our ten fingerprint scans were processed, and evaluated. Other than my short tour of a Bowie State penitentiary, I was clean. Who knew what secrets my Catholic wife might be hiding? The answer is… none. Everything came back fine declaring us suitable for foster parenting.

Along with our fingerprint paperwork, we had to submit full physicals. It was important to be in good health and hernia free before fostering a kid from the community. The physical requirements must have been low as many of the foster parents were overweight grandmothers. Krista whispered in my ear. "You've got to be kidding me. We're probably the youngest and healthiest people here."

"I know. I do not think many of these foster parents would last ten minutes on a cardiology stress test, but I bet any foster kid assigned to their home receives some good cooking. Sign me up for that reality television show."

Thinking of the other grandmothers at foster training I confidently completed my physical examination as required. Some kid had better appreciate the fact that I turned and coughed to provide him with a good home. I had better not get any lip about future high school sports physicals.

The training went on, held in a long, rectangular seminar room at the non-profit foster care agency. All of the parents lined up along a conference table, binders in hand, to complete the additional training that included adult and child CPR, as well as first aid certification. The agency hired a young energetic instructor who came in and taught us how to *save lives!* He reminded me of a young version of the old man who sold Krista the juicer. Looking around the room it was easy to see that no one actually wanted to use the knowledge provided by his training. Even so, each prospective parent focused upon the teacher as we blew our breaths into "Annie," the Red Cross blow-up doll. I relished the experience. Marriage had insured that my time spent with Annie was the closest I would ever come to starting a new romantic relationship.

Next, we were on to child CPR lessons. The plastic practice doll, that I affectionately named E.T. was creepier than the doll from the movie *Chucky*. I was nowhere ready to handle a baby, nor was I ready to handle E.T., so I watched as Krista took the doll and went first.

"*Be gentle!* You don't need to smack the poop out of it," I exclaimed as she gave E.T. his required back blow.

"*Shut up!* I know what I'm doing."

"Well if you keep hitting him like that, he'll never be able to phone home."

Being competitive, I looked forward to beating Krista's high score on the CPR exam. On our first round of CPR testing we both scored a ninety-five. I did not win this particular competition, but was happy with the result. The chance of E.T.'s death from his first heart attack was officially only five percent. That meant my own personal survival rate should be the same; I just hope she remembers the CPR training when my heart attack occurs.

The pages of the binder contained an array of information. It talked about the types of problems that foster kids and foster parents face. Common problems, both physical and mental filled the pages of the binder. A general question and answer section was included as well. Information in the packet also had various resources for children with special needs. A number of organization and contact lists were available. Programs advertised horse therapy for kids as well as support groups for parents. I could not imagine what a horse could do for a kid with behavioral issues, but perhaps the extremely bad kids could shovel the manure.

Additionally, the binder contained more forms. The most important form was the checklist of challenges that we were willing to undertake. This list included everything from bedwetting, to fire starting, to sexual abuse. We decided to avoid the latter two. I could handle some soggy sheets but did not feel like attending any additional fire-fighter training. Sexual abuse was a scary topic as well. I was gun-shy from a previous experience with this topic and not ready to face the fondling accusations of a child that might arrive with a predetermined mental disorder.

****

When I was a teenager, I experienced the confusing and frightening emotions that result from false accusations of sexual abuse. One day I was babysitting my nephews and my niece in my parent's backyard. The kids were fond of our spacious wooded yard and enjoyed playing with the neighborhood children. We had a number of small kids their age that lived nearby, and my relatives wanted to find some friends to play with. They asked if they could go next door and recruit two boys from the neighborhood named Jason and Jacob.

Trying to be a helpful babysitter, I walked them to the neighbor's backyard and suggested that they play a game of duck-duck-goose. Boredom set in and they soon looked for something else to do. I suggested a fun game where each person in the circle would take a turn standing up to do something funny. What could go wrong with that plan?

My nephew Rick stood up and made a funny face. My nephew Jon decided to make a funny sound. My niece Chellie did a funny dance. Jacob stood up and pulled down his pants. The kids certainly did laugh. I immediately ordered Jacob to pull up his shorts. Instead, he and his little friend Jason held a streaking contest. I grabbed my kids and left! We were no longer going to play with the local perverts of the neighborhood.

A few hours passed and my sister's kids had gone home when the doorbell rang and I received an unexpected visit. It was Jacob's mother and she was in hysterics. She was about to break through our glass storm door and rip out my throat. "Get out here you sicko!" she screamed.

With an expression of confusion and shock I replied, "What's going on?"

"You know!" she replied. I had absolutely no idea why this woman was standing on my front porch calling me a sicko. Did she somehow know that I still liked to play with Matchbox cars? She continued, "Jacob came home naked and he said that you told him to do it!" Now I knew where this was going.

I explained the situation and respectfully stated, "I told him to do something funny. He decided to run around naked. *I never* told him to drop his shorts."

"I'll be back!" she exclaimed as she stomped away. Even though I knew I was innocent, I had a horrible feeling in my stomach. Someone had accused me of being a sexual deviant. I was fourteen and I had not even had a date. She returned a short time later once she had shaken the truth out of little Jacob and she gave me a sincere apology. It was heartfelt and honest, but it made no difference. I could never look her in the eye again and made every effort to avoid her in our neighborhood. That was the feeling that I never wanted to experience again. I feel terrible for every foster child who has experienced sexual abuse, but caring for one who had was not an option for me.

Chapter 7

What Are We Waiting For?

Krista and I had completed our initial foster parent training. The government had determined that we were not criminals and our single family home in Violetville was safe enough to house a child from the bullet-ridden streets of downtown Baltimore. We had passed our physicals and both Krista and I were negative for Hepatitis, Tuberculosis, and every other form of rare infectious disease, including Dengue Fever. The tests seem a bit excessive but necessary in our cautious, lawyer-driven society. No rabies in the dogs either. They tested free of disease, enduring many rigorous tests, included a stick shoved in their backside. My dogs now require group therapy, but their sacrifice to society provided the documents approving our home for foster care.

The foster agency and our government were now in possession of all our information. They knew our yearly income, our monthly bills, our citizenship, our proof of employment, our criminal-less background, and our dog's poop test results. Summer had arrived and we were now officially licensed foster parents. We even received a little foster parent license that we could frame. I thought to myself, *Foster Care must be desperate if they'll take me.*

My wife and I were excited about welcoming a child into our family and we stood ready for the droves of children waiting in line for our foster home. "Hey Krista, has the foster agency called yet?"

"No."

"What the heck? When will the children come forth and join our foster utopia?" A month later and the phone still had not rung. "Hey Krista, has the foster agency called yet?"

"No!"

"When are they going to dial our number?"

"I know! I was under the impression, *because the agency told me*, that foster parents were in desperate need. Why haven't we received a call?"

It seemed as though there were more considerations, politics, and bureaucracy that goes into placing foster kids than we had ever imagined. To understand this, we had to understand "The Steps" within foster care. So before our foster care fairytale could begin, we had to learn just a little bit more about additional factors that affect the foster care system.

****

Four distinct groups of foster kids are living in foster homes or residential treatment facilities. Each child fits into a placement according to his or her individual behavior and personal life story. I will refer to distinct groups called "Steps." The highest step is Step Three. The lowest step is Step Zero. The first group, or Step One, includes the average children that simply need a foster home due to neglect, abuse, or abandonment. Abandonment may have occurred for one of many reasons, including the death of the biological family, or because the birth parents simply went AWOL.

The children of Step One are considered healthy in mind and are thriving. They fit into a standard foster care environment with standard foster care parents. These parents have the minimum required amount of foster parent training. They may have been trained by, and report directly to, the Department of Social Services. Many of these parents found the DSS website and clicked on the tab labeled Adoption and Foster Care. This level is like *Introduction to Foster Care,* or *Foster Care 101.*

It always amazes me when I hear about people flying to China or Russia to adopt a child. There is usually one waiting for them twenty minutes away from their home. In fact, parents with a desire to adopt do not have to lose their life's savings to a possible adoption con artist. They can go to a website to sign-up as foster parents, and receive government funding to take a test ride with a friendly neighborhood spider-kid.

The argument that I have heard from adopting parents is usually associated with the fear of loss and their own emotional attachment concerns. They fear they will become emotionally attached to a child, and then lose the child to a biological family member. This is a legitimate concern. Adoptive parents may have to perform a couple of two-week babysitting gigs before meeting a child in need of adoption. After all, reunification is the first goal of foster parenting, but reunification is just one of three goals.

Goal number two is conversion of the foster home to an adoptive home, and goal number three is to move the child to someone else willing to adopt him or her. Two out of the three goals of foster care is adoption by someone other than the biological family. 66.6% is not so bad, is it? In actuality, what often happens is this: Junior or Juniorita transitions to his or her foster parents with an estimated stay of six months, but before you know it, birth mom and dad go AWOL. Then the original six-month visa suddenly morphs into a lifetime stay.

Responsible people have a hard time grasping the fact that some biological parents just do not care about their own kids. This is probably due to a fact that most responsible people have never been hooked on heroin. There are so many kids in the adoption process that Baltimore City performs adoptions a courtroom at a time. Any parent wishing to adopt should not worry so much about finding and keeping a kid; I would worry more about foreign adoption costs or scammers.

Here is a hint for anyone wishing to adopt through the foster care system. At each DSS agency there is a person called a *placement coordinator*. He or she is responsible for matching kids with potential parents. The trick is to tell this coordinator about an interest in long-term care or adoption. I guarantee the placement worker will light up with joy. In fact, he or she might even hop on the table and perform a river dance. Many kids in foster care need ongoing care or an adoptive resource. If all Americans interested in adoption would adopt through a Department of Social Services, there would not be a single U.S. orphan left in America. Heck, we could probably adopt half of Mexico's orphans too.

At the other end of the spectrum, there is much opportunity for anyone wishing to get involved in foster care and not adopt. Volunteers can sign up with their local Department of Social Services to become "respite" parents. They can do short babysitting gigs with the kids stuck in foster care while their full time foster parents train or relax on a Caribbean island. Respite care is a great way to lower oneself into the wild world of foster care. I highly recommend signing up as a respite care parent to anyone interested in helping the abandoned kids of the community, yet fear commitment. The kids in Step One foster care need temporary parents.

Let us skip ahead to kids in Step Three foster care. Contrary to the Hollywood image of American adoption, there are no old fashioned orphanages like Oliver's home for boys, or Annie's hard knock life with Ms. Hannigan. These places today are referred to as residential living or group homes, but I will refer to them as they once were... *institutions*... since I cannot stand politically correct name changes. Institutions are the intermediate placement locations that DSS and our government use to house the abandoned children of our country. They are a fancy form of no-kill shelters and you would not want your child living in one.

I have found that the best institutions are those sponsored by philanthropies such as the Church. The state-run facilities have less to desire. They are the unadvertised buildings sitting along the side of a highway or a country road. We drive by them every day, to and from work, never thinking about what or who is inside. They are located in business parks along I-95, or buried in a grove of trees along Dulaney Valley road. They are in plain sight, yet hidden from our minds.

Inside, the abandoned children of our society sit waiting. They are waiting for a biological parent to get out of jail. They are waiting for a foster home placement to open up. They are waiting for an adoptive resource. They are simply waiting, disappointed when visits from biological family seldom occur. Depending upon need, they are bused to school, go to therapy, and attend camp-like group sessions while being monitored by their temporary family, otherwise known as "the staff."

There must be a better environment for children, but this is the current government solution. These children sometimes become permanent residents of their institution. When they are designated for an ongoing life inside of an institution, they are at Step Three. Step Three foster kids are the permanent residents of the U.S. residential treatment facilities.

Stepping down, the children of Step Two foster care are where Krista and I come in. As therapeutic foster parents, we trained to serve the Step Two population of children. They are the children identified to receive additional services, yet do not require the full services provided by an institution. These kids are more likely to end up institutionalized or placed into group homes than the kids of Step One. If a therapeutic foster family or trained institutional staff cannot handle the needs of a Step Two child, he or she winds up permanently in an institution.

The placement of a child often depends upon the rap sheet of the child. If there is a history of setting fires, then he or she is pretty much destined for a spot in a state run facility. A history of continued aggression within therapeutic foster homes can also land you into a room without a view. When the economy is good, the option for "kids in need" is as good as it gets. I would like to use the description "better," but better than what? I guess that life for these kids is "better" when the economy is better, but when the economy is bad, lookout. When the economy is bad all sorts of things hit the fan.

When the U.S. economy slides, so do the options for abandoned children. The nonchalant term used by the state to describe decreasing services is "stepping down." "Stepping down" refers to the technique the state uses to reduce the funds used for foster care. Step Three, or institutionalized care, is the most expensive form of care. When the state allocates money to an institution, it can be in excess of hundreds of dollars per day per child. Now that is some big bucks.

Step Two care does not cost nearly as much. Pulling kids from institutions and placing them into therapeutic foster homes can save *a lot* of money. Then again, placing Step Two kids into Step One homes can save a lot of money too, *and* it will open up more spots in Step Two homes. Then

there is more room to save more money on the expensive Step Three kids…
or better yet, *make* money on the expensive Step Three kids.

Confused? The only time it is financially beneficial for the state to
place kids in Step Three care is when those kids are placed in a state run, state
funded facility. That way the government has the funding designated for its
own program. If you inflate a budget then you can request more funding for
that budget. Does that happen in the government agencies?

Stepping Down: Let's put Step Three kids into Step Two homes
and put Step Two kids into Step One homes. In other words, let us move
the fire starters into Matt and Krista's guest room and the Step Two
therapeutic foster kids into Dick and Jane's basement. The resulting affect
empties the therapeutic foster homes as standard Step One foster parents
will unknowingly volunteer to foster a Step Two therapeutic child. The
problem is… Step Two therapeutic foster parents *cannot* handle the needs of
Step Three institutionalized kids so the Step Two homes end up empty. The
system attempts to place dangerous children into therapeutic foster homes,
and the parents must refuse them.

"Hey Krista, has the foster agency called yet?"

"Yes."

"*What?* Did you say yes?"

"Yes."

"Tell me more. What did they say? Do they have a kid in need of
our home?"

"A placement coordinator named Sue called. She asked if we could
house a fifteen year old boy with a history of aggression, violence, and animal
mutilation."

"Are you kidding me?"

"No."

"Well, when is he coming?"

"Ha ha, obviously I had to say no. If I remember correctly we signed
up to handle kids with special needs, not kids with special skills like shiv
carving."

The kids that are at Step Three are obviously there for a reason.

****

Months later, I was still wondering why our phone had not rung
with the news of a suitable placement. Perhaps it was because we had not
checked fire starting, animal abuse, sexual abuse, and shiv whittling on our
checklist of acceptable problems. There had to be at least one available foster
kid who did not fit into those four categories. After receiving a few more
calls about teenagers with minor felonies, we were not as optimistic about
our future as foster parents.

So what happens to the Step One kids that used to be in Step One or standard foster care homes? Oh, they went back home. Their taste of a drug free lifestyle ended the day the economy went south. As the Step Two kids are "Stepped Down" into Step One homes, the thriving children of Step One foster care are sent home for round two of neglect and abuse at the hand of their loving birth families. It's like telling a kid, *"You're doing so well that you deserve some time off in the ghettos of Baltimore... don't worry... you'll be back... we just need some time to save a few bucks then perhaps we'll have a spot for you again... hopefully you won't get sold for drugs in that time... good luck!"*

The kids sent back home belong to the fourth distinct group of foster kids, or Step Zero. There is no Step Four. As a foster child, you are in an institution, in a graduate level foster home, in a basic foster home, or back home at ground zero. Ground zero is the place where all the problems began.

In a good economy, you transition back to ground zero because your birth family got it together. In a bad economy, you transition back to ground zero because you no longer get funding. You had better gather up your coping skills and get ready for round two of abuse, neglect, starvation, prostitution, and/or beatings. It is hard to imagine the blunt facts of the abandoned foster child's life, but this is the reality that many children in and around the area of Washington D.C. and Baltimore City face.

How does the government justify sending kids back into such dangerous and detrimental conditions? Simple, there is a catch phrase for it. They come in handy during a recession. The original catch phrase, *"Placing Out"* is from back in the late 1800's. This year the new phrase is *"Place Matters."* Catchy, is it not? I could not have thought of a better one myself. It suggests the theme that you matter, the theme that where you come from matters, the theme that this magical *Place* is more important than the actual bullets that are flying over your head. Try not to worry; in this place, it is safe to go outside for approximately five minutes past dawn.

****

The Department of Human Resources Secretary announced that *Place Matters* would correct problems in the Maryland child welfare system. To reach particular goals the state focused on identifying permanent families for foster children. How does the state define permanency? How do foster parents fit into the equation that equals *Place Matters*? Are there other factors like budget considerations motivating the Department of Human Resources?

Maybe the real motivation behind *Place Matters* is to have a documented excuse for sending kids back into the war zone. It would be a clever design to reduce liability while stepping kids down from Step One to Step Zero. A child might be doing great in a Step One foster home placement, in fact, too great. It is time to send them back into the ghetto, not because it saves money, but because *Place Matters*. You start at the bottom pushing kids down, and then you can make room at the top. To save money, the government wants to reduce the number of institutionalized placements, even if it means placing career criminals into the homes of volunteers.

They even announced awards for the various DSS agencies pertaining to *Stepping Down* and *Place Matters*. Our governor recognized the winners at the State House on September 17, 2009. Here is a surprise. Baltimore County DSS reduced the number of children in foster care by thirteen percent. That sounds wonderful except what is really happening is a slash and dash. Get the kids back onto the streets or pushed into adoptions. Use all the tricks of the trade like coercion and bribery to make it all happen. I even heard rumors that persons received bonus payments and promotions based upon the adoption success of their caseload. Could that be true?

Even though I appreciate the services of the DSS and the good honest efforts of many DSS employees, I still question their methods. Another surprise: Baltimore City DSS increased family reunifications by twenty-two percent. That particular Department of Social Services has mastered the art of *Place Matters*. They also managed to win the award for reducing the number of children placed into group homes. That rate was down by thirty-two percent. Amazing... keep on Stepping Down the road.

On a side note, child murder statistics did not factor into these awards. From 2002 through 2006, homicide accounted for fifty-nine percent of all fatal injuries among Baltimore City children. Over sixty-five percent of those homicides were from gunshots. In fact, during this time period, Baltimore City children suffered around twice as many fatal injuries as the State of Maryland or the United States as a whole. Why are we sending these kids back home? Baltimore City is slashing prices and the State of Maryland is sending out award announcements. Never mind the means to an end. Congratulations!

Finally, another reality is a little thing referred to as "Performance Based Funding." Performance Based Funding does not exactly advertise the fact that it ultimately denies funding to public non-profit foster agencies, but it does. When it does, the government then acquires and manages that funding. If you say the word "*audit*" to the director of a public non-profit foster agency, he or she might have a heart attack on the spot. The non-government foster agencies face audits several times a year, by multiple levels of government. First the state, then the Feds, the audits never end. The agencies use internal auditors to keep up with the government auditors. The government auditors can provide cause to shut them down. Of course, it is all *in the best interest of the child.*

With overbearing requirements, the public non-profit agencies disappear and their funding becomes reallocated for larger state run facilities. The Performance Based Funding merchants sell their product as beneficial. The philosophical pitch goes something like this: "If private agencies are held responsible for their services at a higher standard of accountability, then children will receive better services." Yes, but who now holds government agencies accountable?

At this rate, foster family programs will be extinct by 2030 and we will have prepared large mini-prisons for the abandoned children of America. Many predetermined bad decisions have been justified in the best interest of the child. This is only one more example. I wish there was an available foster placement for every time I have heard the phrase, *"in the best interest of the child."* Somehow, the best interest always equals the best interest of the budget, but it is time for me to get off my soapbox and tell the story of my foster family. Here it goes…

Part II – Let's Get This Party Started

Chapter 8

Advice From The Father

A couple of months had passed before we received a placement call matching our list of child requirements. In the meantime, we had given up waiting for *"the"* phone call and kept ourselves occupied with the busy agenda of a normal daily routine. During the fall, we spent our time walking in the woods of Liberty Reservoir with our two young Border Collies in tow. The dogs had enough energy for the both of us. Krista was in her last semester at Loyola College and she had nearly completed the courses required for a psychological license. My wife simply needed to acquire the license work hours in order to be eligible for the state licensing exam. This, as well as other aspects of our life had nearly eclipsed our status as future foster parents.

Near the end of the summer, my father died suddenly of a heart attack while on a camping trip at our family reunion. It was the first time I had decided to forego the mini family reunion held each year in Lake Raystown, Pennsylvania. When the phone rang, Krista and I were packing for another trip, with plans to head towards the green grasses of Emerald Isle, North Carolina. Those plans changed the moment I received the call from my mother. She was in Pennsylvania with my father and the rest of my extended family. The moment I raised the telephone receiver I knew something was wrong. I thought I was about to hear that my grandmother had fallen ill. I totally did not expect the news that I received. A feeling of shock and sorrow overcame me as my mother uttered the words, "No, it's your father."

I went into denial. "What are you talking about?" I mouthed. The old man had beaten cancer, beaten diabetes, and more than once... had even beaten me. He was the old oak forever shading my life with stability, the battleship that would never sink. Who will bring me jumper cables? Where will I go when I am lost? How... could he have died?

****

Growing up I did not receive much advice from my father. Most of his sentences were primarily composed of a mixture of grunts and gestures. He was not much of a teacher, or even much of a talker. From him I learned how to change the oil in my car, fix a flat tire along a busy road, and swing a baseball bat in my backyard, but not much else. The advice I frequently received were the words, "Matthew, *feed* your dog." He really could have shortened his directive phrases into simple, one-word commands like feed, listen, and turn.

Along with commands like "Matthew, *listen* to your Mother," or "Matthew, *turn* to channel five," I really got most of my advice from fathers around the neighborhood. My best friend's father taught me the canonical phrase, "Don't bring a girl home unless she's Catholic." Oddly, he did not seem to think much of the Catholic Church although he did marry a pious Catholic woman. Either way, it appears that it worked on me at some level since I ended up marrying Sister Krista.

Another neighborly father taught me the benefits of college education and something described as a good government job. It appears as though I inadvertently followed through on his advice as well. My own father simply taught me to work hard every day and then come home for a rigorous evening of scheduled television programming. As the years passed, I quietly watched his life and took note that he always helped anyone who asked. Like a case of poison ivy, I think his bad habits rubbed off on me.

My old man never used words like love or faith. He did not fill me in about the birds and the bees, on the benefits of educational achievement, or on the topic of religious beliefs. I did not have much of an understanding pertaining to faith. Was *faith* some variant of *love*? How exactly does one define *faith*? How does one define *love* for that matter? My father had acquired his beliefs from the streets of post-depression Chicago. His "lessons learned" did not pertain to the delicate teachings of faith or love.

Raised by God-fearing Protestant parents, I attended church every week. My parents took me along, and I went to enjoy my weekly church mint. The church mint was the little treat I received somewhere around the offering portion of the church service... *if* I had not acted up. As my parents dug into their pockets for their churchly donation, they pulled out their mints as well. My mother's offering was a Breath Saver and my father's, a Velamint. I had been through the rigorous teachings of communion and confirmation, but all I had ever discovered was that I preferred Velamints. I liked the square shape and solid center while the Breath Saver reminded me of a communion wafer.

Everything I learned in church seemed fine. Heaven, life everlasting, and forgiveness for sin, it all sounded beneficial. Still, I really had not grasped the concept of *faith*. What was *faith*? I was nearly thirty years old and had not witnessed death or lost anyone close to me. Is this where *faith* comes in? Is it a belief we grasp onto when confronted with the realization of death, or is it something more? Was Faith only the attractive co-worker that sat two cubicle rows to my left? I did not search for *faith* in the foothills of Tibet, and I did not find it in the intricacies of my dark soul. *Faith* introduced itself to me... in a dream.

****

One night, a few weeks after my father's death, I climbed into bed and said goodnight to Krista. As I shuffled into the sheets, one of our dogs, Sassi, curled up at the bottom of our mattress. Sassi closed her eyes and soon fell asleep. Moments later, I followed suit, and fell into a deep slumber of my own.

Around three in the morning I was abruptly awaken by the beat of a wagging tail. Sassi was sitting upright at the bottom of the bed moving her tail back and forth, as if she was greeting someone. The dog had her nose up in the air and looked like she was receiving a pat on the top of her head. She let out a deep whine of joy. The cry was very familiar, one that she only uses in the presence of an old friend.

At that moment, infused with adrenaline, I sat up, completely awake. The vague details of a lost dream had come rushing to the forefront of my mind. I vividly rehashed a vision that that was now flooding into every part my being. I shook Krista and exclaimed, "Wake up, wake up! Something just happened?" My wife pulled her head up from under the covers.

"What is it?" Krista was not usually one to wake up in a good mood, but she rolled over to see what was going on.

"Look. Look at Sassi." I directed and pointed at our dog sitting at the bottom of the bed. She was still sitting upright but no longer in the middle of her own personal experience. The dog turned her head and looked back with a nonchalant glance.

"And *what* am I looking at?" Sassi's moment of salutation had ended. She no longer looked like a dog having a meet and greet with an invisible friend. There was no evidence of a supernatural occurrence, no smell of incense or sulfur, just the pungent scent of dog. Krista turned and gave me the same silent glance as Sassi.

"Never mind her, I'll tell you about that later. I just had the most vivid dream of my father." I sat awake as my wife shook off the cobwebs and fully awoke from her slumber. She valued every moment of sleep she managed to squeeze in between the rifts of my snore.

"Tell me." Krista had more experience when it came to religion or things pertaining to the afterlife. Over the years, she has visited various religious shrines such as Lourdes in France and her life was rooted in belief and faith. She sat up and attentively listened to my dream.

It really was not like much of a dream at all, more like a moment in time, filmed on location at my childhood home. In this vision I had been working in the yard and casually stepped onto the screened patio of my former residence. The patio room, alongside the kitchen, sat just outside of an entrance to the house. It was a cool summer evening and the crickets had not yet begun to chirp.

As I entered the room, I saw my father sitting on the chair, in the spot where he often positioned himself. He enjoyed watching the television that was set up in this outdoor version of a living room. This was his way of getting fresh air. My old man kept up with his favorite shows while enjoying the beauty of the great outdoors and the smell of the mimosa that bloomed in the front yard. Coincidentally, my father died during a television commercial while camping at the family reunion. At least he had his priorities straight.

I looked down and saw Sassi lying on the same spot of the floor where my childhood dog Leisure often laid. At that moment, I realized the numerous personality and physical similarities between my former and present pets. Then I realized something else. I looked over at my father and spoke to him, "Dad! What are you doing here? You're dead!"

He answered back, "I know, but that's not important right now…" It sounded like a Leslie Nielsen line from the movie *Airplane*. I cut him off and continued speaking before he had time to finish his sentence.

I began questioning him further, "What is heaven like? What is it like after you die?" He held up his hand giving me a physical gesture that delivered the message, *slow down.*

Then he repeated, "I know, but that's not important right now. You'll know everything in time, and this is not the time…" I cut him off again.

"Not the time? How are you here?"

My father then answered me with a phrase he had repeated more times than Archie Bunker referred to his son-in-law Mike as Dumb-Dumb. He said, *"Patience Matthew… patience,"* and then I woke up.

Krista and I sat up and discussed my dream. It felt like more than the mixed remembrances of some previous day. Sassi resumed her spot on the bed and curled up in a ball between our feet. "What *did* my father mean? Back from the grave and his one word bit of advice is *Patience?*"

I could remember his sermons on patience since before I lost my baby teeth. My entire life had felt like one long stint of waiting. I waited for my first job, waited for my first car, waited for my first house, and waited for my wedding. When does the waiting end? *"So much for patience—now I've got to wait to die before I can find out what the old man was talking about!"*

I called out to my father, "What is the next item on my long list of waiting?" I could not wait to find out

Chapter 9

What's His Name?

We were still waiting for the phone to ring. When would DSS dial our foster care hotline? We had requested the placement of a boy or girl anywhere from kindergarten through eighth grade. Notice that preschool children did not fit into this category. I did not like the thought of wiping some stranger's butt, even if he or she was only three years old. Additionally, we were hoping to avoid anyone that would fit the description of a violent teen, so we opted out of teenagers all together.

The description we received was for a seven-year-old child who needed temporary placement for approximately six months. The placement coordinator gave us the breakdown on the kid's situation. The child was noted as having Attention Deficit Hyperactivity Disorder, Reactive Attachment Disorder, and possibly psychotic. That third one sounded fun. Once we agreed she gave us some more basic information including the fact that the child was a boy. The initial details of a placement description are often extremely vague. Anyhow, we looked forward to meeting… him.

A little boy had spent the last several years in transition, passed from one biological family member to another. His birth mother kept watch over him with the assistance of his grandparents who were currently living in the Patterson Park area of Baltimore. Members of the immediate family were all involved in the habitual use of heroin. Apparently, the use of this drug made caring for an energetic young boy and his siblings very difficult, and the boy's mother had a number of other children spread amongst the relatives of each paternal father.

Eventually the boy's mother left him to the care of his grandparents and went back to the streets to enjoy her preferred teenage lifestyle. At the age of three, he had developed a strong bond with the maternal grandfather that cared for him.

Unfortunately this would not last. An unhealthy lifestyle had caught up with the middle-aged man and one day his heart failed. The little boy was left broken hearted. The child had lost his best friend and caregiver as well as his primary source of support. The grandmother was battling addiction, and the boy passed from one family member to another. Heroin had become the family's curse.

The next stop for the boy was somewhere in a suburb of downtown Baltimore. At age five, he lived for a time with his birth father. The man known to him as Gerald Mean Jean preyed upon his fears. There were reports of abuse – including harsh beatings, threats of fictitious alligators, and a night where the boy slept on the front porch of the house. A neighbor's report may have been the trigger that removed the boy, or perhaps it was leather belt beatings and other forms of mental and physical abuse.

At the hands of his birth father, the boy was unsupported, degraded, and abused. Negatively compared to his half brother Troy, the boy experienced new forms of degradation. Mean Jean's five-year-old son from another relationship was the preferred sibling of the home. In a normal environment, the two might have been perfect playmates, but in this reality, he was the focal point of Gerald Mean Jean's degradation. After DSS removed the boy from his birth father's home, he never heard from the man again.

The boy moved on to live with his maternal great uncle, Uncle Jim. In the Baltimore suburb of Lutherville, Uncle Jim had managed to free himself from the family scourge. He also freed two others, the little boy's maternal aunts, Becky and Heather. Uncle Jim and his wife Aunt Pat had their hands full raising two teenage girls. The two young aunts adopted by Uncle Jim, had been raised by he and his wife since the girls were toddlers. Now teenagers, the girls were enough to keep the young couple busy.

Uncle Jim and Aunt Pat had done their part to help, and they were in no position to raise another generation of their extended family. They reluctantly accepted the initial DSS request to house the boy, but it was only temporary until a suitable placement could be determined. DSS knows that bonds often occur between blood relatives and they hope that a kinship placement will result in adoption. It often does. In this case, the highly active young man and the two teen girls were too much for one couple to tackle. Even more, the young couple desired to have their own biological children. Soon after the brief stay, the young boy moved on.

The boy had run out of suitable relatives and ended up at a nearby institution called Saint Xavier's Center. Here a professional staff was able to manage the needs of his ADHD, RAD, and psychosis. The little kid had become increasingly fragile on the verge of a nervous breakdown. Three medications subdued the effects of his multiple diagnoses.

At St. Xavier's Center, the rap sheet on the boy was relatively short. After all, he was only seven. He only made one attempt to escape and occasionally reported seeing invisible dinosaurs. That sounds normal for a seven-year-old, except this kid really thought he saw dinosaurs. The Center's staff introduced medication for *the hallucinations or perhaps the hallucinations were the introduction from the medication. Nobody really knew. They did know that without the meds he had far more outbursts than he did under the meds. After three months at St. Xavier's Center, it was time for the boy to transition after identifying a matching foster placement. The assigned social worker reached out to the network of non-profit foster agencies and the placement coordinators started making calls.*

I was at home one afternoon when I received a call from our placement coordinator. We were finally getting "the call" from the bench, taking us into the complex game known as foster care. What would it be like to meet our first child? Would it be like the musical *Annie* where she was uplifted by the overwhelming lifestyle of Daddy Warbucks? Would the kid humbly ask us to hang him up like a picture in our bathroom? Perhaps everyone involved would break into a lavish Broadway musical dance routine. I anxiously questioned our placement coordinator, "So... when is he coming?"

She answered, "You'll need to talk to the county DSS worker to find out the details. Her name is Gail Witherspoon. Give her a call later today. She will be expecting to hear from you. She can completely fill you in on the details. For now the plan is to transition the boy to your home where he will remain for approximately six months, or until a biological adoptive resource becomes available."

I hung up the phone and immediately dialed a number the placement coordinator gave to me. The voice of a composed and confident woman answered the phone, "Hello. This is Gail Witherspoon."

"Hi Gail, I'm Matt Hoffman. I'm the new foster parent calling about the boy at St. Xavier's."

"Oh, yes... Mr. Hoffman. So you and your wife are all ready to transition this child to your home?"

"Yes we are!"

"Okay. First let me talk to you about the transitional process we would like to take..." She continued talking for around five more minutes as I listened to her version of the preferred DSS method of transition.

Eventually I cut in, "So when do we get started?"

"Hopefully he will transition after the holidays."

"*The holidays?*" It was only September. We had completed our foster training back in the spring. In the summer, we received nothing more than DSS requests to foster the likes of Charles Manson. I was tired of waiting. This was our first legitimate placement and now we were going to have to wait three more months.

Sometimes DSS likes to transition slowly and this boy was one of the slow cases. According to the placement coordinator, he was only coming for six months, yet it would take three whole months to transition him.

That seemed odd. I wondered if they knew something that we did not. I wondered if he was coming for a lot longer than six months. Once again, I had a feeling that I was descending into a pot of boiling water. A thought came to me, *Patience Matthew, patience.*

The social worker continued to fill us in on the extended history of the boy and his current situation at the institution called St. Xavier's Center. It turns out that we would get to meet him in a couple of weeks, once he had settled into his medication. That sounded encouraging. He had been at the institutional home for several months and according to the worker was still adjusting. Once our initial introduction was complete, we would be able to schedule more visits with the little boy until we reached his "transitional goal."

His official moving date was set for after the start of the New Year. The process seemed very slow and cumbersome. Like a child's caterpillar race, it sounded like this kid could go in any direction. Still, we had a child on the way and the social worker gave us his name, Jared. I thanked Gail and our conversation had ended.

****

There were still plenty of distractions to keep us busy while we waited through the transitional process. My mother was going through a transition of her own. After forty plus years of marriage, she was without her husband and still grieving. At the same time, she was trying to maintain my childhood home. Due to my nighttime work hours, I was able to visit regularly and talked with her almost daily. My siblings helped as well. My sister and her teenage children handled some of the yard work, including the disposal of the autumn leaves. I would stop by the house to do little chores like cleaning the gutters or cleaning off the outdoor patio. My mother was making strides as well. She had found solace in riding the lawn mower and enjoyed rounding up piles of grass and leaves.

My father's closets slowly emptied as I hauled his old clothes to the downtown Lutheran version of Goodwill located in Federal Hill. Years of clothing and items overflowed from the back of my pickup truck into the front doors of the donation center. My mother did her best to let go of what she could, but she held onto a lot more. She made unusual requests to avoid disposing of almost every item. Articles of clothing, such as my Dad's used tighty-whiteys shipped off to my nephews. Apparently, my mother found comfort in the thought of her hairy little grandson Stephen wearing her deceased husband's underwear. Steve denied wearing them.

My older brother received many of the other clothing items. Fortunately, I was too big to squeeze myself into dad's overall suspenders. Recycling my father's old clothes helped my mother grieve while my brother looked dapper in his new Texas tie. I did my best to comfort my mother. She would break down in tears and holler out the words, "He left me with all this crap! I have told him for years to get rid of it all! I knew he would leave me with everything!" Was she kidding? She was the biggest packrat the Great Depression had ever seen; my dad was just along for the ride.

To comfort and reassure her I would say, "We'll handle it. It takes time." All of my years watching afterschool specials had finally paid off. We would get through this difficult time together, just as soon as she stopped reminiscing about her former sex life with my father. I did my best to delegate that duty to my sisters. It is no wonder they did most of their support over the phone. Unlike me, they considered their youthful days with our mother as *"a poor placement."*

****

The foster care definition of "a poor placement" means exactly what it sounds like, a poor placement. It is a situation where the parent or parents assigned to a child are not a good match. During the foster parent training, I heard many stories about poor placements from the other foster parents in the room. It seems like foster parents tend to gravitate towards two subjects, their current foster kids, and the poor placements they have had in the past. Each story has a different version of a transitional process including the slow monthly transitional process that my wife and I were currently undergoing.

There are three types of foster care transitions: fast, medium, and slow. In addition to the slow monthly transition, there is the medium weekly transition, as well as the fast (and favored) ten-minute transition. According to numerous foster parent reports, it appears as if there is no correlation between transitional style and the overall success of a placement. In theory, a long transition might be best for matching parent and child, but evidently, the ten-minute transition was just as likely to be successful. It all depends on the individual parents, the individual child, and luck. I would have preferred to experience a ten-minute transition, but we were on track for the monthly variety.

The monthly variety was the favored transitional method of social workers and DSS, but it was not necessarily the favored method for the parents involved. You could spend two months doing visits and getting to know a kid, just to have he or she abruptly sent to live with a biological family member. A court injunction, a surprise mystery relative, or just about anything could happen over a monthly timeframe. The weekly transition is much better. You quickly get a sense of the kid and then the ball starts rolling. *Move 'em in, move 'em out, rawhide!*

Then there is the ten-minute transition. It alone has the element of surprise. You open the front door and your new child is standing there on your front doorstep. This was my preferred method of transition. I do not like to think too much about anything. *Let's just get'er done.*

Throughout the training, parents talked about the kids that ran away, the kids that fought, and the kids that stole. Occasionally I would hear a story about a wonderful child with the qualities of a real son or daughter. Which type of kid would we receive; the one who runs away, fights, and steals? Is there any other kind? Foster care is an ongoing violin solo of optimism. The desired monthly transition method is in the minds of agency placement coordinators who try to make it happen. Sometimes reality gets in the way.

Child placement planning is much like a game of roulette. It works like this... The DSS coordinator checks all of the DSS resources. When there are not any available DSS resources, they make calls to the non-profit agencies. The placement coordinators at the private non-profit foster agencies attempt to assist the DSS placement coordinator. This coordinator then reads a list of foster homes looking for the first available placement legally allowed to handle another child. It does not matter if the child is eighteen and the available placement is requesting a two-year-old. They might find a way to get that kid into a crib if necessary.

It comes down to this: All of the forms you complete and all of training you receive flies out the window. When the little bouncing ball of the roulette wheel stops on double zero it is your turn. You may be a standard Step One foster parent and still receive an un-standard Step Three foster child. Perhaps, in an attempt to avoid receiving an oppositional defiant child you checked off the box indicating that you did not want someone labeled with Oppositional Defiant Disorder. Yet you still end up fostering a young Mike Tyson. That would be a good example of *"poor placement."*

Chapter 10

St. Xavier's Infant Asylum

We received the date for our first scheduled meeting with Jared. The social worker assigned to the case gave us instructions for the meeting. We would meet in the lobby of St. Xavier's Center in Rosedale, Maryland. It is a branch of Church Charities, which supplies housing and services to children between the ages of three to fifteen. With the help of the campus staff, they handle between one to two-hundred kids with severe behavioral issues and emotional problems.

The residential treatment facility originated from a corporate body initially named St. Xavier's Infant Asylum of Baltimore. Does that sound creepy or what? It invokes an image of psychotic toddlers running around with bloody knives or the place where Hannibal Lecter spent his rehabilitation time in the film *Silence of the Lambs*. Even as such, if you had to be pulled from your biological family and placed into an unfamiliar setting, the modern day St. Xavier's Center would be a good place to start.

We were excited about meeting Jared and heard good things about the St. Xavier's Center from our parish priest, Father Bill. It turns out that our very own priest had spent time working with the children at the residential treatment facility. (No priest jokes here please.) Father Bill had positive feedback concerning the St. Xavier's Center and was excited to hear about our foster son, Jared. The good Father did a little reconnaissance and gave us the scoop on Little J. He described him as a soft-spoken child with a propensity for dinosaurs.

****

It was mid October and the trees outside of the St. Xavier Center had started to turn shades of red, yellow, and orange. As my wife and I pulled into the parking lot, I absorbed the serenity around me and commented, "This place doesn't look so bad."

I imagined a place once referred to as an asylum would be a bit more rundown and depressive. This place reminded me of the Daisy Hill Puppy Farm where Charlie Brown found his beloved pet Snoopy. It was nothing like the black and white mess hall I envisioned from the theatrical version of the musical *Oliver*.

Krista spoke up, "Yea, it's a pretty nice place. I've been here before."

In her teenage years, she had driven by it every day on her commute between home and school. St. Xavier's Center sat just outside Lake Montebello surrounded by trees and green rolling fields. The country setting of the campus was peaceful and tranquil. Aesthetically, it was a great place for any foster child. It had been working out well for Jared. His social worker had informed us that his behavior improved since his arrival at St. Xavier's Center.

We entered the main lobby and walked up to the receptionist to begin the registration process. In order to gain access to the facility we filled out some paperwork, turned in our driver's licenses, and signed in. Being an amateur detective I scanned over the names listed along the sign-in sheet. I recognized that Jared's birth mom had visited just a few weeks before. The list was not very long. It appeared as though there were not many visitors to St. Xavier's at all.

According to the social worker, things were going well for Little J. He had only had one setback since his last visit with his birth mom. It appeared as though a lack of biological visits might actually benefit a confused little boy. For now, being "out of sight and out of mind" was working out for the best.

The St. Xavier's receptionist was a stern looking middle-aged woman with glasses hanging from the tip of her nose. She took the sign-in sheet and disappeared down the hallway. Krista and I waited in a small lobby that displayed hanging Baltimore Raven Halloween decorations. As I paced around, I took note of the Raven cutouts and football décor that had been set up for Halloween. It appeared that the Ravens donated money and decorative supplies to St. Xavier's Center.

About ten minutes later the receptionist returned and called out to us, saying, "Follow me down to Jared's cottage."

"*Cottage,*" I jokingly replied. The receptionist did not find the hint of sarcasm in my voice very amusing; many receptionists do not. Cottage must be a St. Xavier's term, derived to make the institution sound almost comforting. Perhaps cottage *is* more kid-friendly than the word, unit. "*Hey Kid! Go back into your unit!*" That sounds somewhat Orwellian while "*Go back to your cottage*" sounds almost fun. That is exactly what these cottages were… pseudo-fun institutional units.

We followed the receptionist as she led us past a cafeteria and down a long hallway lined with doors. The place smelled like a hospital and the halls echoed like an auditorium. You could hear the muffled sounds of staff members shouting orders to the kids of their friendly neighborhood cottages. We listened as the receptionist gave a short tour of the facility while she described the services and location of the cottage where Jared awaited. Perhaps he was in there waiting for our arrival along with his friends the three little bears. Actually, Little J did not know that we were coming, who we were, or what we were doing there. Our tour guide instructed us to maintain an "observer type" presence at all times.

We stopped after a short distance as the receptionist showed us the facility's medicinal closet. It was like a mini-pharmacy where the nurse lined up water and medication cups for the kiddies. We continued down the hallway, now relatively silent. It was currently after dinnertime and the kids were already prepared or preparing for bed. By this time, they were ready to play quietly behind the thick unit doors. We turned the corner and walked down one last hallway, eventually reaching our designated cottage door.

The receptionist knocked on the door and a unit staff member walked over and opened it. The staffer was a burly African-American man who reminded me of Krista's co-worker, Desmond. I was beginning to think that the organizations that care for special needs children were recruiting their staff from the NFL. This man could have easily played as a defensive lineman for the Washington Redskins. Filled with excitement and anticipation, Krista and I entered the room.

As we stepped in, we surveyed the scene and smelled the aroma of microwave popcorn. The unit was cozy, yet felt confined. The space partitioned into two large areas had separate hallways leading towards a number of bedroom units. I could see a staff member in the play area engaged with a couple of kids. She appeared to be college age and was probably accumulating hours for a psychology license or degree. The young woman bantered with the children while explaining the guidelines of video game sharing. Video game time was a big reward for good behavior on the unit.

Krista and I stepped further into the main room with the Washington Redskin staffer standing behind us. He discretely pointed over to a little boy who was sitting by himself playing with plastic dinosaurs. The boy was thin and pale, with blond hair and blue eyes. Deep tired circles rested just below his large eye sockets. His skin appeared almost transparent from the lack of sunlight. I could see the color of light blue veins running along his neck and arms. He reminded me of a malnourished Chihuahua. As we approached, he looked up over his left shoulder and smiled with an awkward grin. I noticed a tiny diamond stud earring in his left ear as Krista leaned over and whispered, "Oh, that's got to go." I nodded in agreement.

"Do you want to play with me?" he asked.

"Sure," I replied as I sat down on a plastic child-sized chair. He was holding a dinosaur in one hand while arranging a plastic fern tree with the other. There was a pictorial layout of directions sitting on my side of the table. Looking at the scene before me, I recognized that he had set up his Dino-land to match the one displayed on the cover of the box. Krista stood next to me watching as I picked up a plastic dinosaur. "What's this one called?"

"Steak-e-o-sore-us."

I held up another toy, "And this one?"

"Try-ser-a-tops." Then he took the plastic fern and placed it into the scene in accordance with the picture. He began to use both hands to move the dinosaur figurines around the prehistoric setting. "Rooooaaaaaarrrrr. This one is a T-Rex. He's my favorite," he commented while ramming two toys together. I looked back at Krista with a sarcastic smile, using my expression to communicate the message, Ooooo-Kaaaaayyy.

I turned back to the little boy, "I like triceratops. They live in families and use their horns to protect themselves from meat eaters like the tyrannosaurus." My big brother instincts had already kicked in and I was trying to teach the kid a lesson. It went right over his head. The little boy had a glazed look behind his dilated pupils. I realized that being on three medical prescriptions probably meant that he was as high as a pterodactyl. Too bad I did not bring a pack of Ho Hos, as the kid would have been in stoner heaven. I would make sure to bring them on the next visit.

The kid did not have a clue as to why we were there and probably would not even remember anything about our visit. No wonder he was reportedly seeing invisible dinosaurs; he was drugged up and playing with toy dinosaurs every night before bed. I have seen equally scary things after a bottle of cheap wine. I looked around the room to survey the environment. Even though it was day's end, I could see colorful trees and the green fall grass from the window of Jared's unit. At least the kid had a good view. It was much better than the view from any windowless public school.

The young female attendant ushered some children off to bed. Due to our visit, Jared enjoyed extra time speaking with us. After a few final words with Little J concerning the lifestyles of the green and prehistoric, Krista and I said goodbye. We walked back towards the door and waved farewell to him. It was time for Jared to clean up and head off to bed and Krista and I wanted to talk to each other privately. We said goodnight to the staff and moved through the doorway to the outside hall. As we walked away something about Jared seemed very familiar to me, but I could not put a finger on exactly what that something was.

The walk back to the main lobby, riddled with turns and dead ends, seemed endless. We found ourselves lost several times on our way to retrieve our driver licenses. Once we had distanced ourselves from the muffled sounds of the unit, we were free from any prying ears. Then Krista asked, "Well, what do you think?"

"I think we need to get that kid a tanning bed." I always avoided any heartfelt conversations, and kept this one on a humorous level.

She continued, "He's a little younger than I expected, but he seems alright." Even though Jared had just turned eight, he came off more like a four-year-old. When we filled out the foster care paperwork, we listed our ideal age range somewhere at the middle school level. Jared did not fit into that range. Krista and I pictured ourselves in the role of big brother and big sister, not mommy and daddy. My personal experience as a substitute teacher involved middle school children and I had myself fostering a child around that age.

I continued, "At least he is old enough to wipe his own ass. With that in mind, Jared seems fine to me." Krista agreed. I called the caseworker to inform her of our positive experience with Little J. She told me that we would have another visit in just a couple of weeks.

****

The weeks passed and we returned to St. Xavier's Center for a second visit with our future foster son. It was now November and the lobby was set up with corresponding Thanksgiving decorations. The Baltimore Ravens Halloween décor had vanished and made way for a new motif that included paper turkeys. We signed in and headed down the long hallway once again. This visit was going to be a little longer and it would give us more time to sit with Jared while he wolfed down the bag of Funyuns I brought, which would go well with a November issue of High Times.

Today we were going to tell him exactly why we were visiting. We entered the unit and found him playing on the main room video game console. It was early in the evening and the overhead lights were beaming with maximum wattage. Krista motioned to Jared and invited him to sit with us at the nearby play table. He obliged and came over to join us. Once he sat down, we began filling him in. I started by simply stating, "Hey J!"

"Hi," he replied.

"Do you know Ms. Gail?"

"I know Ms. Gail Witherspoon. Is she here today?" He started looking around the room.

"No, but she's been telling us about your situation. She told us that your mom is going to be busy for a while, at least until she finds a job and a good place to live. Until then Ms. Gail says you would like to live with a family. Is that right?"

He responded, *"Yea!"* in a Dennis the Menace kind of way. He seemed generally enthused about this upcoming prospect. We told him about ourselves, and our dogs. His eyes lit up with excitement when we showed him pictures of Sadie and Sassi. Through his medicated persona, he was as excited as any stoner watching a Pink Floyd concert.

"Do your dogs bark?"

"Sometimes," I replied.

"Why?"

I looked over at Krista hoping she would offer a suggestion, but she chose to remain silent. "Well, they bark for different reasons."

"Oh… Do you have snow in your yard?"

"We have snow in our yard when it snows."

"Good… because snow means Christmas."

"Well actually, Christmas is…" Before I could finish Jared had interjected.

"I want it to snow so that I can have a Christmas tree."

I looked at him with a smile, "Sure… we'll work on the snow thing."

He was ready to pack up and leave for Santa's Workshop until we informed him that his transitional process includes two more visits here at the cottage. The next visit included a trip to McDonalds. It was not Candy Land, but he was still excited about a visit with Ronald McDonald. Then, the final visit would include a sleepover at his future home. "Sleepover!" he excitedly exclaimed.

The next visit was a few weeks later and Christmas was just around the corner. On a chilly night, my wife and I went back to St. Xavier's Center for our evening outing with Little J. We signed in, signed him out, and hopped into my truck. It was only a short drive to the Cold Spring Lane McDonalds restaurant located just north of Baltimore. The little boy sat comfortably in the backseat of my Chevy Silverado.

The first thing I noticed about my potential foster son was that he never stopped talking. I quickly learned the AYRT or "Ah-ha, Yea Rotation Technique." With each proclamation or question, I answered back with a corresponding "Ah-ha" or "Yea." Sometimes I would mix in a, "That's cool." In just a few minutes, I had developed a perfect wheel of rotational answers. It was like some sort of natural parenting tool that preexisted somewhere deep within my biology. Krista was in charge of actually answering the questions. She was better equipped to decipher the thick sounds of "Baltimorese" jutting from this kid's mouth. Some of her extended relatives still talked with this exact same accent.

At our wedding, a pair of her Baltimorese cousins attempted to initiate a conversation with me. I simply smiled and nodded in agreement. I think at one point I may have agreed to join them at the Hippo Club, and now there was a little boy in my backseat spewing the local Baltimore dialogue with more "Yoouse" and double negatives than an old waitress from Café Hon. I felt like I was in the middle of a John Waters film. Was this kid the offspring of the *Cry Baby* character, Hatchet Face?

We soon arrived at McDonalds and pulled into the parking lot. Krista unloaded Jared and held his hand as we walked into the restaurant. It was dinnertime but the lines were not too long. The smell of French fries and grease encompassed the place. Little J stood alongside of my wife as I waited in line and looked up to read the menu. What would we have today?

Using my best Baltimore accent, I said to Krista, "Look *Hon, d*ey have eggnowg miwlkshakes. Goowd stuff." I continued to scan over the board as Krista had already decided on her standard McDonalds meal – a double cheeseburger, fries, and a coke. We reached the cashier and it was our turn to order. The young woman behind the register began her rehearsed greeting, "Welcome to McDonalds. May I take your order?" She delivered that line as well as any 1980's McDonalds commercial.

I looked up. "I'll take a number one with diet coke and… a double cheeseburger meal with regular coke and…" Then I looked down at Jared and asked, "What do you want big guy?"

He stood there dumbfounded with a blank stare. It looked as if no one had ever asked him this question before. I had only been a parent for the last twenty minutes and had no clue that a part of the parental job description was ordering for children. Nor had I considered the fact that he could not yet read. After a moment of waiting I asked, "What do you like – cheeseburger, hamburger, or chicken nuggets?"

He nodded on the chicken nugget prompt and pointed towards the picture of a happy meal toy. Turning back to the cashier, I finished ordering, "… and a chicken nugget Happy Meal." I had just learned the most important lesson of parenting today, ordering fast food at McDonalds. It was so simple. For the next ten years all I would have to say is "Nugget Happy Meal" and *voila!*

Of course, McDonalds had to throw a wrench into my plan by creating the Mighty Meal, but even I could adapt to that. What I cannot adapt to was the change from Double Cheeseburger to McDouble. That will forever be a thorn in my side. We sat down and ate our first meal with Little J. This whole parenting business seemed like a piece of cake – no wonder my parents were able to handle five. After consuming the fast food, we headed back to the St. Xavier's Center and said farewell to Little J.

****

In preparation for the final visit with Jared, Krista and I upgraded the upstairs loft of our modest home. The upstairs loft area of our house divided into two sections. The back was an enclosed bedroom with a double bed and a dresser while the front was a play area with a twin bed, a hockey game table, and a television with video games. It would be a nice place for Jared to keep his toys or play with future friends. The twin bed could serve as an extra bed if he wanted to have a sleepover. Krista agreed because she loved the idea of sleepovers. They were her way of reliving the days of her youth.

There were two reasons why the loft area of the house was perfect for foster care. One, the entire area sits above the master bedroom and the guest bedroom. Therefore, my wife and I could hear any movement that any kid makes. The second reason is that the loft bedroom is far from the kitchen, and all of the sharp utensils like forks and knives. This way I would have plenty of warning in case I needed to prevent a reenactment from the movie *Psycho*.

The other bedroom designated for foster care was our downstairs guest bedroom. That is where I had recently taken residence because of my snoring habit. I had a snore that could scare any lion off the African savannah. In our first year of marriage, I realized that neither earplugs nor white noise was powerful enough to deter my roar. I also discovered it was the reason my father spent most of his years sleeping in his own guest room.

****

It was a mild December day when we drove back to the St. Xavier's Center for our final visit with Jared. This was going to be the last visit before his official transition to our home. We signed in and I scanned over the list of names. The last visitors on the list were Krista and I. No biological relatives appeared anywhere on the list. We sat down and waited for the staff to retrieve Little J.

This time the lobby appeared decorated with Christmas decorations. A Christmas tree adorned the open space filled with Ravens paraphernalia. There were Raven Christmas bulbs, purple lights, and black bows tied to the branches. A short time later Jared entered the lobby to join us. We zipped up his coat, signed him out, and loaded him into my truck with his overnight bag. He was excited to see his new home. As we took the twenty-minute drive home, the little boy continued with nonstop chattering and repetitive questions. Krista did a great job of finding the answers to his flighty inquiry. I think the cocktail of psychotropic medications were working on him again. I thought to myself, *The happy-pill train to dinosaur land is the first thing we should advocate against!*

As I drove the truck I listened to the little boy ramble in the backseat. Something seemed so familiar about Jared. I finally realized what it was. He reminded me of the Looney Toons character "Ralph." Jared was the daydreaming cartoon kid that only appeared in a few Looney Toons episodes. I had seen each one of the episodes numerous times as a child, back when Jared went by the name Ralph. The Ralph character always had a distant glazed look while sitting in his cartoon classroom. While in the classroom, he would drift off from one daydream adventure to another.

If you have ever seen the movie, *A Christmas Story*, the Looney Toons character Ralph was very similar to "Ralphie," the boy who shot his eye out with a Red Rider BB gun. They looked the same, and so did Jared. If someone strapped a pair of glasses on Little J, he would fit the role of Ralphie quite well. I imagined his tongue would one day be stuck to a metal pole, or I would find him in the backyard hunting a fictitious villain named Black Bart. To further support my comparison, Jared was currently in the backseat proclaiming fantastical comments. Each one was far off from everyday reality. "Are there alligators living in my new closet?" he asked.

What, did this kid grow up on a swamp? Using her best sympathetic tone, Krista gave him an appropriate answer, "Oh, sweetie... only the hungry alligators."

Just kidding, that would have been my answer, but I knew when to keep my big mouth shut and let Krista perform her motherly duties. After all, I wanted to be able to get some sleep tonight. The last thing I needed was a crazy kid in my house running around from invisible alligators at three o'clock in the morning. We continued driving home as the road noise began to drown out the rest of Krista and J's conversation.

The alligator conversation resulted from a fear tactic used by his birth father, Gerald Mean Jean. Fortunately, his new loft bedroom did not even have a closet, just a dresser and a rack for hanging clothes. More "off the wall" concepts presented themselves each time I talked with the boy. At the age of eight, he was still under the impression that *everything* on television was real. Krista and I did a lot of explaining concerning this topic. It required many conversations pertaining to Superheros, Godzilla, and the talking Pillsbury Dough Boy. I doubt this kid would ever eat Parkay Butter.

Jared inquired, "What about Godzilla?"

"Jared, that's a guy in a suit."

"Wow... that must be one *really* big guy."

"Yea, in his spare time he plants apple seeds and markets paper towels."

"What?"

"Nothing Jared, nothing."

We arrived at the house and Jared was enthralled with his new room, particularly the Playstation video game console. I had picked up a bunch of kid-friendly games for him and he immediately began playing a game called Spyro. Spyro was a game about a purple dragon that runs around finding jewels. If I had known earlier that this kid would become obsessed with dragons, dinosaurs, and shiny rocks, I might not have bought it for him. He truly loved video games and probably did not notice anything else about his room. Jared grabbed the controller, turned on the game system, and exclaimed, "I want to be Spyro when I grow up! He's my favorite."

"Well, you can't actually grow up to *be* a video game character."

"What?"

"Never mind, maybe you can. What do I know?"

The introduction of our dogs, Sadie and Sassi, was only a momentary distraction from the purple dragon named Spyro.

"Will they bite?"

"Only if you grow up and turn into a purple dragon."

"What?"

"Never mind Jared... never mind..." Jared spent a short time with our dogs before seeking out another form of entertainment; he preferred imaginary animals to real ones. We then took Jared on a walking tour around the house. He headed right for the family room and began jumping on the couch. I yelled, "Hold on kid! Rule number one: *no... jumping... on... the couch!*"

Jared obviously needed to burn some excess energy so I led him outside to the backyard. I half expected him to introduce me to the new purple dragon that now lived in the shed. We tiptoed through the dog-tulips and crossed a small footbridge that sits at the edge of our property. I had seen other neighborhood boys in the area and decided to search for them. Perhaps Jared could make a couple of friends on this short overnight visitation. We looked around a nearby baseball field but no children appeared. Playmate free, we walked back to the house where Jared's new video game oasis awaited. The sleepover went smoothly and Jared looked forward to his upcoming six-month stay.

The next day we returned to St. Xavier's and checked him back in at the lobby. We left Jared with pictures of our dogs, our house, and ourselves. He took them back to his little St. Xavier's cottage after we said goodbye. Christmas was next week and Jared's official transition date was finally set. It would happen immediately following the holidays.

Chapter 11

Somebody's Knocking On The Door...

A baby with the unique first name Eloiro was born in downtown Baltimore at Bon Secours Hospital in 1983. He was the first child of a young couple living somewhere along Monument Street where he spent his early years living in city subsidized housing. In 1984 a little brother, Wallace was born, and then another brother, Nevar the year after that. Eventually, twin sisters, Diynah and Carlyn were born as well and Eloiro was the eldest of five children, three sons, and two daughters.

Around age four, Eloiro transitioned into foster care with his youngest brother, Nevar. The youngest brother was born mentally challenged and Eloiro was the sibling selected to join Nevar on a journey into foster care. Their mother maintained custody of the three other children, Wallace, Diynah, and Carlyn. Even at the age of four, Eloiro believed that it was his duty to take care of his mentally handicapped brother Nevar, and believed that this duty was his role in the family. Reasonable or not, Eloiro felt tied to this fate.

It was not long before the realities of foster care separated the two brothers. The younger brother went to a therapeutic placement home and Eloiro was destined for standard care. He spent most of his life living with one foster family being beat repeatedly with everything from belts to bats. Various objects throughout the home were weapons used to smack him across the backside or wallop him against the head. Unbelievably, it took over a full decade before his abusive foster mother lost her license. The abuse did not hit the spotlight until there was trouble between Mommy Dearest and her husband. Eloiro's foster dad could take no more of his abusive wife and initiated divorce proceedings. Unfortunately, his foster dad did not maintain a foster license, so Eloiro transitioned once again.

The next several placements led the young teenager to a number of homes throughout Baltimore City and Baltimore County. He lived with single moms and grandmothers while making new foster siblings along the way. After an odd turn of events, he wound up at our front door.

In 2001, the night before Christmas Eve, my wife and I relaxed inside of our childfree home. It was around eight in the evening and my friend Charlene had stopped by for a short visit. We took turns posing with the dogs to take seasonal pictures in front of our Christmas tree then sat with Charlene to talk in the living room. Before the conversation started, the phone rang. I leaned over to check the number on the caller identification box. Even though it was an unfamiliar number, I decided to answer the call.

On the other end of the line, I heard the voice of a stressed out social worker. A child on her caseload was in a dire situation. Abruptly moved from his current placement, the foster agency was desperate to find an available home. Due to the holidays, the normal placement coordinator was unreachable. The worker on the phone frantically asked us for help. This was our first experience with the ten-minute transitional method, and there is no better time than two days before Christmas. In accordance with her procedures, the worker read back a detailed description of the situation. This description is an introductory verbal rap sheet. She began to read…

"Placement needed for a seventeen-year-old high school student. He has no negative medical history and has a limited psychological history, including ADHD diagnosed when he was younger. Already through several placements, he has transitioned due to abuse, neglect, and/or abandonment issues. He has been in foster care for somewhere over twelve years."

The worker also pointed out the fact that he was African American, and had never before resided in a Caucasian home. "You may run into issues related to culture." Normally, agencies attempt to place a child with a family of similar background, but *"Place Matters"* does not always factor in when dealing with a Christmas Eve ten-minute transition. A child's background did not matter to us either.

I responded. "I know, but that's not important right now. Why the Christmas move?"

The social worker continued, "The current placement has become… *afraid* of him." Her voice resounded with disbelief. I could almost hear her eyes rolling in the back of her head.

"Afraid?" Before I could continue speaking, she had cut me off and was already in mid-sentence. She spoke rapidly in a tone that emitted disappointment and disgust.

"Eloise decided to cut school yesterday and hid in the downstairs furnace room in order to avoid class. I cannot blame him."

I interjected, *"Him?"*

"Yes him, I'm talking about Eloise."

"So Eloise is the boy's name?"

"Yes. The boy's name is Eloise. The spelling of the name is different, E-l-o-i-r-o, but everybody pronounces his name, *Eloise*... but that's not important right now."

"Okay, sorry. Please continue."

"Anyhow, I cannot blame *him*. If I went to Northern High School, I might want to avoid class too. Mind the fact that the current foster mom is an elderly grandmother. Anyhow, the grandmother went downstairs to do her laundry or something like that, and was startled when she found Eloise hiding behind the furnace. He was downstairs hiding and reading comic books. For crying out-loud, the kid was reading comic books! Ms. Cullen went into hysterics and now she fears for her life. She darn near called 911 on the poor boy and now claims that she is so frightened of him that she will no longer remain his foster mom. I tried to convince her to give him another chance but she will not budge. I did manage to talk her into letting him stay one last night, but that is all she is willing to contribute. Eloise is a great kid! He loves fishing, basketball, and art. He especially loves to draw and sketch."

In her emotional state, the worker had broken standard protocol by divulging the names of the involved parties, but who could blame her. It was two days before Christmas and who plans to search for an emergency child placement just before the holidays? I put her on hold for a moment to confer with Krista. After hearing the story, my wife did not have any objections. Who in the world could say no to a child on Christmas Eve? Besides, how dangerous could this young man be if he reads comic books, sketches, and goes by the name Eloise? My great aunt had damn near the same name. I imagined that Eloise, like my great aunt, was beyond harmless. I removed my hand from the telephone receiver and asked one final question, "What time *tomorrow* should we expect him?"

"In about one hour?"

I covered the phone, looked to Krista, and whispered, "About one hour."

"I guess," she said as she threw up her hands.

I responded to the worker, "See you then." Krista and I did not know what to expect and did not have much time to think about it. Our guest Charlene could see that we had much to take care of so she bid us farewell and headed home. Krista and I sat on the living room couch and looked at each other as we came up with a plan.

"Where should we put him?"

"I guess in the guest room," Krista answered. I had a better idea. Even if Eloise, the fish-catching, art-loving, basketball player, *was* harmless, I still wanted to be able to hear his every move. I also wanted to stake my claim on the guest room.

"What about the upstairs bedroom, in Jared's future room?"

"Fine, but where will we put Jared?"

I explained, "He can go in the playroom area on the single bed and we can make that area his bedroom. He will like being closer to his toys, and it's more open to the rest of the house. That way we can hear both kids through the ceiling, if they do start moving around."

"That sounds good to me." Thank God, Krista was easy going.

I joked, "Besides, if the older kid *is* dangerous, then Jared's sacrifice will give us time to escape with the dogs."

With this plan, everyone would be happy. The "scary" boy with the old woman's name would have his own private room. Jared would be closer to Spyro, and closer to us. I would have my own private snore chamber and Krista would have her own full suite with attached private bath. Oh yea, and the dogs would have plenty of room on that king sized bed of hers as well.

Krista agreed with my plan and exclaimed, "We've got to get moving. Christmas is only a day away! What are we going to get this kid? We've got to get him something." She was right.

"Well, the worker says he likes fishing and art. I will run up to the store and get some stuff. I'll have it wrapped and under the tree faster than the Grinch can steal Christmas."

Thirty minutes later, I was back. The Ames department store supplied me with a tackle box, a basketball, and a bunch of drawing supplies. We quickly wrapped them up and stuffed them under the tree. A friend Mike was running errands in the immediate area. He helped me out by picking up some Raven's gear from the nearby mall. I wrapped up the clothes and shoved them under the tree as well. We were now ready for our first Christmas with our new son, one we had never met. Somebody named... Eloise. How in the *hell* is that spelled anyway?

****

It was crunch time, time to transform myself from a light-hearted party dude into a responsible foster dad. I wondered how I would do in the role of foster Dad. I dug deep into my dark abyss of youthful experiences. Perhaps I could use the knowledge, the guidance, and the skills I once absorbed from my own parental role models. I took a moment to think about that... perhaps not! I did not want to scar this kid for life. If I carried out our family tradition, this kid might end up applying to psych wards instead of colleges. Even worse, he might end up in a psych ward wearing my dead father's underwear.

I thought back to the parental approach I learned from my mother and father. The first lesson I learned is that parenting takes planning. I will never forget the first time my parents sat me down at the dinner table and informed me of their own plan as my father uttered the words, "Your mother and I have decided your future over dinner last night."

It must not have been a very long future because it did not take them much time to map out the precarious details. My dad could scarf down a meal in less than ten minutes and it appeared as though he found time "to plan" in between the meatloaf and the Harvard beets. Perhaps they had chosen a wife for me just before they ate dessert. According to my parents, my destiny was to join the Coast Guard. Their intention was for me to avoid the future draft for the Gulf War. Currently, there was no draft for the Gulf War, but my parents must have had some sort of inside information.

Yes, my first foster kid was about to become subjected to the dysfunctional methods of my unordinary upbringing, but I believed that I could improve upon the parenting skills learned from my predecessors. In fact, I had already made one improvement. Eloise's current Christmas presents did not include any of the canned goods that I often found stuffed into my stocking. Nor would he be opening boxes of cereal wrapped in Christmas paper, no Christmas Captain Crunch for this kid. My survivalist mother would be gravely disappointed. She felt that dry goods were an appropriate gift for just about any starving college student.

Perhaps she was just trying to send me a message. After all, she was tired of my frequent raids to her food pantry, but whatever the case, I had improved upon my parent's method of gift giving once I came to realize that my mother was teetering on lunacy. The other lesson I learned from "Mommy Weirdest" pertained to vacuuming in my bedroom in the wee hours of the morning. I believe that by doing so, it was her intention to motivate me. In my mother's world, the vacuum cleaner equaled "Carpe diem." What did I know? They were parents to five children and I was just the fifth test subject of their bizarre experiments.

After fifteen more minutes, there was a knock on the door. Our inaugural moment of foster parenting had arrived. It came a few weeks earlier than we originally expected, and the child was not exactly *the person* we expected. When it comes to foster care, you need to "go with the flow." After all of our spectacular foster training I was now ready to parent a neglected, abused, African-American, teenage, boy… or at least I thought so. So far, I had successfully influenced the lives of two Border Collies; one was currently hiding under a bed while the other was in the backyard gnawing bark off a tree.

I opened the door and welcomed a young man and his social worker. She was a tall slender woman wearing wire-rim glasses and a kind smile. He was a short, muscular, young man wearing an expression of guarded anxiety. His emotions hid behind a blank, expressionless stare. This kid had one hell of a poker face.

My wife and I helped the young man with his "Foster Gucci" suitcases. The public would identify these suitcases as plastic trash bags. It was my first introduction to the ongoing tradition of moving foster children with their belongings in a black Hefty trash bag. Together we hauled his two bags up the spiral staircase, through the loft, and back into the upstairs bedroom. We left everything on the floor of the room and headed downstairs to regroup in the living room.

The social worker sat down and started a brief conversation to ease Eloise into his new placement, but it was obvious that she had to get going. After all, it was the day before Christmas Eve. Minutes later, she said goodbye and exited through the front door. She assured us that she would call the next day to see how things were going.

Eloise sat down on the floor with his back against the wall and his legs and arms crossed. He had wedged himself in between the Christmas tree and a brick platform that housed our woodstove. Krista offered him a beverage and dashed off towards the kitchen to see what she could scrounge up for a snack and a drink. She left me to deal with the awkwardness of the situation alone. I sat on the couch, across from the young man, and initiated a conversation. Other than the sounds of Krista fumbling around in the kitchen, the house was silent. I started with, "So, Eloise... that is an interesting name. How do you spell that?"

He cautiously replied, "E-L-O-I-R-O." Then he said, "The RO is silent."

"Shouldn't there be an S at the end of your name if it's pronounced, Eloise? In fact, the way it's spelled I'd say it's pronounced, E-LOY-RO."

More confidently, he responded, "No, it *is* pronounced E-LO-IS. That's the way my mother used to say it."

I thought to myself that his mom must have had a little problem with sobriety, but I knew better than to argue with a teenager about his or her name. I had a niece that recently changed her name from Shelley to the trendier version, *Chellie*. She never responded well to CH-ellie pronounced with a hard C-H.

Sitting across from this young man and using a name similar to my great aunt's name genuinely felt awkward. In my mind, "Eloise's" were older women who kept dishes filled with old-fashioned ribbon candy. He certainly did not fit the bill. I made a suggestion, "Mind if I call you Elo, and just drop everything else? Has anyone ever called you that before?"

"No, but it's not bad. You can call me that if you want."

"I want. Cool. Then you can call me, *Dad!*" He cast a look of surprise and his eyes bugged out of his head. Then I continued, "I'm just kidding. My mother pronounces my name Moth-hew, but I go by Matt." I saw the hint of a cracked smile. "Krista is the one in the kitchen making us a batch of gourmet food."

"Really?"

"No. I am just messing with you. Nobody cooks around here. So I hope you've got some culinary skills." His defensive position loosened up. He dropped his arms into his lap, and looked more comfortable.

He cautiously, but enthusiastically responded, "I'm a pretty good cook."

"Sweet, I'm a pretty good eater. I look forward to eating some of your cooking." Krista returned to the room, handed Elo a drink, and sat down next to me on the couch. We continued with some small talk as he gave us the details of his exodus from Ms. Cullen's home. He had skipped school and he began to tell us why. According to Elo, Northern High School was replete with drugs and locked down classrooms. He described a scenario where a student fell from a bus window. It sounded like a very pleasant high school experience so naturally, Elo skipped out.

We decided that our first goal was to get Elo out of Northern High School and enroll him somewhere else. The broken ice had now melted and we were starting to feel comfortable around one another. I threw out a line of advice, which I should have copyrighted. I said, "We've got a great life here, but we have a few rules. Follow these rules and you will have an awesome life. We eat good food, we have good times, we take great vacations, but you only get to enjoy them… if you are still here. To stay here you have to follow these three rules: no fights, no drugs, and no sex, at least none that I'll ever know about." Sitting next to me, Krista listened to my rules and decided not to comment.

My plan was to parent using the good memories of my past, and not the bad memories of my parents' past. I wanted to put myself in the shoes of a kid and then foster parent from there, no matter how bad the inside of those shoes might smell. I had never experienced abandonment, I had never experienced abuse, and I had never been black, but I had been a teenager struggling with the issues of life.

As far as what we had in common, we were at 40%. In any casino, two out of five were still good odds, so we would start from there. Besides, since I was a late bloomer I imagine my maturity level was only a few years beyond his. Over the next couple of weeks, we came to know Eloiro Jax Winford, or Elo, better. He began to open up and educate us about his life in foster care. He had been through several short stays and one longer placement. None of it sounded like very much fun.

I was just glad that he made it to us in one piece, and so was he. The social workers and my wife recommended therapy, but he refused. Instead, he would sit and talk to me about his distaste for therapy, all while pouring out the details of his incredible past. I watched how Elo expressed the sadness of his abuse. He would talk about the torture he faced with a slight smile, transferring the pain into subtle comedy. The true emotion, the true meaning, hid below the surface. It was very reminiscent of my own method of transference. Now with three out of six, our commonality percentage had risen to 50%. We were finding out that we had more in common than either of us had originally thought.

****

Two weeks later, my wife and I informed our new foster son about the imminent arrival of his new foster brother, Jared. Elo, laid back for a teenager, did not seem to mind one way or another. Over his long and short term placements he had lived with foster brothers, foster sisters, as well as the biological children of his foster families. He missed many of his siblings and occasionally spoke to them over the phone. The young man expressed a desire to reconnect with them as well as reconnect with his old foster dad, Mr. Freeman. Today would be the first day he would "connect" with Jared, and vice-versa.

Krista, Elo, and I hopped into my truck and headed towards St. Xavier's Center. Today was the day that Jared would finally check out of his modern-day orphanage, transition into our home, and meet his new foster brother, Elo. It had been less than a month since Elo's arrival but it felt natural to have him around. Due to our lack of culinary expertise, Krista and I went out to eat often and our new teenage son never turned down an invitation to join us. He never missed a meal. Over our dinners, we had become accustomed to the familiarity of our trio. Today we would add a pinch of Jared to this recipe we called our family.

We arrived at St. Xavier's Center on a cold day in January 2002. The skies were gray and the brisk winter wind was blowing strong. Elo and Krista bundled up in their winter coats and I put on a new stylish jacket, another gift from my generous in-laws. We checked in at the lobby, decorated with only a sign-in sheet as well as Jared's social worker, Tina. She was a sweet woman who rose almost seven feet tall. Tina was taller than the Christmas tree that once stood in the spot where she was now standing. Her bright earrings were ornamental and her hat could have doubled as the star on top of a tree, but the long black coat she was wearing was not as bright as the string of Christmas lights that once illuminated the spot where she now stood.

Tina was not here to decorate the lobby; she was here to do her job, which was helping transition Jared to our home. We listened closely as she gave us the informational breakdown concerning the transitional process, which included bits of information pertaining to Jared's medication and upcoming therapy appointments. We were about to begin a very busy time of our lives. Krista continued to listen to Tina as Elo and I started to look about the room.

The attention deficit in our minds had led us away from the topic at hand and towards just about anything else in our view. The Center had not yet set up for Valentine's Day, and my imagination pictured hanging hearts with Baltimore Raven pictures glued in the center. Perhaps there would be a big poster of a football player like Jermaine Lewis or Matt Stover with a message stating, "Be My Valentine." Almost in a trance, I turned to Elo and said the first thing that popped into my mind. "Elo, do you want Jonathan Ogden to be your valentine?"

He gave me a confused look and replied, "Whatchu talkin' 'bout Willis." Cool, I had officially fallen into the Mr. Drummond category, a reference from the old television show *Diff'rent Strokes,* and just in time. Willis was about to meet Arnold.

As if on cue, Jared entered the lobby with some Hefty bags of clothes and a tub of his precious dinosaurs. *What a relief, I would not have to go dinosaur shopping later today.* Krista and I introduced Jared to Elo as we all stood together in St. Xavier's lobby. Jared had a clueless look upon his face and Elo wore an expression of humor mixed with worry. Elo silently looked over Jared and gave him a slight nod of recognition. Then, without prompting Elo grabbed the bags of clothes and headed for the door. Perhaps he did not want to hang around too long in the group home just in case anyone got any ideas.

I carried the tub of dinosaurs while Krista held Jared's hand. We crossed the parking lot, climbed into the truck, and Elo buckled Jared into the backseat. Krista and I buckled up front, and I started the engine. Elo commented, "I've got a funny feeling about this one." He was referring to Jared.

We arrived home and loaded into the house. Elo dragged the bags of clothes up the stairs and into Jared's loft bedroom. The little boy followed along with his tub of dinosaurs. Little J was glad to have the twin bed in the play area that sat just outside of Elo's room. He looked up at Elo and said, "We can play together." His voice often sounded like that of a possessed child in a horror film.

Elo answered back, "Whatever you say kid." J's room came with a television and video game console while Elo's did not. Jared went right for the video game system and Elo headed into his room. I started back down the stairs to see what my wife had to say about our interesting day when I heard *"Ouch!"* bellow from upstairs.

I called out, "What happened?"

"The little squirt just kicked me!"

"What did you do?" They had only been up there for a few seconds. What could have possibly happened?

"Nothing, I was just coming out of my room and he ran over and kicked me in the shin."

"Next time … make sure you block!" I was not ready to play referee for an eight-year-old and a teenager. I blew it off and opened the fridge looking for a beer. It was late on a Saturday afternoon and five o'clock somewhere. My own friends were coming over for some game time on the other video game console that sat in the family room. I knew Elo would come down and join us soon enough and he could explain his side of the story then.

Chapter 12

God Fearing Folk

After the first year of initial foster parent instruction, there were 29 new mandatory hours of annual training required to maintain our license for foster care. In years past, the number of training hours was 19, which seemed like more than enough, but the new governor managed to disagree. He or the new administration determined that ten additional hours would better ensure the quality of foster care. He or they could not have been more wrong. What the new administration did not understand is that the majority of foster training is more or less, useless. Not to mention the fact that foster parents are required to work full time jobs outside of their foster care duties. Between work and caring for a child with special needs, there is little time for any additional annual training.

Fortunately, my wife was already receiving twenty of the twenty-nine hours of Continuing Education Units or CEU's for her license as a psychologist. Unfortunately, I was not receiving jack. I find it humorous that the average therapeutic foster parent is required to train fifty percent more than a licensed psychologist. Psychologists also get to include collaborative meetings towards their CEU hours, while foster parents can only submit hardcore "official" training sessions. The specifications for trainings are more stringent for foster parents than they are for your local neighborhood psychologist. It is funny; the state considers "psychologist" as a person with a job... but not the title, "foster parent."

I was ready to get moving, "Come on hon. It is time to go. The training starts in forty-five minutes!"

"I don't even know why I have to go. I'll get my hours though my LCPC license."

"Oh come on. You talked me into this foster parenting business, at least come with me for the first continued training session."

Krista retorted as she followed me out to the car. "Why do we need this continued training anyhow? Supposedly, this is not a job. I thought only jobs required continued training."

"Well, apparently this *is* a job... even if it isn't a job."

Those of us without official titles or nannies consider childcare a second job. In order to deter parents from using foster stipends as income, the state requires that all foster parents show proof of employment and W-2's. The majority of foster parents are single, and it is even more difficult for them to keep up with the balancing act of life, childcare, and foster parent training.

"Perhaps foster parenting should be considered a career in itself," Krista replied. "We're talking about one person caring for two or more children that have multiple physical or mental diagnoses."

"I know. I wish the persons writing foster care licensing requirements had done a little more research. The fact that foster kids are usually born to someone else should be a consideration. Why is it that being a foster parent is not considered a full time job? Is this where the government committee on disillusionment steps in? It seems like the state wants everyone to believe that foster children are the responsibility of the foster parents who care for them, and for the sake of political correctness, the foster parents go along with it."

"I know. Your brother-in-law Dennis told me that some states allow people to perform foster parenting without holding another "primary" job. Considering the fact that birth parents cannot, or will not do their parental duty, I do not understand why foster parenting is not simply a personal career choice. Then these children might actually get the care they need."

"Exactly, why should someone have to work at Boston Market while caring for children with special needs?" In a deep persuasive voice I continued, *"Hold on Michael. Your intravenous feeding is going to have to wait. Mommy has to pass out rotisserie chicken to fulfill her state requirements."*

"Perhaps dropping the W-2 foster care requirement would be in the best interest of the child. If it is not a nationwide requirement, then perhaps Maryland should consider the big picture. In this case, it seems like Maryland has got this requirement all wrong."

****

Krista and I arrived at the location of our sponsoring non-profit foster agency. The downtown training room was set up like a classroom with rows of desks. I looked around the room and noticed that all of the attending parents had squished together into the last two rows of tables. It was as if they were attending a Pentecostal Snake Handling Service and did not want to be too close to the snakes. My wife and I stumbled into the front row and sat down. With a look of confusion, I turned to my wife, "Why is everybody in the back? Is this a training session with a Bangladeshi Snake Charmer?"

"I don't know. It is strange. Maybe everybody knows something we don't."

We were the only couple seated in the front row. Other couples came in and immediately grabbed seats close to the exit. I looked back at several rows of seating which remained empty before the overcrowded back rows.

"Well, I guess we'll find out soon enough. If these people aren't here for the presentation, what *are* they here for?"

"Like you said… I guess we will find out soon enough. Perhaps parents just show up to earn the required hours of training?"

"If you're right, then it wouldn't even matter if the speaker was a ninety-year-old talking about foot odor."

"I guess not."

I looked around the room at groups of unenthusiastic student parents. "I think this is going to be very interesting."

A woman walked to the front of the room and addressed the group. "Sorry everybody; I have bad news. We will not hold the training on autism tonight, but we are already working on other arrangements. Please sit tight and a presentation will begin shortly."

This was the first sign of one of the many problems with foster parent training: Some speakers simply do not show up. I quickly deduced that volunteer speakers were difficult to recruit. Most of the speakers have other jobs and the foster agencies are desperate to find someone to donate time. Around the fifth time we had a training cancellation, I considered raising my hand. Perhaps I could talk about the problems with foster care, but that would be pointless. Everyone in the room was already an expert on the subject.

Back at our first training session, the foster care agency went ahead with their usual workaround. The training coordinator volunteered to perform an adlib training session. We found out that this happens more often than agencies would like to admit. Foster agencies are jumping through hoops to offer training and keep parents on track with the state required twenty-nine hours of training. These training sessions often come in two- or three-hour classroom jaunts scheduled on evenings after school or work. Many of the agency employees donate their personal time in order to perform or attend the trainings. Some do it for their own required training hours, while others volunteer and simply go beyond the call of duty.

Another parent entered the back of the room with a young child holding a coloring book. An employee of the agency spoke up, "I'm sorry Miss, but you cannot bring a child to this training. This training is for adults only."The frustrated parent offered a look of disapproval, turned around, and exited through the door, clutching her child's hand.

This presents another quandary of foster parent training: Most training does not offer childcare. Yet the issue is that foster parents cannot legally leave children alone with anyone other than a licensed foster parent. This is a problem. If everybody has to be at the training, who stays home with the kids? Both parents have to complete their required training hours, so a husband-wife team has to alternate training nights. It is a scheduling nightmare, and difficult to maintain. I will not even comment on the scheduling issues that a single foster parent must go through. Luckily, many agencies are attempting to offer childcare to address this issue. It was a good thing for us that Elo came along: He was old enough to stay home and babysit Jared.

I turned to Krista, "It's a good thing you'll get your training hours through your psychology training."

"I know. That way you can go to training while I stay home with the kids." Krista delivered a taunting smirk.

"Lucky me," I sarcastically replied.

As a workaround, foster parents can request a licensed foster care babysitter. This person is a respite care parent. Apparently, according to state requirements, Respite Parent is not a job either. Respite care means that someone with a foster parenting license babysits your kid. Funny, that sounds like a job to me.

Per year, each child comes with a number of available respite care days. Sort of like a benefit offered at "a job." This benefit does not work as intended because the people doing respite care have to be at the trainings as well. It is only helpful when you want to take a vacation and leave the kids at home. From what I have heard, summer is the busy season for respite care parents.

The training coordinator stepped to the front of the room, "Okay everybody. Let us get started! Tonight's training session is about transitioning a child into adult care." Then a social worker introduced herself and began the presentation. "Transitioning" is the foster friendly word for "moving." Little did I know that I would hear about this topic each year.

Variety is the next problem pertaining to foster parent training. There are only so many topics available to discuss before you start listening to the same sermon. Topics usually pertain to one of the numerous disorders common to foster children. Sometimes the speakers cover various topics, such as advocating for your child or assisting them with their homework.

Krista whispered in my ear, "Tell me why we have to do this training?"

"All I know is that the State of Maryland mandates the training. This way some lawyer can say, 'See… all of the foster parents have been trained.' It's some form of a legal disclaimer. If not, society runs the risk of having disgruntled birth parents join forces with money-hungry lawyers. I have been lucky enough to experience it firsthand. There are so many frivolous lawsuits initiated by the drug community that if you take one ambulance-chasing lawyer and add a dash of deadbeat mom, you get one real expensive tax-funded defense case. Birth families offer various forms of abuse which extend to the legal system."

"What's that about?" Krista asked.

"Well, I knew a lawyer who didn't chase ambulances – he chased something else, and that something else is attached to each and every one of the strippers for which he provided his pro *bono* services (no pun intended.) He was literally getting "Tit for Tat." The man enjoyed spending his spare time exchanging services with the local strippers of East Baltimore. He would help them with anything from drunk-driving charges to foster care services. Unfortunately some unlucky kids wound up back under the care of their drug-dosing stripper moms."

In many cases, foster care truly is the best life for some kids.

****

Krista and I continued our first foster care training session. We learned two things from the evening's topic, "Transitioning Foster Kids to Adulthood." One, transitioning was a huge pain in the ass, and two, you had better start transitioning early. The waiting list for funding for adult care was literally years long. What do these kids do while they wait for funding? Perhaps I would find out.

The rest of the training session continued with random stories, redirections, and complaints from a number of student parents. The substitute trainer and social worker attempted to give instructions associated with the subject at hand. The social-worker/presenter explained, "In order to allow time for DDA to process and approve required funding, you'll need to fill out the required paperwork as soon as your child turns the required age of eighteen."

Approve? I thought that funding was already available to these kids. I would think that the Developmental Disability Administration, or DDA, would be ready to receive known disabled children under their current umbrella of funding. It was not as if they had never met these kids before.

There were obvious problems with the system. Some of the kids have been under the care of the state for the past eighteen years. After all, these child cases, currently funded by Child Protective Services, or CPS, are the wards of DSS and the Department of Human Resources. You would think the agencies could make a smooth transition all by themselves. It should not take two sprinkles of magic pixie dust from a foster parent.

Should the state identify the monetary needs of a transitioning child before he or she ages out of the system? Should the state transfer the funding of a child from one government source to another? I think so! No, that would make too much sense. Instead, they have foster parents fill out lengthy complicated forms and then instruct foster parents to sign off on authorization. Foster parents follow these instructions and sign away, never mind the fact that they cannot legally do so. Why? Because the foster parents are not the legal guardians of the child, DSS is. The useless forms come back denied. It is a wonderfully designed circle of tax dollar spending.

As the speaker began to veer off the topic, I whispered to my wife, "What the hell are these people talking about?"

A foster mother in the back called out. Perhaps she had something to contribute to the funding topic at hand. She began to ramble, "I have this one child. He is crazy. He just wants to run around and never come home. One time he decided to cut off all his little brother's hair. I don't know what he's thinking. I think he's got that OPD thing. He's always fighting and running. I need to get that boy on some more meds."

The attending foster parents often have plenty of comments to make, and many of those comments often make absolutely no sense at all. Sometimes the parents even get into arguments with one another over any number of trivial issues. Their comments and arguments are completely unrelated to the topic of discussion. I watched two foster moms argue about whether or not it is okay to call a teenager "baby." One mother clamored, "My babies always need a break when doing their homework."

The second mother answered back, "You need to stop calling those teenagers, *babies*. I heard that if you do that, they will never grow up."

"I can call my kids babies if I want to! They will always be my babies!" the first mother angrily exclaimed. It was like a bad episode of Jerry Springer. Fortunately, the fight fizzled out before it turned into an all out brawl. The speaker redirected the parents and the training eventually continued.

Herein lies another problem with foster parent trainings: We students are often not on par with the subject at hand. Perhaps if that day's topic had been "The Psychology of Childhood Nicknames," our conversation would have made more sense.

The foster parents of Baltimore City are good, simple, God-fearing folk. Sticking them in repetitive training sessions is not helping anyone, especially them. Perhaps completing a checklist of courses might be a better approach to foster parent requirements. Once a particular course is complete, no one would ever take it again. It would be orderly and designed, like that of a college degree. In ten years, I would have enough training hours to receive a PhD in specialized childcare. Some of the parents surrounding me in this training session had already been foster parents for over twenty years.

I turned to Krista. "What was the governor thinking about when he signed the increase in training hours?"

"I'm not sure, but it couldn't have been the benefits provided by these additional training hours."

In many ways, the state government has made conditions worse for foster agencies and foster parents. As the budget tightens, so do the audits. If agencies are in violation of their requirements, then the state government has a valid reason to deny funding. If that happens then the state might budget all of the tax money to compliant state run programs. I imagine there would be a lot less audits once the money is solely in the hands of the auditors. As always, it is all about the money.

Chapter 13

School Daze

After the weekend of Jared's arrival, I began the task of enrolling both kids into school. I worked nights, so I handled the job of running around to the schools during the day. Jared's social worker handled the details of enrolling him into a Level 5 school called Charlesbrook, an elementary school with a multi-age magnet program. Students found themselves placed into classrooms dependent upon their educational level and not solely by grade. Level 5 meant that Jared required 'substantial educational intervention.' He had missed kindergarten and most of the first grade so he was far behind the age-appropriate curriculum. I enrolled him as a first grader, but Jared was still learning on a kindergarten level. With any luck, the bus would pick him up at the corner of our street.

Elo's educational story had traversed several chapters before it ended with him settling in at the local high school. First, we traveled to Northern High in northeast Baltimore City to have Elo removed from their roster of students. The school looked rundown and in disrepair. We walked towards the front of the building. At this point, the school administration believed he was just another kid who had gone AWOL. Rumor has it that this was a frequent occurrence at Northern High.

"Well, here we are. Welcome back!"

"Yep, it looks just like I remember."

The school was everything that Elo had described. As we walked towards the entrance, I looked at the buses parked along the front of the school. This was the place where Elo had described a kid falling from a bus window. We entered the front lobby where a security officer took my driver's license and my information. The guard asked me, "You his social worker?"

I smiled and replied, "No. I'm his dad." The guard gave me an odd look and pointed us in the direction of the school guidance department. I wondered about the kind of guidance one received from Northern High School: "Don't go to the bathroom alone, keep your head down, and watch for stray bullets, or, don't... do... drugs... unless you buy them from the school store?" I followed Elo down a hallway alongside of the school cafeteria and caught an out-of-place scent. It was the smell of marijuana.

"I told you so." Elo looked back at me and smiled. Anytime somebody said those words to me, I was not any place that I wanted to be.

I should have requested that Krista run this little errand. Northern High School was right down the road from her old alma mater, Mercy High School. I imagine her all-female Catholic high school had a very different population of students. The halls of Northern High were completely empty and the doorways into the rooms, closed. It looked like the place was on lockdown.

An administrator paroled the hallways, perhaps searching for the source of the marijuana winds. Elo and I eventually came to a doorway with a paper sign marked "Guidance." A heavyset woman, the guidance counselor, sat squeezed in behind an old metal desk. I whispered into Elo's ear, "Is that the lady who decides your future over dinner, or the lady who serves you Sloppy Joe at lunch, or perhaps *both?*"

Elo replied, "Hopefully neither."

A row of chairs next to the woman's desk served as a waiting room. I sat down and informed her of our intention to discharge Elo from the high school. The counselor gave him an insidious glance of envy. He was the lucky one who was getting out of Northern Penitentiary on good behavior. The counselor was currently helping a young woman with plans to enroll in beauty school and we were all sitting in this tight room together. Other than a snide expression, the counselor failed to acknowledge our arrival.

Due to my personal exposure to Broadway musicals, compliments of my wife, the song *Beauty School Dropout* had popped into my head. It was a show tune favorite from the musical *Grease.* I sat there waiting and wondered how many girls at this school went by the nickname "Pinky."

About forty-five minutes later the guidance counselor was ready to assist us. The young beautician exited the small room and we pulled up two chairs at the desk.

The woman abruptly asked, "What are you here for?"

I replied, "Elo is transferring to a school in the county and needs the discharge paperwork from Northern."

"Here, fill these out." The woman slid a packet of forms across the table.

She took all of Elo's information after we filled out the forms. Moments later, the discharge was official and he was no longer an inmate of Northern High school. He could finally retire his orange jumpsuit and his life was now moving in a positive direction. He knew this new transition was for the best, and coincidentally it occurred just in time. Soon thereafter, Northern High School was officially decommissioned.

The next step was to enroll Elo at Overly Manor High School, the school near our home. His social worker assisted in the enrollment process. Overly Manor was right down the road from our Violetville postal stop, and the kids there were average middle-class students. In other words, they used filtered bongs to smoke their marijuana. The process to enroll Elo was easier than the process to release him from Northern High School. His new principal was a no-nonsense man who gave us a stern warning about the rules of his campus. He sat behind his desk and exhaled deeply while reading Elo's rap sheet. My foster son had a propensity to get into fights over the past few years, all documented in his paperwork. Fighting was almost a prerequisite at some of his former schools. The principal scoured over the papers before him and uttered, "I don't tolerate any fighting in my school. I hope you don't plan to come in here and start any trouble."

I immediately spoke up in Elo's defense. "Sir, I'm sure you'll find that Elo is a great kid. He hasn't been in a single fight since I've known him." I had known Elo less than a month, but my statement still held true.

"Who are you – his social worker?"

"No, but I've been getting a lot of that lately. I'm his foster dad, Matt." Elo sat quietly with his shoulders slouched. He had the mannerisms of a rejected young man. "You're not going to fight anybody… isn't that right Elo?"

Elo looked up and shook his head left to right. "No Sir!" he forcefully replied while keeping his eyes low like a dog displaying a submissive posture. His voice was solemn and filled with concern.

I spoke up again. "He's a lover, not a fighter."

The principal's demeanor lightened with a smile. He answered with a laugh, "Alright then. I will see you next week. I'll be keeping my eyes on you."

Elo looked up and assertively replied. "Yes sir!"

As we rose and walked down the hallway, I could feel the weight of concern lifting from Elo's shoulders, and mine as well. He did not want to let me down, and he had not. For me, I was just glad I could check school enrollment off our long list of "things to do."

So far being Elo's foster parent had been rather simple. He was a great cook, and I never even had to worry about any social worker visits. The Baltimore City worker had not shown up except once since the day that Elo first arrived on our doorstep. The private agency worker, Arlene Fitzpatrick, completed the monthly agency visits and she was as sweet as pie. I always enjoyed our monthly meeting with Arlene.

****

We reached the end of the month and Elo had taken on a few duties around the house. He was handling the trash and bringing in the mail. Elo delivered the day's mail directly from the mailbox to the kitchen. I stood in the kitchen speaking with Krista as Elo dug through the refrigerator. The monthly newsletter from our foster care agency had arrived and was laying on the countertop. It contained a myriad of information such as the dates for upcoming foster parent training and other bits of news like "The Foster Parent of the Month." Secretly, I hoped it would be me!

My wife and I were curious to see if we even made the runner-up list considering our Christmas Eve transition for Elo, not to mention our lengthy transitional efforts concerning Jared. Krista raised the newsletter and read back the announcement for all to hear, "And…the foster parent of the month for January is… Ms. Cullen!"

"What!" I exclaimed.

Krista turned to Elo and asked, "Wasn't that your last foster mom?"

He replied, "Yep."

I added, "The one that *threw you out* on Christmas Eve!"

"Yep," he replied again. I am not sure how long I stood there with my mouth hanging wide open, but I am sure it was long enough for flies to reproduce on the back of my tongue.

I continued, "You've got to be kidding me! Is this how you win foster parent of the month by kicking kids out on Christmas Eve?" Krista and I stood in utter disbelief, but Elo did not seem to be surprised. He had been in the role of foster child for far too long and had seen hypocrisy at its best. Krista and I were still relatively new to the system and hopefully optimistic – in other words, naïve. I should have known that awards require more than merit alone. Like many aspects of life, awards go to the person who complains the most or who knows the right people. Nothing made sense in this wild world of foster care.

"Man I wish I could playback some of the jacked up things I've seen and gone through during the holidays," Elo later stated. "It's enough to make any man, woman, or child cry. I'm just going to leave it at that."

****

A month later, I received my first call from the school principal that managed the hallways of Overly Manor High. He had bad news concerning Elo and asked me if I could come down to see him at the end of the day. Nervously, I drove to the school for my second meeting with the principal. He invited me into his office and offered me the seat next to my foster son. Elo looked up at me with an egregious smile. I had the feeling bad news was on the way. The principal had some great things to say about Elo, but in the end gave us the cold, hard facts. I sat back into my chair as he began his explanation.

"Elo has been a great student here at Overly Manor. We love having him and he has been true to his word, absolutely no trouble at all, but we have run into a snag. There is a legal stipulation that does not allow Elo to remain here at Overly Manor. There is a student here at Overly Manor that had a previous relationship with Elo. He is a former foster brother, and the two of them cannot remain in the same school. After speaking with the student's legal counsel, we agreed that Elo must transfer. Our staff has researched the matter and it appears as though the information is correct. I am very sorry. Again, it has been a pleasant experience having Elo at our school. We are all very proud of his progress in the short time he has been with us." Elo sat back into his chair wearing a depressed look of rejection. This was another bump in his road of life, a road in desperate need of new pavement.

"Thank you. I understand, and we appreciate the explanation, but what do we have to do now?"

"I've taken care of it. The paperwork, already submitted to Keylong High School, is waiting for you in their guidance department. He can start there on Monday but you will need to go see a guidance counselor to work out the details of his class schedule." Elo shook the principal's hand one last time and we walked out of the front door together.

Once we reached the car, I asked Elo about this unusual issue concerning a former foster brother. He gave me the details of an old foster placement. The former foster brother made a false report of abuse directed towards Elo. Fearing the foster father, the actual abuser, the boy said that Elo was the person guilty of abuse. Even though I only knew Elo for two months, I had no doubt that he was the innocent scapegoat of this story. He had never lied to me, and I do not think he ever would.

The incident in his former foster home was not the first time Elo took responsibility for some irresponsible adult. That all started the day he landed in foster care with instructions to look after his little brother. We moved on and it was time for round three of Elo's enrollment in the Baltimore County Public School System. I was getting a lot of practice and it seemed easier as we went along. This time the new principal was expecting a well-behaved young man, and he did not even sit us down to run through Elo's rap sheet.

Keylong High School touted its academic achievement and Elo would have to deliver. They advertised their exceptional SAT scores across the school marquee. Honor student enrollment was at an all-time high and Elo would have to raise his game. With only four months of school left, our goal was to make sure graduation happened. The main problem was that Elo's previous twelve years of school did not intend to make sure graduation happened, at least not to Keylong High's standards – so my wife and I would have to do extra tutoring to ensure a spring graduation.

We worked to help Elo with his final course credits. He needed to pass his final English class in order to graduate. Without success in English, he would not be able to receive a High School Diploma that spring. Thank goodness, Krista was a former English teacher. Back then, the motivation to write was not in me, so it was up to her. Before Elo could walk across the stage, the school required that he write one final ten-page paper. Ugh!

Chapter 14

Disney Fixes Everything

Along with everything else going on in our world, we were simultaneously working on another huge aspect of foster care – namely bio-visits. Unlike Elo, Jared's foster plan was only temporary. The current goal for him was biological reunification; Jared was to return to his birth mother once she was fully functioning and back on her feet. To do so she required proof of permanent residency and evidence that she had overcome whatever problem or habit she had previously faced.

A bio-visit, scheduled later in the week, was just around the corner. Krista and I discussed the visits and decided that I should be the one to handle them. We theorized that it would make more sense for a father figure to bring Jared to an appointment with his birth mom. This way there would be no chance of hearing the words, "You're not his mother! I'm his mother!" My goal was to build good rapport with birth mom for more than just the obvious reasons. We needed her to sign off on many forms, including the reduction in Little J's psychotropic medication. I was hoping to see the clear blue eyes that hid behind the boy's glossy overlay.

Thinking back to my own bio-family, I imagined that the upcoming bio-visit had the potential of a Jerry Springer episode. Being a large alpha male, I was the safe bet if the meeting turned into a smack down with the boy's relatives. The social worker set up the first meeting, which was to take place the following week at the DSS central office. My job was simply to arrive at the office, take Jared into a little room, and leave him with his assigned social worker.

The most important factor of the bio-visit was to tell Jared as little as possible. As far as he knew, he was just going for a visit with the social worker. It would be a nice surprise when birth mom magically appeared. I had the option of watching through the room's two-way mirror, and accepted this opportunity so that I could eavesdrop with a view. I was curious to see, and possibly meet, the mother of the little boy under my care.

The social worker met with Little J while I waited for a half hour in the room next door. Eventually the worker ended the meeting and told us we could leave. She bid farewell and gave Jared a wave goodbye. His mother had not shown up, but Jared was not sad because he never even knew that she was supposed to be there. This visit was simply a fun day at the DSS office. Perhaps next time we would go to the zoo.

****

After hearing Elo's story about life on the streets, I decided to give Jared my own version of downtown survival camp. I taught him how to cross a busy street, how he should pay attention to those around him, and explained that he should "never talk to strangers."

He replied, "I don't know any strangers."

"Exactly."

"Exactly what?"

"Never mind Jared... never mind..."

He learned the importance of using a can opener in case he ever found himself in a position that required one. I stuffed him full of meals and created a junk drawer of food we referred to as the "snack drawer." Here he could eat as much as possible, whenever he was hungry. He was a scrawny little kid and I wanted to bulk him up before he returned to the streets of Patterson Park.

I damn near considered buying him nunchucks for his own protection and eventually enrolled him in a Kung Fu class. Next, I helped him memorize our home phone number and taught him the important use of the numbers 9-1-1. I informed the naïve boy about the nasty facts of life, including the reality of bad people in the world.

"Jared, you need to understand that there are bad people in the world."

"Like Swiper from Dora the Explorer?"

"Well, not exactly. Swiper is a cartoon fox. What I'm talking about are people like kidnappers."

"That's silly. It is okay for kids to nap. I took lots of naps at the cottage."

"Never mind Jared... never mind..." My goal was to prepare Jared for his future lifestyle, to harden him up, and to make him more like Elo. In Jared's case, this was not going to be an easy task.

Elo joined the conversation. "Jared, napping has nothing to do with kidnappers."

"What do you mean?" Jared inquired.

"I mean, a nap is a siesta… and kidnappers are creeps who steal little kids."

"So you are saying that a C-S- something, is a creepy sleepy person?" Elo shook his head in disbelief. "Forget about it Jared."

Reluctantly I rejoined this comedy of errors, "Elo, sometimes you just have to draw a line with Jared."

Jared had an answer to my comment. "Ha! I don't even draw!"

I rolled my eyes, walked away, and drew a line for myself.

Elo was sometimes frustrated with Jared, but he was still a great role model for his little foster brother. He regularly gave Jared the 4-1-1 on the reality of life in foster care. His first bit of advice was, 'Never leave Matt and Krista!' My wife and I both took this as a huge compliment considering the fact that Elo had been around the fostering block.

****

As we moved through our first winter with the boys, school was going well for both kids. Jared received passing grades and had no behavioral problems in his new classroom. Things were not the same for the classmates around him. The first sign of problems in class appeared in the form of a new shirt that had come home from school on Jared's back. For the first time since he started at Charlesbrook, he returned home from school wearing something other than a dinosaur t-shirt. This new shirt arrived with a note attached. It read, '*We apologize for the shirt. You will find Jared's shirt, soiled and packed inside of his book bag. There was a problem with another child and a container of Jell-O.*' Jared had met his first bully. Perhaps being in a Level 5 school was not such a good thing for Little J after all. I asked him, "Are there a lot of kids throwing Jell-O at school?"

He answered back, "No but they're thowin' all sorts of stuff."

"Like what?" I asked.

He continued, "Chairs, desks, pencils, food… all sorts of stuff." Things were wild and crazy at Charlesbrook Elementary. A couple of weeks later his class picture arrived and that picture did tell a thousand words. I could see a wild look in the eyes of the children in the portrait. If nothing else, Charlesbrook might help to make Jared tough.

****

Soon it was time for the next bio-visit with Jared's mom. We had already taken Little J to his pediatrician, and pending a few signatures, we had authorization to stop two of his three happy pills. Krista picked out Jared's clothing and fixed his hair before I loaded him into the truck. It was time for the next visit with the "social worker."

Twenty minutes later, I hauled him into DSS and left him in the visitation room. I went to my post in the room next door and stood behind the two-way mirror. This time birth mom had arrived. I sat in the observation room and watched in fascination as the social worker and birth mom spent time with Little J. There was not a huge explosion of emotion as I originally imagined. It had been well over six months since their separation but no one broke down into tears. Birth mom quietly entered the room, said hello, and watched Jared as he played with the toys. She directed him to come over and gave him a hug.

Birth mom was the taller female version of Little J. She stood around five and a half feet tall and appeared younger than a teen. I did the math in my head. She gave birth to Jared at fourteen or fifteen and he was now eight, so she must be somewhere around the age of twenty-two. Her soft voice, gentle smile, and dirty blond hair were the same as her son. As she spoke, she moved around the room, and I recognized her mannerisms. They were the same as Little J. He walked over to her, gave her a hug, and went back to playing with his selected toy.

The social worker asked Jared questions about school and his new home, like "How do you like living with the Hoffmans?"

"I get to play with Spyro."

"Oh, is that one of their dogs?"

"No."

"Then who is Spyro… a cat?"

"He's a dragon."

The worker replied with a raised eyebrow. "Oh, okay."

The little boy gave puzzling but positive replies to each question as he continued playing with his toy. A half hour later and the visit had ended. Everything had gone well. Birth mom departed and the social worker sat down for a few more questions with Little J. His mom gave him a little gift which he enjoyed opening and would forever covet. He tightly hugged an odd T-Rex dinosaur with an oversized head. The toy appeared to have some special needs of its own.

****

Everything was going well at home with the boys. Elo and Jared continued to perform notably in their new schools and Krista and I had no reason to complain. We both believed in the methods of positive reinforcement and our first big reward was about to be announced. My wife and I booked our vacation timeshare for Daytona Beach and Disney World. Neither of the boys had ever been outside of Baltimore and I could not wait to take them somewhere exciting and new. I wanted to show them, especially

Elo, that the world had more to offer than Baltimore's Inner Harbor. Spring Break arrived and we had eight full days to travel down to Florida and back. We loaded up the truck and got on our way driving south into the dusk.

Before the sun had set, we had traveled the first hour towards Florida. We came upon a magnificent site that rests along the Washington Beltway, an awe-inspiring bit of architecture called the Mormon Tabernacle. The building's tall white towers spiral almost thirty stories into the sky, the exterior sheathed in one hundred and seventy-three thousand square feet of Alabama white marble. From the top of the tallest spire, a golden statue of the angel Gabriel is sounding his trumpet for all to see.

I pointed to the Tabernacle and called back to Jared who was sitting upright in the backseat, "Look! The Magic Kingdom! We're there!"

Jared's eyes lit up with excitement as he cried out in a high-pitched squeal, "Yeah! When do we get to see Mickey Mouse?" Elo bore an expression that illustrated confusion. Both boys began to peer through the windows of the truck's passenger side.

"We'll get there in about sixteen more hours! *Yeah!* That is the Mormon Tabernacle! *Yeeeeaaaah!*" I was repeating an old prank my father had once played on me. Twenty years later and I finally tricked my own little sucker.

Elo chimed in with his infinite wisdom, "I knew that."

"Sure you did Elo. Sure you did."

Jared chimed in, "Sixteen more hours? How much longer is that?"

I responded simply, "Patience Jared, patience."

****

Krista and Jared slept in the backseat while Elo kept me company in the front of the cab. He was a night owl and happy to stay awake while I drove through the evening hours. At home, he stayed up late, cooking, and feeding scraps to the dogs. He had managed to turn Sadie into quite the beggar, far worse than any begging dog of Athens.

As we drove through the night, we had long philosophical discussions about life and death, the rich and the poor. The only other sound was the hum of the truck wheels along the asphalt. The travelled road presented heartrending material for discussion including, unfortunately, a highway road accident that left dead bodies in its wake. As the sun rose, we had much to reflect upon.

"Why are you doing this?" Elo asked.

"Because I'm the only person awake that also happens to have a driver's license." Elo was referring to this trip to Disney World. I had only been his foster father for a few months and to this day, no foster parent had ever taken him anywhere significant.

"You know what I mean ... . All this."

"I just want to give you something that my parents gave me, other than canned goods. I want you to see that there is more to life than the streets of Baltimore. For example, there is Main Street in downtown Walt Disney World. Besides, I love to travel and now I have an excuse to go back to Disney World. The last time that forsaken Dumbo ride screwed me over. I waited for an hour, then it started to rain Aristocats and Plutos... and then they shut the ride down. Dumbo still owes me a flight with his magic feather. In fact, I can think of a few dumbos that still owe me a flight with a magic feather." Elo laughed and seemed content with my explanation. I was not about to get gushy with him. He was far more emotional and deeper than I was. What I explained to Elo is that which lay on the surface. I have always been comfortable staying on the surface.

What I did not explain was the underlying motivation for participating in foster care and my reason for taking him to Disney World. The reason I was doing "all this" had more to do with my personal belief in karma. Raised in an odd, yet privileged manner, I wanted to "give back." Both sides of my family had struggled through the Great Depression and each had their own story of neglect, abuse, and abandonment. Perhaps I could help an orphan rise from the pit of the abandoned and abused.

As we continued driving along I-95, I inadvertently drifted off into thought, thoughts that were below the surface. *My father's mother, Hattie, had lost her parents as a young girl and she spent much of her youth in a German orphanage. She eventually managed to escape the dubious fate of post World War I German orphans by catching a ride on a ship towards Ellis Island. Now that took courage... although I do not think she had much of a choice. Working as an indentured servant, she found her way onto the streets of Chicago and later she spent much of her life volunteering to care for the sick at a local hospital.*

After she died, my uncle discovered a secret safety deposit box. Inside was a sum of money, several news articles, and a note. The note detailed specific instructions for spending the money on her funeral, as well as financing for a countrywide family reunion. The news articles had titles such as 'Mar. 18, 1918: Unknown Illness Kills Forty-six at Fort Riley, Kansas,' 'Oct. 31, 1918: Kaiser Wilhelm Falters as German Casualties Reach All-Time High,' and 'Nov. 11, 1918: Woodrow Wilson Signs, Ending War!'

Even though I hardly knew Grandma Hattie, I still yearned to connect with her. I only met her several times before she died. I remember a time when she came to stay with us, back when my father was battling cancer. At age eight, I wanted nothing more than to impress her. After rummaging through a costume box, I dressed myself as a German soldier. The cap I adorned was an old World War I infantry helmet. I paraded into the living room and Grandma Hattie dropped to her knees. She sobbed profusely and tears poured down her face. There were many things about Grandma Hattie I never understood, including the ways I could make her proud. Then I snapped out of my reverie and emerged back in the present, still driving south towards Florida.

Our conversation remained on the surface. I turned to Elo, "Speaking of Grandmothers, Grammy will be joining us in Orlando."

"Speaking of what, huh?"

"Yea, we're picking up Grammy on Wednesday at the Orlando Airport."

"Oh… cool. Good times with Grammy."

From a tired haze I replied, "Yep… Good times."

We fell silent as the drive continued. This vacation was as much about me as it was about the kids. I could get back to Disney World and my mommy could finally take me on the Dumbo ride, but there was more to it than that. Over the last four months, my mother and Elo had developed a friendly relationship. It was nice to see both of them enjoying each other's company. Elo needed a grandmother, and my mother needed a friend.

What a pair they made. They both liked to cook, and my mother talked endlessly for hours while Elo enjoyed listening. For whatever reason, they matched up well. It warmed my frozen heart to see them enjoying each other's company. My mother particularly enjoyed her senior citizen outings to the local Bob Evans with her new foster grandson.

After daybreak, Krista awoke and took the wheel for the rest of the journey. We had about two more hours before reaching Daytona Beach and I slept in the back until we arrived at our beachfront hotel. Visiting Daytona Beach and Disney World on the same trip was like killing two birds with one stone. The boys could have their first trip to the beach as well as their first trip to see Mickey Mouse.

Perhaps Elo would even get a taste of *Spring Break.* I know that I planned to do some Spring Break sightseeing. Afterwards we would head over to Orlando and hit some of the area amusement parks. In Daytona, we had a great time in the ocean and an even better time in the waves, just after I taught Elo and Jared how to swim within the safety of the warm hotel pool. Krista enjoyed lying out in the sun. She read and relaxed while I kept the boys busy on the beach.

After three days at the beach, we packed up and took a short drive to Orlando's Airport. We picked up Grammy and headed to our hotel complex on International Drive. The next few days, filled with rigorous hikes through Orlando amusement parks, kept everyone busy. We hit a number of parks and Grammy's wheelchair came in handy. Her handicapped status pushed us to the front of each long Spring Break line. Elo pushed her around in the wheelchair and the joke of the trip was referring to Grammy as 'Ms. Daisy.' Elo smiled and laughed. He seemed to have transitioned smoothly into this vacation lifestyle.

My mother's first trip without my father had gone smoothly as well, and she had an overall good time. Krista particularly enjoyed an animal safari at one of the parks. Jared liked the robotic dinosaurs displayed in Dinoland, USA. The kid was in dinosaur heaven. I was just glad to see everyone happy. This trip was what everyone needed, but even the wonders of Disney World and the serenity of the beach could not completely mask the problems of life in foster care. At one point on the trip, each of our boys had a run-in with confusing emotional issues.

Near the end of the trip, Elo simply broke down at the dinner table. We were having a family meal in a nice Italian restaurant along International Drive, and the scene was right out of an Olive Garden commercial before Elo had his first foster care flashback. As we ordered our meal, he cried out, "I can't eat here." I brushed off the waiter and asked him to return in a few minutes.

"Why?" Grammy asked, "Why can't you eat here?"

Elo said nothing. He sat tense and silent, contemplating his position in this carefree world of happiness, fun, and family outings. It was too much, too soon, and too good to be true. What would happen if it all ended tomorrow? Elo stood up and exited the restaurant.

Immediately, Krista rose, following behind him. Minutes later, she returned alone. "He just needs some time to himself right now."

Our meals arrived and we ate them in awkward silence, while Elo took some time to reflect. I hoped that he could adjust to the many changes going on in his life. Four months ago, he was hiding in a basement to avoid classes at Northern High School and now he was eating posh food on vacation in Florida. Elo, an impoverished young man who had only known the struggles of the inner city life had become overwhelmed.

Suddenly, he found himself engulfed in change – he was about to graduate high school, had just experienced his first Spring Break, and was living a different life, with a different family, for an undetermined period of time. Additionally, his new family was white. He was adjusting to cultural changes as well. We had different rules and different expectations for him then he had previously experienced. It was no wonder he felt insecure and was flipping out. Was this new lifestyle really for him? Unlike today's entitled generation, he wondered, 'Do I really belong here?' His classmates and peers certainly thought he did, but did he?

****

In the other corner, Jared confronted his confusing foster issue near the end of the trip. We had packed up and were driving home on the road towards Maryland when Jared had his first foster child revelation. After spending two days in a dinosaur dream world, he began to open up. The substance of his usual ramblings had slightly improved, so to find out more about Little J we asked some questions about his birth family. Coincidentally, the bulk of his ethnicity stemmed from Polish and Irish descendents, very much like my wife. We ran into a conversational snag when I inadvertently informed Jared that his Polish birth father was Gerald Mean Jean. He was under the false impression that his father was a completely different individual. Jared believed that the father of his half sister was his father as well, but the proof was in the pudding.

I pointed out to Jared, "You and Gerald Mean Jean have the same last name."

"*No!* That's not right!"

At that moment, his world came crashing down upon him. The realization of his true birth father had more than one effect. First, it meant that his birth mom had not been completely accurate about his short past.

"*How could she not have told me?*" he pondered.

It was probably to save him from some ugly truth. Second, it meant that the man who fathered his sister, Logan Hammersmith, was not actually his real dad. All along, he thought he knew his actual birth father. Third, it meant that Gerald Mean Jean was his own flesh and blood.

The little boy broke down into tears as he cried out, "*No!* It isn't true!"

I responded to him candidly, "I'm sorry to say that it is, and I'll tell you something else…everything that I am going to tell you will be the truth. Other adults may lie to you, including friends and relatives, but I will not. You will only be able to make good decisions if you know the truth. Other people may not always make good decisions, and lying is *always* a bad decision. With the truth, you will at least have a chance to make your own decisions, good or bad."

Tears poured down Jared's face as he turned and hid in the corner of the truck's backseat. As I watched him through the rearview mirror he glanced back in my direction, giving a look drenched with contempt. In that moment, he hated everything about me, and hated every word that had come from my mouth.

Elo motioned towards Jared, attempting to comfort him, but Jared shrugged away and curled up in the corner of the backseat. Over time, Little J perked up, and began to act as if nothing ever happened. He sat with glossy eyes and a content smile, determined to live within the confines of his false reality.

I did not want to teach Jared that life was not the Cinderella story of his imagination. I did not want to teach him that in reality *life is not fair*. Sometimes the truth hurts, but Jared needed the truth. I could not sugarcoat the sad fact that addiction and irresponsibility had transformed his life. It would be easy for both of us to avoid the truth, but if I did not take the blinders off Jared's eyes, then I would be guilty of blinding him myself.

At age thirty, I was still learning various truths about my own family – the abandonment of my grandmother, the struggles of her children, and ongoing generations of alcoholism. The details of my own family genealogy inspired me to be a source of truth for my children. Jared believed in a false reality derived from generations of family addiction and shame. I would want someone tell me the truth about my life long before misinformation transforms into permanent memory. Many children in foster care live under thick clouds of lies and misinformation and I felt obligated to ensure that my children would not.

Chapter 15

The Dad Ate My Homework

Spring Break was over, the kids were back in school, and instructions arrived for Elo's final term paper. This was the big project required for graduation. Since my wife had been a high school English teacher, she was able to help Elo with the paper. She and Elo worked away on the body of the paper. A week later, they were near the end of the project. They sat working on the paper using a computer located in our guest bedroom and the two fit into the room quite perfectly. Fortunately, there was no room for a third writer.

The only thing left was to complete the loose ends of the assignment. These loose ends included a table of contents and a bibliography. Burned out from the paper, Krista requested that I take over for the final stretch. The table of contents was no problem. I breezed through, typing away as Elo read back the titled sections of the paper. The bibliography was a different animal. I composed what I knew to be a working bibliography. When writing papers in high school and college I had never had a problem writing a bibliography, but this teacher's standards were extremely high. It took a few hours but Elo and I came up with what I considered a functional bibliography.

Joyously, I informed Krista that my part of the project was complete. "It's all done!"

Krista entered the room to look over my portion of the assignment. This was never good, but inevitable. The former English teacher was coming with a ruler in hand to check the quality of my work.

She sternly inquired, "What the heck is this? Did you even read the instructions?" The answer to that question would be *no,* but I was not about to admit that to her. She continued to look over the document while pointing out the obvious flaws.

"It'll work. It works for me. Does it work for you Elo?" Elo cautiously nodded his head in approval.

"Well it won't work for his teacher! Look at the list of requirements. It has to be exactly... what... the... teacher... says. She is ten times stricter than I!" That is like saying Genghis Khan was stricter than Stalin. If this teacher was an English Nazi, Krista was her *kamerad*. I scanned over the list of requirements. It was longer than the Declaration of Independence *and* more confusing to boot. This teacher was prepping her students for a job with the Library of Congress and all I wanted to do was make sure Elo did not end up with a GED.

Krista continued, "You're just going to have to start over."

She fiddled over the rules of the proper work-cited bibliography format as my frustration grew. After hours of working on this section of the term paper, I was not about to *start over*. I did what came naturally – or at least what came naturally to me. Before Krista could utter another word, I reached out and snatched the requirement paper from her hand. I crumpled it up, stuffed it into my mouth, and began to chew away. I would be damned before I would write this thing a second time and I would rather eat it then listen to Krista read off the teacher's requirements. As long as this ridiculous list of instructions existed, Krista would force me to rewrite the bibliography.

I muffled out, "Screw 'er damn 'nstructions. I's good 'nough!" I was fired up and red in the face. My audience fell to the floor laughing hysterically as I munched on the midday snack that came about because of my frustration.

Krista broke into tears of laughter. "Don't swallow it!"

I had every intention to do just that, but she was right. I spat out the clumped ball of sopping words and walked out of the room! "Screw it!" I said.

Krista tried to pull herself together and muster a straight face. "What are we going to do now? We can't go get another set of instructions."

"So what, he'll lose a few points on the bibliography! I am sure the main paper, *that you worked on,* will give him plenty of points."

She knew I was right. "Okay, but what will he tell his teacher? He's supposed to hand in the requirements page with the paper!" Elo looked at me for an answer.

I said, "If she asks any questions he can say that the foster dad ate it! After all, he'd be telling the truth!"

The next day Elo turned in the paper. As I predicted, he only lost a few points for the improperly formatted bibliography, and the teacher never asked him why. Even considering the complex homework assignments, fostering Elo was still the easiest job I ever had. I wondered if the city social worker would ever show up. Evidently, he was an easy case for her as well. With the numerous ongoing appointments we had for Jared, I certainly did not mind her visitation no-shows. Elo had one appointment with his agency worker once a month. Jared had two social worker visits, a bio-visit, and a monthly medication appointment. Next, each foster child's lawyer visited as well. Later, there would be sibling visits. To keep up with all the visitors I needed to install a revolving front door. On top of the visitors, my wife and I were also trying to schedule in our ongoing training. Before we could blink, it was a new year and new training hours were once again required.

****

The time had come for another bio-visit with Jared and his birth mother. As usual, I drove him to the DSS office for his date with the social worker. This time the worker wanted me to sit in on the visit. The main goal of foster parenting is reunification, but this is not always the best scenario for a child. In Jared's case there was the possibility that his birth mom would not successfully achieve the goals laid out for her by the Department of Social Services. I was growing attached to Little J and wanted the best for him either way. If Jared's mom was not ready to take him back, he could stay with us for as long as he needed to.

Today, I would directly interact with his birth mother for the first time. Jared and I sat down in the visitation room. The small, dimly lit room echoed a bit and was full of scattered toys. There was also a shelf of old board games like *Trouble* and *Life*.

"Is my mom coming today?"

She was running a little late and I could sense his growing anxiety. "I think so."

"Is she bringing me a present?"

"Uh, I don't know. I guess we'll find out."

She arrived about twenty minutes later and was apologetic about her lateness. She was very pleasant and Jared began searching for his newest gift. She handed him a bag with a toy and he immediately started playing with it in the corner.

Along with the toy, she gave Little J a crayon stick-figure picture that she had drawn of Jared and his half sister Stephanie. In the picture, they were sitting on a swing alongside birth mom and a male figure labeled Logan Hammersmith. She and Logan were obviously the parents in the picture. They were standing next to a stick figure house. I held the picture up for J and told him that we could put it into a frame once we got back to our own stick figure cape cod.

Overall, the visit went well. Birth mom was very gracious and thanked me for my service as Jared's foster dad. She was glad that he now had a positive male role model in his life. The visit went much better than I expected. No bouncers were required and nobody went out in handcuffs. Birth mom was very friendly!

I soon realized that the social worker incorporated me into the visitation for a specific reason. She wanted birth mom and me to work out visitation for ourselves and gave us the option to manage our own visitation at a local mall or a nearby McDonalds. This also meant the social worker was no longer required to reserve a room at DSS, and it freed up time on her visitation schedule.

We all agreed on the new arrangement. It was the best scenario for each of us. On the next visit, Jared and I could simply pick up birth mom at the Owings Mills metro station and go somewhere local for a short visit. This meant the visitation commute would be shorter for me as well. That was one more benefit of the new arrangement as regular trips to the Baltimore County DSS office were inconvenient and cumbersome.

****

Along with foster parent duties that included schoolwork and arranging visitation appointments, there were other issues related to everyday parenting. We had trouble with two particular situations: the school bus driver and neighbor relations. Both were unpredictable and both were a big pain in the ass. In our case, the Baltimore County bus assigned to Jared was extremely undependable. It never came at the same time, and sometimes it never came at all. When it did actually arrive, and arrive on time, it was as if Jared was receiving a little present.

When we complained to the school, the driver would deny our accusations. It was his word against ours. Some days I would actually see the bus miss our stop as it barreled down Wilkens Avenue. I would call the school to complain but the complaints came to no avail. The driver would lie straight-faced and tell the school that he stopped at our bus stop. He missed our stop purely on incompetence. I do not *think* it was actually intentional. If you missed the turn onto our street, there was no turning back on the main road. Jared and I would then hop into my truck and drive the six miles to his Level 5 magnet school. My job was to fill in for the bus driver.

The next problem was our neighbors. Jared enjoyed playing with children in the neighborhood and we hoped that he would make a few new friends. He seemed to be doing well socially after the psychotropic drugs had disseminated from his body. Increasingly social, he was ready to make some new friends. I figured that the children of *normal* families would be a good influence on a child in foster care. In our case, I was wrong.

Three boys in the neighborhood were the same age as Jared. The best of the three was a little boy named Tunde. With his family, he had moved to the United States from Africa and into our small Violetville neighborhood. He was the caretaker of the group, a positive influence on Jared, and a good playmate.

The other two boys were another story. One child, Bernard, was the unfortunate product of a fatherless home and a drug den. His mother and older brother were both hooked on heroin. I was shocked to find the heroin epidemic hiding in my own backyard. Bernard's family was doing just about anything they could to support their fix. Drugs are not only a problem for kids in foster care.

The older brother had worked a job taking down dead trees before his habit earned him a needle to the afterlife. He had spent time in foster care but eventually stepped down to Step Zero. Going back home did not work out as well for him as planned. The older brother died two years later from an overdose. Meanwhile, younger sibling Bernard had a crime-ridden future engraved into his DNA. He was a sharp little kid with wit, and a serious but amusing personality; he was very likable. I had hoped that I could become a good role model for him. A few years later, Bernard ended up in foster care too and eventually landed in kinship care.

The third kid in the neighborhood was a complete disaster, a future model citizen that moonlighted as a serial killer. Move over Anthony Perkins, here is Sammie. Sammie had already led Jared and his gang on several adventures that included breaking and entering at a dangerous construction site. He would often lead the boys beyond the busy thoroughfare and all the way across an eighteen-hole golf course, stealing balls along the way. This kid had bad news written all over him. I had already noticed that a number of Jared's toys and video games were mysteriously disappearing. I suspected that our sweet little Eddie Haskell named Sammie was responsible.

As any good parent would, I decided to venture out and talk with his parents. That was my first mistake.

The father pulled back several large attack dogs and invited me in to search Sammie's room, "Go ahead. Take a look."

Sure enough, I found several of Jared's video games hidden under his bed. Sammie cried as his dad smacked him into full submission. I did not want to involve myself in any Child Protective Service reports and got out of there before I witnessed something worth reporting.

As I walked out the door the man informed me, "If you come knocking again, you won't be reclaiming Jared's missing valuables."

I thought that was an odd statement to make, but I guess what he meant was, *'From now on, you're on your own concerning my son's behavior.'* I guess I would have to think again concerning the good influences of *normal* families.

I limited Jared's play with Sammie to the outdoor yard. Once he was no longer allowed inside my house, I saw a lot less of him. Strangely, things continued to disappear. One day I returned home and found that the interior of my house painted with a can of paint that I had mistakenly left lying on the kitchen floor. I figured out why things were disappearing. Sammie had been stealing from us even when we were not home and this time Sammie had left his mark. He could not resist the opportunity to paint my walls when tempted with a can of paint. The paint left a trail of size three shoeprints back towards Sammie's house. Once again, I went to the boy's home. The father slammed the door in my face. I guess I would have to finish Sammie's new paint job all by myself. Perhaps it was time to consider moving.

****

May arrived and it was time for Elo's prom and graduation. We hit the mall and picked up his tuxedo selection, an all white Prado Tuxedo. He looked like Mr. Peanut in his pictures as he posed with each of our black and white Border Collies. Even though he was going stag to the prom, Sadie and Sassi were his primary two bitches.

Prom came and went and Elo's next big event was graduation. He and I filled out the invitations to his upcoming ceremony and I made sure to inform all of his social workers. We even sent an invitation to his long lost Baltimore City worker. Perhaps she would finally make an appearance. Graduation Day arrived and both the agency worker and the AWOL city worker appeared.

The first thing the city worker asked was, "Where's the party?"

She was referring to the buffet spread of caviar, cocktail shrimp and liver pate. Elo's party was not going to be that fancy. Our plan was to celebrate at TGI Fridays. Perhaps a Cobb Salad would be to her liking. I was sorry to have disappointed our unexpected guest, but that would have to do. After all, we had no relationship with this worker and Elo had not seen her since his arrival at our home. Considering that there were only seven of us, I only prepared for a small party at the nearby restaurant.

Ironically, now that Elo was eighteen years old and no longer required visits, the city worker had finally shown up for her first monthly visit. She made the most of her time as she inhaled a plate of hot wings with several glasses of iced tea. After her meal, she bid us goodbye, and we never saw her again.

****

Another month passed and I took Jared for our first self-scheduled bio-visit with birth mom. We coordinated the meeting on our own and his birth mom was supposed to be at the Owings Mills metro station at two in the afternoon. We would then take her to the nearby Burger King for a little *quality time*. I informed Jared of our itinerary as we climbed into my truck. We drove the short five-mile distance to the metro station and pulled in to wait for his mom.

I parked the truck facing the entrance of the metro station as Jared instantly asked, "Where is my mom?"

"We're about fifteen minutes early so it will probably take a little while before she gets here."

We climbed out of the truck and walked towards an opening that leads under the metro train station. I could smell the warm, spice-filled air caused by the nearby McCormick factory. The flavors of the day appeared to be tarragon and lemon thyme. This particular metro station is above ground and the trains seem to drag the aromatic breezes as they arrive overhead, especially on clear sunny days. We watched and listened to the rumble of the trains as they pulled into the station. His birth mom did not appear to be on any of them but it was still early.

I killed time by looking over the metro map posted outside. Jared looked around the shrubbery for bugs or anything else that could occupy his time. Gentle winds, provided by the metro trains, caused the flora around Little J to sway while grasshoppers leaped from plant to plant. I discovered that dirt, bushes, trees, and every creature living in or on them were great distractions for Little J. It was a quarter after two and I finally decided to wait back in the parked truck. I called Jared over to join me on the walk back to our vehicle. He cried out, "What about my mom?"

"She's not here yet. Let's just go chill out in the truck while we wait."

His expression turned into a look of worry and perhaps frustration. He was no longer concerned about the bugs living in the bushes nearby.

I continued, "Don't worry buddy, we'll wait for another half hour in the truck. She'll probably be on the next train."

Jared stomped on an ant as he backed away from the spot where he was playing.

Another half hour passed as we waited in the truck. I sat in the driver's seat talking with Little J about school and bullies and the perplexities of life that were unrelated to biological families. I wanted to take his mind off his birth mom. Jared shared stories of food fights at school and talked about his fellow students. The kid who threw Jell-O at Jared also held a victory dance on the cafeteria table afterwards.

For a while, our conversation distracted him, but eventually Jared's mind returned to the present fact that his birth mom had not appeared. It was three o'clock in the afternoon and I was ready to give up.

"Hey buddy, I don't think she's going to make it today." I said.

He burst into tears. I reassured him, "We'll try again next month. Something must have come up. Try not to worry about it." There was nothing I could say or do to keep him from worrying. I looked at him. He was thin, pale, withdrawn and stressed out, much more than any eight-year-old child should ever be. He hid his face in the backseat of the truck and worked his tears into the upholstery below the window.

Chapter 16

"I'll Fro Chairs"

It was spring and walking our dogs in the nearby woods of Liberty Reservoir was one of our favorite pastimes. Elo and Jared joined us on our little adventures. They both developed an appreciation for nature and the great outdoors. Elo liked walking with the dogs among the high pines that lined the fire trails. The trails weaved around the clear body of water where Jared searched for freshwater clamshells along the beach. He always wanted to bring home every type of shell he found. Jared's shell collection even included the oyster and crab carcasses from our dinner outings.

To this day I do not know why children covet every relative carcass they come across, although I myself was known to keep an odd collection of turkey wishbones as a child. I secretly kept a number of poultry wishbones hidden in my closet, just in case a wish might come in handy. Years later, when I discovered the box, I only wished that I had thrown them out. By the time I grew up, they had lost their magical appeal.

As a family, we hiked through the deep woods and discovered little beaches where we threw sticks out to the dogs. Our Border Collies had transformed into Labrador Collie Retrievers. With no sheep to herd, they found new duties that fulfilled their desire to work. As summer approached and the school year ended, the reservoir woods became our family therapy room...for the dogs as well.

Once the kids finished the year of school we began receiving calls from social workers who had a number of respite care requests. Now that summer had arrived and foster parents stayed home with their children, everyone was ready to use the available ten days of respite care. Our license qualified us to foster for two full time therapeutic children, but also allowed us to house additional temporary children, children referred to as respite visitors.

Our first respite visitor was a teenage boy named Vance. He had multi-faceted psychological diagnoses as well as an incurable non-fatal disease but the boy's greatest setback was his overwhelming personality.

"So Vance, how is life in your foster home?"

"Cool. My foster dad's a tool so I pretty much do what I want."

"Like what?"

"You know. Whatever."

"Aren't you afraid of being removed if you act like that?"

"No. I know how to handle my foster dad."

Sarcastically I replied, "I'm sure you do."

Vance was the quintessential "know-it-all," a teenager filled with ten times the normal level of teenage bullcrap. I entertained Vance's fabricated tales and extensive knowledge on everything while Elo found that it was best to avoid him. You see, Elo was a know-it-all teenager as well, but Vance had far more drama to share. Krista took to Vance immediately. I did not mind having him around.

Vance became a presence in the neighborhood and kept a watchful eye on Jared. Our new temporary teen spent his time outside tinkering with an old rider mower when he was not doubling as the family tattler. Elo on the other hand spent most of his time in the kitchen or in front of the television. His television addiction was the reason I stopped watching TV all together. Eventually I cancelled cable as I came to despise MTV with a passion. In the meantime, we were receiving more requests to provide respite care for Vance and he was at our home at least every other weekend.

On top of the usual bio visits, we began corresponding with Jared's great uncle, Jim, and great aunt, Pat. Jared had stayed with the pair just before he became a ward of the state. They were the members of his biological family who had adopted Jared's aunts. Uncle Jim was willing to share useful information pertaining to Jared's extended family. He was an inside source of information and our best means to investigate the details of our foster child's case. DSS really did not know squat. What they did know they did not always share with us.

Uncle Jim knew the real story of Little J's life including those portions not incorporated into the DSS rap sheet. The uncle informed me that heroin was the family curse and had been so for decades. Another interesting fact that DSS neglected to mention was that Jared had been transitioned from Uncle Jim's home because of animal abuse.

"How is Jared doing with your dogs?"

"Okay. He really doesn't pay much attention to them."

"Good. Just make sure that you pay attention to Jared."

"Why?"

"Didn't DSS tell you? Jared had to leave our home after we caught him provoking our dog."

"No. DSS forgot to mention that little detail."

"Like I said… just make sure you pay attention to Jared."

We had crossed out animal abuse on our list of compatible behavior. DSS slipped that one under the rug. Fortunately, Uncle Jim's pug named Rocky had survived his traumatic ordeal with Little J.

Uncle Jim filled us in on the family history, "I'm glad to see that Jared is doing well. Most of our family, from grandparents to grandchildren, spent time in foster care at some point."

The family was involved with foster care dating back to the earliest days. Jared was at least a third generation foster child. Most stories ended tragically with tales of neglect and abuse. Uncle Jim managed to escape the cycle of drug abuse while saving two of his nieces in the process.

There was another bright spot in Jared's family, Uncle Frankie. He had recently overcome a battle with heroin and had just fathered a son. The baby was his second son and he and the baby's mother celebrated with a wedding ceremony at the downtown courthouse. Uncle Jim's wife, Aunt Pat, was currently filling in as their babysitter while Uncle Frankie worked from nine to five. He was holding down a good job, taking care of his family, staying clean, and doing better each day.

Uncle Jim looked at Little J and said, "Jared, you are the spitting image of your Uncle Frankie."

Jared remembered Uncle Frankie, nodded, and smiled. Uncle Jim's declaration meant the world to Little J. He longed for a real connection to his mother or to any other biological family member. Now Uncle Frankie could be his biological male role model. Our visits with Uncle Jim were very beneficial to Little J. They were also good for us and good for the entire bio family. Little J enjoyed spending time reconnecting with the members of his biological family and he especially enjoyed hearing about Uncle Frankie. I never actually met Uncle Frankie but on a visit with Uncle Jim, Jared showed me a picture. Frankie *was* the spitting image of Jared.

Little J held up the picture and proclaimed, "I'm just like Uncle Frankie!"

****

Now in my early thirties, I had adjusted to the responsibility of mentoring three young men. Elo graduated high school and began looking for summer employment. He filled out job applications with fast food restaurants scattered around the area. Our respite child Vance was coming and going. He filled us in on his latest outlandish gossip. Jared was busy playing with the kids of the neighborhood and his demeanor continually improved after a successful June bio-visit with his birth mom. He was acting much more confident, and far less anxious. To Jared's relief, his birth mom attended a recent bio visit at the Owings Mills metro station. He had been tortured for forty-five minutes because she ran late, but she did appear. We had a nice short lunch at Burger King where they spent time catching up on school and talked about his new neighborhood friends.

I really liked Jared's birth mom. She always displayed genuine remorse for her tardy arrivals. She was very sincere; she just was not capable of getting anywhere on time. The young mother was a caring person who simply did not contain enough discipline for the meticulous duties of motherhood.

The number one skill needed for good parenting is dependability. You have to be dependable to get your child to school, you have to be dependable to get your child to the doctor, and you have to be dependable to provide food, clothing, and shelter. Dependability does not come easily for everyone, particularly for some 22-year-olds. At 22, I was reciting the creed of my college fraternity while standing on my head and drinking beer through a tube. I imagine that dependability is even more difficult if you are a parent battling some sort of addiction.

****

After ten months of intense foster parenting, Krista and I decided to try a weekend getaway without the kids. Elo could stay home with the dogs and we could use respite care for Jared. Our foster agency arranged the respite time for Jared at a nearby foster home with a couple named Mr. and Mrs. Carter. We packed Jared's clothing for the weekend and I dropped him off. It was just eight miles down the road.

The foster mother appeared courteous but described a strict ideology of old school parenting techniques, "We expect the children to maintain appropriate discipline at all times. They will handle themselves appropriately and respond respectively."

Discipline was a keyword in her description of caring for a child. My wife and I mixed a dash of discipline into our child rearing routine, but this couple's method was extreme. A little eight-year-old boy named Quinton was already under their command. The boy was nervously awaiting his next order as I dropped Jared off with an overnight bag.

Mrs. Carter continued, "Mr. Hoffman, did you pack the clothing I requested for church?"

"Yes I did."

"Yes what?"

I looked at her inquisitively, "Yes I packed the clothes you requested for church?"

She responded, "Yes Mrs. Carter."

"Ooooooookaaaaaay, yes Mrs. Carter."

"Don't be cheeky with me! I believe we will see you promptly at seven o'clock on Monday evening?"

"Yes…" I hesitated then completed the correct reply, "…Mrs. Carter."

"*Good.*"

I turned to Jared and stated, "Look here Jared, you have Little Quinton to play with while we are gone. It will be fun playing with him. We'll be back after three nights so count the sleepover nights and we'll be back before you know it."

Jared said nothing but did not exactly look thrilled. He watched from the front door as I headed down the steps and back to my vehicle. I waved goodbye with my free hand as I backed my truck out of the driveway. He stood at the window with his two hands pressed against the glass. I saw the look of a sad puppy facing his first session of crate training. With a hint of doubt, I thought to myself, *I'm sure he'll be fine.*

Everything went smoothly for us on our vacation. We returned home to find that Elo had not thrown any Risky Business-like parties and my next order of business was to pick up Jared from the respite care home. When I arrived at the home, he appeared physically healthy but mentally askew. It was as if his mind had reverted to a condition reminiscent of his days spent at St. Xavier's Center. He had a strange blank stare and spoke in a hollow, monotone voice. I started the truck and he sat in the back in a hazy trance. He was mumbling strange nonsense, as if just dosed with each of his previous medications.

"The clouds are missing in the building under the park, where the glass broke in my hair," he said.

"Hey J, what are you saying?"

"The nice ladies take the glass out of your hair."

"What?"

"That bullet made me bleed, and it put glass in my hair."

"I know. Listen… when we get home you can play Spyro for a little bit and then we will order sushi for dinner. How does that sound?"

"*Suu-sheeee!*" he exclaimed.

Something was off-kilter and I wanted to distract him, bring him back to reality. For some reason, raw fish seemed to do the trick. Jared sometimes reminded me of the character Gollum from *Lord of the Rings*, especially when he talks to himself or chomps into sushi the way Gollum chomped into the side of a raw fish. Physically, his thin frame and large eyes made him look a lot like Gollum.

After ten months of stable living, Jared was not ready for an overnight stay with strangers. On the ride home he flashed back to age four and a time when he experienced a drug deal gone bad. From the backseat of an old Chevy Impala, he witnessed the gunfire that shattered glass above his head, leaving him covered in broken pieces of the windshield. Under duress, he often reverted to this story. For whatever reason, it was comforting for him to share this enduring trauma.

Jared was a fragile egg, much more fragile than I imagined, and my wife and I decided to avoid respite care from that point forward. A few days later, the content of his conversation had exponentially improved.

He managed to describe the strict environment of his temporary respite care placement, "We didn't get to stay up after dark. They just said get in bed and we had to go to bed. We could not wrestle or go outside. When we made noise, we went to a time out. I never want to go back there."

Elo joked with Little J concerning his shell-shocked state of mind. "Try staying in a home like that for ten straight years," he stated. "You're lucky nobody beat your ass."

Jared looked at Elo with a clueless gaze as if to say, 'What could Elo possibly mean?'

****

Summer was almost over and school was just around the corner. Elo would be starting his first semester at Catonsville Community College and Jared was going back to Charlesbrook. By now, Jared was becoming more than just educationally delayed and confused about his life. He was almost nine years of age and was beginning to realize the hard truth about foster care. His birth mom had not shown up for the latest meeting at the Owings Mills metro station and his emotions were now moving into a dark place.

Jared never considered any of his birth mom's no-shows as any fault of hers. It was always my fault because I had not waited long enough for her to arrive. Never mind the extra hour that I had already stayed there. The social worker directed me to sit for a maximum of fifteen minutes, but I always went beyond the call of duty. Little J did not know how to manage his disappointment, which manifested itself as anger directed towards everyone else.

Elo would try to help with little comments like, 'Get used to it kid.' He was referring to the generalized disappointment that came from bio family interaction or lack thereof. Elo had hardened his emotional shell a long time ago and only wanted the best for Little J. His philosophy was, 'toughen up kid, before things really get bad.'

Every now and again, Elo would appear jealous of Jared's good fortune and would treat Little J rudely, but Elo would also complement my wife and me with statements like, 'I wish I had you guys back when I was eight.' Krista and I appreciated the positive feedback we received and understood that much of his life must have felt like a raw deal. In return, we tried to give Elo and Jared the encouragement and emotional support they needed. Right now Jared required as much support as he could get.

A failed bio visit ignited Jared's first major outburst. After we returned home from a "no show" bio visit, he had a temper tantrum and nearly broke the glass table in our living room. Like a good father, I told him to go to his room for a classic 'time-out.' Emotionally he was in a bad place. First, he felt abandoned after his recent respite weekend left him alone with Little Quinton and a pair of non-friendly foster parents. Second, I had not waited long enough for the arrival of his hallowed birth mom. In an act of rebellion, he decided to decline my request for a time-out with an emphatic 'No!!'

This was the first time my fatherhood was tested and I was ready. Yelling is my specialty. I come from a long line of hollering banshees. My father yelled so loud he could have called me home from beyond the grave. Now it was my turn. So I put on my best display of patriarchal bear-like behavior and let out a, *"What?"*

It was the first time I ever emulated the parenting technique learned from my father. I bellowed out a deep roar that literally made the glassware of our dining room hutch chime together. I created my own earthquake as I stomped my feet and moved towards Jared. With a demonic voice, I breathed the words, "You had *better*, get your little *butt*, *up*, in that *room!*"

I had never seen a kid move so fast in my life. He looked like Speedy Gonzales spinning away from Sylvester the Cat. Like a squirrel scrambling up a tree, he traversed the spiral staircase up to his room. The kid was now motivated and flew up the stairway as if his pants were on fire. Even so, he was not done. He had stored up enough pent up anger to call my bluff. From the top of the stairs, I could hear the sounds of crashing legos and the words, *'I'll fro chairs!'*

I looked though the opening of the loft and saw him dragging out the chair that sat next to his bed. Now he had really pushed my buttons. I found myself standing upstairs and holding him by his armpit and his ankle. It was as if I had somehow teleported into that exact position.

In a sarcastic yet jovial voice I exclaimed, *'I'll fro you!'*

I used this moment to emphasize my physical and mental dominance. Then I set him down onto his bed. He looked at me with a shocked expression. Perhaps I was a little more like Little J's birth dad, Gerald Mean Jean, than he originally thought. I did not want to completely scare the crap out of the kid, but I was not about to become the pushover of an eight-year-old child.

As I trudged down the spiral staircase, I could hear Elo snickering from behind the door of his room. He was repeating Jared's words while laughing, 'I'll fro chairs. That's awesome!' From that day on Jared took his time-outs peacefully. He never 'frew' another chair, and later that day the mild mannered boy even offered to give me a foot rub. My empty threat worked like a charm.

****

It is against the law for foster parents to use any form of corporal punishment although it is legal for a biological or adoptive parent to use an open hand to spank a child's backside. Foster parents have to discipline while working around the legal rules pertaining to physical punishment. Spanking, not allowed by law, is not a technique described in the foster parent handbook. When the use of positive reinforcement fails, I have found that the next best option is an empty threat. You just have to sell it well. If you need an empty threat to work you had better make it look official. It is the ultimate child-rearing bluff.

Over the years, our family culture has adjusted to meet the requirements of an empty threat. We have become very loud and overly dramatic. When bedtime arrived, you would think each child in my home was on a death row march down the Green Mile. Theatrics might have had an overall negative effect on my family; that is yet to be determined. My daughter has won three roles in professional theater, and she is only six. As a whole, I recommend taking a course in theatrics to compliment your successful foster parenting techniques.

****

Returning to anarchy, Little J's rebellion did not end with the table and the chair. It reared its ugly head once again the next day. While we enjoyed a quiet Sunday afternoon at home, Jared was outside rebelling in the backyard that sunny pleasant day. I was inside competing with Elo on the family video game console and could hear bickering from the backyard. Our temporary foster son Vance burst into the room. Vance had been outside 'modifying' our rider mower while Jared was playing in the yard with his friend Tunde.

In full dramatic style Vance blurted out, "You wouldn't believe what this kid just did!"

He was referring to Jared. J was standing behind him, ready to plead his own case.

I paused the video game and looked up rolling my eyes, "What?"

Vance exclaimed, "He purposely threw a stick at the dog!"

Krista and I were already on high alert concerning animal cruelty since Uncle Jim informed us about an unpleasant incident with his family pet, Rocky. This new information about Jared became our latest concern. Sadie, the targeted dog, already had enough problems with generalized anxiety and this certainly would not help.

If the dog spent any more time hiding under beds, Krista would make me hire a dog psychologist. My wife was already under the spell of dog trainer Cesar Millan and was ready to devote more time and money towards his latest book. She had just finished another dog book called, *How to Speak*

Dog' and was ready to start writing checks.

Sadie was an easy target for abuse after an unpleasant incident with a neighborhood dog. As a puppy, she had been the casualty of a dog attack and now suffers from Canine Post Traumatic Stress Disorder or CPTSD.

I asked Jared, "What were you trying to do to Sadie? Were you trying to get back at me by hurting our dog?"

He looked angry as he replied, "I didn't do it!"

His denial held no merit. It was his word against Vance. Vance was a sixteen-year-old with nothing to gain from tattling, other than pure enjoyment. In other words, Jared was guilty. He spent the rest of the day in his room not throwing chairs. Krista and I kept a watchful eye on him for the rest of the year. I warned him about our other dog Sassi, Sadie's sister. "Sassi is like McGruff the crime dog. Have you ever heard about McGruff the crime dog?"

Jared answered with a cautious, "Yes."

"If you try to hurt a dog again, Sassi will take a bite out of crime. Do you understand?"

He looked over at Sassi who was now lying on the couch. On a good day, she is dangling from a tree branch in the backyard. She entertains herself by tearing off the limbs of a tree. It looks very threatening but currently she was asleep on the couch lying on her back with her legs sticking up in the air... her underbelly fully exposed. She did not look very dangerous at that particular moment and she certainly did not look like any sort of fierce guardian. Perhaps pulling Sassi into one of my empty threats was not one of my better ideas. Jared did not know what to think, but moving forward he might think twice about hurting Sadie, the sister of the wild-eyed Border Collie known to the neighborhood as Frass.

I turned to Krista and half jokingly said, "You know, Jeffrey Dahmer started out by hurting animals."

My wife was legitimately concerned, and so was I.

Chapter 17

Extending The Extended Families

The new school year was just a week away and I planned one final summer vacation to visit my extended family at Lake Raystown. Little excursions served as positive reinforcement for the boys because trips were a big part of my parenting style. I have always regarded travel and nature in high esteem. Elo was making great progress and making good decisions while Jared was dealing with some tough issues for an eight-year-old. I planned to expose them both to the rigors of nature and to my extended family at our summer reunion. In return, they might develop some newfound family relationships.

Prior to packing for the trip, Elo and I ran to the store to pick up a few items for the campout. My wife insisted that we would need more 'S'more' supplies. She wanted enough graham crackers, chocolate, and marshmallows to feed an army of Stay-Puff Marshmallow men and I wanted to buy a supply of Reese's Peanut Butter Cups to appease my sister Cindy who manages the whole reunion. My new collection of kids would soon overrun her camping lot next to the lake and peanut butter cups are the drug that could lull her into complete acceptance.

As we pulled into the grocery store parking lot, I discovered that Elo had been making more good choices than I initially assumed. The parking lot was nearly full and I chose a spot near the end of the lot, far from any other vehicles. As we stepped from the truck, Elo pointed to a small one-inch zip-locked bag lying on the ground.

He stated, "Somebody's been having a good time around here."

"What do you mean?" I looked down at the clear zip-lock baggie and joked, "That bag's too small for a condom. That is, unless it's one of your condoms."

Elo picked up the bag and placed it into my hand. "You see this. *This* is a crack bag."

"And you know because…" There was a pause. He had captured my attention. Apparently, Elo had something important that he wanted to tell me.

"Because… let's just say… I knew people who used to sell it."

"You sold little plastic baggies," I joked. He was not joking. I looked at him inquisitively and asked, "How long ago?" The thought crossed my mind that I might just find a magic baggie lying around the upstairs of my house.

"I don't hang around anybody involved with that stuff now."

"Good! Keep it that way. I hope you *always* make good decisions from now on."

"Oh, I will!" His eyes were wide open and his expression was confident and direct.

I cleared my throat and spoke again, "Did you ever use crack?"

"*Hell no,* I'm not stupid!" He was smart enough not to use drugs, but had been around it in the past.

"I was just a kid. I didn't know what I was doing, but I knew better than to end up like a crack head."

"Good! Let's keep it that way." As we walked into the entrance of the store, I dumped the baggie into the trash. Elo had been making good choices as long as I had known him and that is what mattered to me. I had not witnessed one single act worthy of a rap sheet. So far, his rap sheet only contained the records of past fights and the behavioral issues from his childhood. Since I had known him, he had graduated high school, was about to start college, and was growing more responsible each day. As we entered the store, I joked to break up what felt like awkward tension, "Do you think they sell little baggies like that in this store?"

He laughed and replied, "Actually, there *is* a guy in the meat department that can hook you up."

"*What!*"

He laughed again. "Damn Matt, I'm just messing with you."

"What the hell kind of joke is that?"

"That's called a funny joke, the kind where I laugh. Actually, I have no idea what that little baggie from the parking lot is for. For all I know it could be for a Happy Meal toy."

Elo had learned from the master, but I knew from my own experience that there was always some truth in jest.

****

It was 2002, exactly one year since my father died standing in front of a campground vending machine. My fourteen-year-old nephew Stephen found his body laying 'asleep' next to the bathhouse. Perhaps that is the reason my mother awarded him with my father's prestigious collection of underwear. My family is generally dysfunctional. Even so, they formed my role model for family life and they always modeled family life with flare.

Each family member has some sort of odd quirk or bizarre habit, but we have all managed to stay connected through our sense of humor. It may not be the best family model in history, but it works for us. My sisters, nephews, nieces, and their spouses must have a great sense of humor because they readily adopted my foster kids into the extended family.

My sister Cindy's husband Dennis was particularly enamored to have his first black nephew. "Damn, I ain't ever had a black nephew before. Had a black sheet metal worker once, had a friend with a black girlfriend… heck, I even had a black dog at one point, but I ain't never had no black nephew. Get over here and give your Uncle Dennis a hug."

Elo nervously glanced in my direction. I responded, "Well Elo, aren't you going to give your Uncle Dennis a hug?"

Elo cautiously moved towards Dennis. My burly, bearded brother-in-law wrapped his huge bear arms around the young man, and then exclaimed, "Got him!"

Elo's eyes bugged out of his head and he wore an expression of shocked confusion. Dennis continued, "Matt, you go grab the rope, and Jon, you start up the boat."

Elo exclaimed, *"What?"*

Dennis continued, "Nephew, we're takin' you *waterskiing!*"

Elo let out a deep breath, *"Whoa…* you scared the *hell* out of me!"

My brother-in-law Dennis is a bit of an old school redneck and fortunately Elo has a great sense of humor. I half expected Dennis to pull out a banjo and start playing 'Dueling Banjos' as a way of welcoming Elo to the family campfire. Dennis had bonded with my foster son even faster than Grammy could sweep Elo off on another private outing to Bob Evans.

Our family reunion is usually more like a comedy roast than a picture from a Norman Rockwell painting, and on this trip, Elo was the guest of honor. Humor does not sit well with Little J. He still requires a heavy dose of calcium to build up his funny bone; jokes fly over Jared's head like a jet flying over an anthill. Little J simply enjoyed his time fishing for bluegills along the lake while the rest of us sat around the campfire cracking jokes.

Uncle Dennis called out, "Jared, you gonna cook up some of those bluegills?"

"Sure!"

"Once you catch about a-hun-derd, let me know and we'll have ourselves a little snack."

"That sounds good Uncle Dennis, I've got six so far!" and Jared ran off to continue fishing.

The boys felt the loving atmosphere of an extended family and I even got a chance to lie down in the exact spot where my father had died. My mother did not appreciate my morbid sense of humor but the rest of my family did.

****

My kids were experiencing the dysfunctional life that is my immediate family. Growing up in the early seventies my often-embattled parents attempted to portray themselves as the loving Von Trapp family from the Rodgers and Hammerstein musical, *The Sound of Music*. My wife did not realize that she married a twisted male version of the youngest Von Trapp child, Gretel. I was the last accident within a group of misguided singing twits.

My entire family got into the fantasy world of *The Sound of Music*. To escape, my mother would spin her *Sound of Music* vinyl record while boisterously belting the songs of Maria Von Trapp. My father enjoyed shouting out orders similar to those of Captain Von Trapp. He would have loved to issue commands with an old sea whistle but used an old sea bell still attached to the outside wall of our home. His own father was a naval sea captain who had run a tight ship over seven siblings. So ordering around children and adults alike was quite natural for my father.

The rest of my siblings got in on the act as well. Each winter holiday, during the yearly television run of the musical, we would gather in the living room with popcorn, candy, and soda. My sisters would act out scenes from the musical score. 'I Am Sixteen, Going on Seventeen' and 'The Lonely Goat Herd' reenacted through the front window of our living room. My older brother munched popcorn and was probably too stoned to play the part of Franz. After all, it was the seventies.

****

The camping reunion created bonds between my foster kids and my extended family, bonds that endured long after the trip ended. Jared had taken a liking to my twelve-year-old nephew Brad, and the two of them enjoyed video games and wrestling together. Elo became good friends with my fifteen-year-old niece Ashley. They liked to talk on the phone about the complexities of their teenage lives. Over the weekends, Ashley also became friends with my respite son, Vance, who quickly became enamored with her. I was a little concerned about their relationship. The young man was a fast talker with fast hands. I did not want his fast hands to be too fast with my niece.

Vance was not my full time foster son and he was not making

appropriate choices in his life. He regularly discussed his desire to obtain and consume alcohol but his intake was limited due to a medical issue with his liver. I believe he was planning a workaround to alcohol consumption that included procuring a bag of marijuana.

"Hey Matt, do you think weed can hurt your liver?"

"I don't know... why?"

"No reason." I hoped that with some mentoring Vance could make the right decisions, but I was tired of hearing about green herb.

A physician had already prescribed the boy enough medication to calm a rhinoceros, but the know-it-all teenager decided to go ahead and represent himself as his own physician. His plan was to stop taking the prescribed drugs and look into another plan of medication. It was the beginning of a downward spiral. I gave him good advice and I wanted him to succeed. I would say, "Take your prescribed meds, don't get into any fights, don't knock up any girls, and I'll help you out. If you don't make good decisions, I'll have to cut you off." I was not about to waste my time on anyone who was not willing to help himself.

The know-it-all answered back, 'No problem,' but a few weeks later, I found out that he had stopped taking his meds. He got into a fight with his permanent foster dad and was sent away to live in a nearby halfway house for teens. It was a form of DSS housing called, 'independent living.' I kept in touch with him and continued to offer good recommendations, but he was *not* on the fast track to success.

Another month passed and Vance wound up expelled from all Maryland state schools. Storing a knife in his locker was another one of his bad decisions. He was then relocated to Washington D.C. and months later called to tell me his wonderful news; he was going to be a dad! I called to congratulate my niece. She was *not* the mother of his baby. She saw that he was making bad decisions and kept him at a distance. Vance was using alcohol and drugs, getting into trouble, and would soon become a deadbeat father. I wished Vance the best of luck, and I advised Ashley to stay as far away as possible. That would be a good decision.

Meanwhile, we spent more time with Jared's extended family. We met with Uncle Jim several more times through the fall and beyond Christmas. It was a pleasant interaction for both Jared and for me. He enjoyed the new dependability of his extended biological family and I got more information about Little J's family. I was particularly curious about his mom, as she had not been showing up for recent visits. Birth mom had done a good job of attending visitation during the spring, but she had been a no show through the summer and into the fall.

Uncle Jim filled in the blanks for us. "Oh don't worry about her. Jared's mom is historically streaky", he said. "Her involvement in the party scene fluctuates with factors such as the weather, the circumstance, and whichever boyfriend is currently around. Her old boyfriend, Logan Hammersmith, is out of jail after serving time for narcotics distribution."

Apparently, they were enjoying some time together, which meant J would be spending more time with us. I was happy with the new situation in which Jared's reservations to stay extended far beyond six months. He and I had developed a father-son bond and Uncle Jim was hoping he could stay with me as well. My wife and I looked forward to our future with Little J. Perhaps he would like to play a sport or would enjoy watching football with me. Maybe he would come in handy when it came time for me to start changing diapers. The future was uncertain.

The Baltimore County social worker Gail set up a visit with Jared's half sister, Stephanie. Offered the opportunity to contact Stephanie's paternal grandmother, Mrs. Hammersmith, I called to arrange a visit, intrigued by the idea of meeting one of Jared's birth siblings. We met his little sister by a lake at Baltimore's Druid Park. The two siblings had a wonderful time reconnecting with one another. They had last seen one another when Jared was about five and Stephanie was about three. She enjoyed bossing Jared around and he enjoyed her doing so.

Stephanie was a sassy little girl with a mischievous smile. Her behavior seemed almost parentified. At age six, she was the dominant personality of her immediate family and possessed an odd, but rather responsible demeanor for a child. Mrs. Hammersmith informed us that the little girl was actually the one in charge when it came to directing birth mom towards making good decisions. She also told us that the little girl went back and forth between a room in the Hammersmith home and the various places her birth mom resided. Sometimes birth mom stayed at the home with Mrs. Hammersmith as well. After the visit, we said goodbye and did not hear from them for a long time. Mrs. Hammersmith gave Jared a picture of Stephanie. He posted the picture on his bedroom mirror just above the T-Rex stuffed dinosaur that his mother gave him a year before.

****

The trees were in full autumn display and change was in the air. Krista had gained weight for the first time since the day I had met her. To put it simply, things were about to get a little more complicated because Krista was pregnant. I do not know if love or some other mind-altering chemical was in the air, but a baby was on the way.

Spring 2003 arrived and for the first time Elo broke one of our house rules. My wife was lying in bed enjoying the symptoms of third trimester pregnancy: tossing, turning, hot flashes, cold flashes, sweating, cramps and nausea. I was twice as miserable working the night shift of a computer help desk. One night the personal line of my office phone rang unexpectedly. It was Krista.

Nervously, she said, "Matt, something is going on upstairs."

"What?" She was not very descriptive, but it was two o'clock in the morning.

"I'm not sure, but I think something is *going on* upstairs." I sat waiting for her to explain further.

"What... is going on... upstairs?"

"I think Elo might have a friend over." I had no clue what she was talking about. Elo was now a 'college boy' and he had always been a night owl.

She kept talking, "I think he might have snuck a girl into his room. What should I do?"

My wife was not accustomed to the rambunctious life of teenage boys. With the exception of me, she had managed to avoid every one of us, all of her life. After she gave me the detailed description of the scenario, I had plenty of suggestions to propose.

If I had been home I probably would have kicked the door open and hit him with a big, *'Surprise!'* but this was not an option for Krista. I mentally squeezed my feet into her shoes and instructed her, "Just ignore everything. He will sneak her out soon. Then I'll talk to him tomorrow." He was nineteen years old and he would not be 'in there' too long. This was my solution and my way of saying, 'Let'im finish.' I just hoped Elo did not end up with any new family members of his own.

Speaking of Elo's family members, we were about to meet the first member of his birth family, his little brother, Nevar. I received a call from Elo's social worker, Arlene, who managed both Elo's and Nevar's cases. Things were going well for each of them at their individual placement and it was now a good time for a bio visit.

****

On a clear Saturday afternoon, Elo's social worker stopped by for a visit with Elo at our home. She had Nevar tagging along with her. The young man hopped out of the front passenger seat of her car and followed Arlene towards our front door. About fifteen years old, he wore a big smile and looked a lot like Elo, but he was lankier with a thinner face and a small gut.

Nevar turned to Arlene and asked, "So this is my new home?"

She responded with the sweet tone of a kindergarten teacher, "No Nevar. This is where your brother Eloise lives. We've come here to visit with him."

"Ohhhhhh Maaaaaann. I want to live up in this place. This place is off the hook!"

The teenager had less muscle than Elo but built with similar facial features. They both had the same mouth, same nose, and each had the same big bright eyes, although Nevar's eyes had the glossy look of a wild man.

Arlene called out, "Hi Matt. Is Eloise around?"

I was standing outside on the front patio watching and waiting as Elo's brother followed her down the path towards the entrance of our home. His thin build and small potbelly were a visual testimony to a diet of pizza and McDonalds. Many foster kids survived on frozen food, Spaghettios, and Ramen noodles.

Nevar was mentally impaired and had recently moved into a residential housing facility that specializes in children with mental disabilities. He was stepped up to 'Step Three' living as he grew in size and was no longer considered harmless in the eyes of his old foster mom. If Nevar got angry, he had the size to do something about it. The teen's rap sheet said that he was mentally handicapped with multiple mood disorders. As a result, he was on a cocktail of psychotropic medications.

I answered Arlene, "Yes, come on in. Elo's upstairs. I'll call him down."

I went back in and hollered for Elo. Moments later, he trudged down the spiral staircase. Arlene took a seat in a living room chair while Nevar began to walk around the house. He was like a dog sniffing out new territory. Elo watched him with a controlled smile as Nevar walked through our foyer and into the kitchen. He was already scoping out the food situation.

The social worker waved Elo into the living room, "Come here and say hello."

Arlene was a caring social worker who obviously poured her heart into improving the lives of foster children. She had known Elo and Nevar for a very long time and her own son was a friend of my oldest foster child. From moving around over the years, Elo seemed to know just about every teenager in the Baltimore area.

"How is Rico doing?" He was referring to Arlene's son.

"Good. He is just finishing high school. How are *you* doing?" As the two talked, I could hear Nevar calling from the kitchen.

"Maaaaaaann, you've got some tight food in the fridge. I'm starving!" Nevar called out. He spoke with a lot of colloquial English terminology.

"Nevar, get back in here. You shouldn't be digging around in their kitchen." Arlene looked towards me and said, "Sorry."

I responded, "No problem. I'll go check on him."

I left the living room and headed towards the kitchen. He had closed the fridge and was walking from the refrigerator towards the family room on the other side of the kitchen. Jared entered from the backyard with the dogs and met Nevar as Elo and Arlene carried on with their conversation. Nevar sat down on the family room floor and introduced himself to the dogs. I watched while standing in the doorway between the living room and the foyer. After he finished with the dogs, the young man got up and walked over to me.

With a big smile he exuberantly asked, "Can I live here? You've got plenty of room."

He had just cased the entire place. It was not that big and I was not ready for his question. I was searching for an appropriate response.

Arlene called out, "Nevar… Matt and Krista already have two foster sons and they are only allowed to have two at a time."

"Oh maaaaaaaaan." He was still smiling, standing in front of me. I did not have a lot of experience with the mentally disabled and simply threw him a shrug. He continued, "Okay, but when somebody leaves you guys I'll be moving in!" The inflection of his stated prediction sounded very matter-of-fact. The tone sounded more like a combination of Eddie Murphy and Bubba from the movie *Forrest Gump*.

"Okay," I responded. The visit went well. Elo was cautious around his brother but always pleasant around Ms. Arlene. He appeared confused by the state of his emotions. I imagine that you do not always know what to say around a mentally handicapped brother that you seldom see. After all, Elo believed that it was his duty to care and protect Nevar but the reality of life in foster care made that impossible.

He tried to offer some advice to his little brother in an Elo kind of way, "Damn boy, you need to make sure you're brushing those teeth."

Nevar took offense. "You aren't my dad!"

It was obvious that there was tension between the two brothers and they did not know how to respond to the unordinary emotions they were both experiencing.

Arlene stepped in with a comment to help dissolve the tension, "Nevar has been doing well in his new residential facility."

"Yea, that place sucks," Nevar interjected. His tone and attitude had completely changed. He went from a big smile to a dark grimace in the blink of an eye. Next, a monologue of complaints ensued. His soliloquy pertained to the staff, the food, and the overall conditions of his new institution.

The bio visit ended shortly thereafter. Arlene ushered Nevar out the door and gave Elo a firm hug goodbye. I walked both of them to their car and waved goodbye as Elo's little brother disappeared from sight. I asked Elo more about his immediate family. I will just say he appeared to be in no hurry for the next Winford family reunion.

Part III – Then Life Takes Over

Chapter 18

Time To Move On

We pushed through the winter and had a normal bio-visit with Uncle Jim and his family. They had not heard much about Jared's birth mom for quite some time. The social workers began to suggest a possible plan of adoption for Little J. Originally, my wife and I did not sign up with plans to adopt, but things had changed and we were open to just about anything. Adoption sat at the back of our minds while we continued learning from our foster care experience.

Over the summer various special needs respite kids came to stay at our home. We performed respite care for two different mentally handicapped teens. One boy named Nicholas liked to talk non-stop. I had never experienced anything quite like it. To remain the center of attention he would repeat the phrase, 'Hey Buddy!'

The kid was a real sweetheart but his insistent 'Hey Buddies' were enough to make a person go insane. I developed a deep appreciation for parents fostering the mentally handicapped. Performing this service requires a new level of patience, more than anything I could ever imagine. Years later, I can still hear the echo of Nicholas's voice in the back of my head. Sometimes I wake up and my first thought of the day is… *Hey Buddy*.

Another young man stayed with us for a different period of respite. He got the guest bed so saturated with urine that the mattress wound up at the dump. Everyone pitched in to help with the special needs of this particular young man. Elo did not appreciate the fact that Krista required his assistance with bathing the young man while I was at work.

I called home from the office and Elo informed me about his day. "Hey Elo, how's it going with the new kid?"

"Never again will I scrub down another human being, disabled or not. Next time, the guy is just going to have to remain covered in piss."

"Thanks Elo, I appreciate it. You earned your keep today."

****

Autumn blew by and the coldest winter of our lives was at hand. Even though we had a baby on the horizon, there were other pressing issues. Elo and I were filling in as caretakers for my mother and my wife had her plate full as well. While I maintained the family home in Columbia, my wife cared for her mother who had fallen ill. In December of 2002, my beloved mother-in-law Beverly lost her battle with small bowel adenocarcinoma, and the world lost a saint. It was a difficult time. My wife needed to grieve as she also prepared for the arrival of our first biological child. Life was nothing we imagined it would be.

The boys needed understanding in this difficult time and my mother needed a full time maintenance man. No one could help us, and no one tried. Burning the candle at both ends, we almost went up in flames. A lot was going on. Social workers introduced the idea of adopting Jared on the doorstep of death and birth. Elo abandoned college and was now seeking a job to fill the void. Jared spent most of his time hiding in the basement and developed a deep relationship with his video game console. Laughter was lost to our home as Christmas passed uneventfully. It was a dark time for our entire family, a dark time of sadness. I began searching for an escape.

As the walls of our family crumbled down, my wife and I reached an impasse. I was merely a caveman and Krista required more emotional support than my crooked brainwaves could supply. She needed her mother; she needed Bev. The relational bond Krista had with her mother was stronger than I could ever understand. It was something I had never experienced nor could ever replace. Their love was a testimony of unconditional love, a deep supportive love.

Bev had given everything to others and had fulfilled many roles for everyone in her family. She was our primary source of assistance, the glue to Krista's family, and the heart of my wife's content. In many ways, she was the glue to our immediate family as well. Pleasant dreams of Bev brightened Krista's mornings but they did not change the fact that Bev was no longer with us. We were on our own and from now on every issue we faced, we faced alone.

My mother was an elderly woman who was still grieving for her husband and was unable to offer any support, so Krista and I looked to each other for ways to overcome our state of mourning. She and I would reminisce about the days when our grandmothers were an integral part of our upbringing. They were the glue. Our mothers' mothers kept us in line and assisted with the difficult task of raising children. Childrearing was a generational team effort, but for our children it would not be the same. Without that glue, would our family fall apart?

As the baby's due date approached, tension grew within the walls of our home. Elo and I found ourselves in our first argument. I do not remember what triggered the fight but it could have been his exodus from college, his lack of employment, or my overall bad mood. Whatever it was, our conversation turned into something else. I remember the fight vividly because I finally heard Elo utter the phrase, *'You're not my dad!'*

Since the day I became a foster parent, I had been waiting for those words. The phrase is memorable from a number of afterschool specials, used at least twice in every TV sitcom ever aired. I had prepared for this moment and expected its arrival, yet I replied to Elo simply, "Your right. I'm not, but I bet you wish I was." Not the comical response I once envisioned, but it did the job in our sad state of affairs.

The fight ended immediately and the argument was over. Elo let down his guard and we moved on, but what were we going to do about the rest of our problems? Without Bev, life was more complicated than I had ever imagined. I wondered if we were on the right path so I did what a caveman does: I went hunting for a solution.

****

They say the hardest things in life are the birth of a child, the death of a loved one, and moving, so why I decided to add moving to our list, I will never know. I became determined to escape our situation and looked to the neighboring state of West Virginia to make a change. Perhaps I chose West Virginia because of the fond memories I had from my youth when I was carefree and spent time on an inner tube floating down the Potomac River. Perhaps I chose West Virginia because my big sister Cindy lived there. She used to care for me as a child and I had good memories from the days I spent under her watchful eye.

Maybe I looked towards West Virginia because the simple thought of living alongside the Appalachian Trail. If I desired, I could whimsically walk out the back door and vanish forever under a thick canopy of natural constitution. Our family was lost in the dark, needed some kind of light, and all I wanted to do was turn back the clock. I wanted to be cared for and I wanted to disappear into nothingness like a deadbeat father that one day goes out for milk and never returns.

Something led me to the foothills of the Appalachians. Maybe it was the mountain views or reasonable prices of West Virginian property, but it was likely a combination of things. I could never really be sure but I began to search for land in the isolated areas of Jefferson County, WV. Maybe I could find a chunk of property for an escape that would accommodate my yearning to leave everything behind and start anew. Maintaining a foster license seemed less significant and the idea of moving presented the importance of adoption. I knew that if we moved out-of-state, I wanted Jared to move with us.

Searching for a new home was an excellent distraction as I looked for a large lot to build my mountain hideaway on. Using the internet, I found available properties that filled my imagination with the fantasy of escape. Many were free of disturbances and free of neighbors. After living eight years in the small neighborhood of Violetville, I was ready to distance myself from everyone, especially neighbors. Krista did not necessarily agree. She was looking for help, remembering the support her family received from the neighborhood where she lived as a child.

My wife enjoyed a happy childhood in a northern Baltimore suburb. Delpha Court was the perfect little utopia of neighborhood relations, at least from behind the rose-colored glasses of a child. Birds chirped merrily and men folk whistled while working on their cropped lawns. The children played outside and the parents all pitched in to help raise them. It takes a village you know. I imagine everybody showed up for church on Sunday, and the kids never saw the corruption that went on after midnight in the village square. Domestic disputes, secret affairs, backstabbing, lies, deceit, and whistle blowing all hide within every *good* community. My wife wanted to find a friendly family neighborhood and I hoped to sell her on the most isolated home I could find. I just wanted to be as far away as possible from everything and everyone.

****

Another season had passed and the cold rains of spring were of no relief to the overall atmosphere of our home. On the weekends, I took the family to West Virginia. Together we climbed the winding roads in search of property along the foothills of Jefferson County. Krista was over seven months pregnant and I had purchased a large conversion van, which kept everyone as comfortable as possible. The vehicle traversed up hills that felt like ninety degree inclines. The locations were remote and isolated. Krista would say, 'If it snows up here, you know we're never getting out.'

I would answer back with a simple reply, 'I know.' She was looking at things from a pregnant person's perspective, but being stranded on a mountain did not sound bad to me. I pictured myself replying to everyone, 'Sorry you all, I'm stuck up here on this mountain. I guess your problem is just going to have to wait... I can't get down there and you can't get up here. I guess every single problem is not my problem today.' There would be no more obligations to neighbors, relatives, bio-families, social workers, or inspectors. It sounded too good to be true.

****

It was the end of March and a new option would become available to our family. This happened when my mother caught wind of our current endeavor. I imagine she went into a full asthmatic panic when she discovered that I was moving away from my original homestead. My older brother had done the same thing with a stint to Minnesota. His relocation did not go over so well. One of my sisters lived deep in southern Maryland, while another lived in Frederick, and yet another in West Virginia. If I moved away, my mother would be in Central Maryland, all... by... herself.

My mother proposed that Krista and I purchase the family home located in a Howard County neighborhood called Allview Estates. Unfortunately, it did have neighbors, but at least I already knew half of them and there were some good folk still holding down the fort. Krista could have her little community filled with fictitious happiness, and I could relive the days of my youth as if I was going back in time. Best of all, my kids could relive my youth while playing around my childhood home landlocked by a river and dense trees.

Allview Estates was a great place for kids to explore. Many of my former playmates had returned to the neighborhood as well, or had never left. There was plenty of space outside so the kids could stay out of my hair. Besides, it was looking more as if Jared would be staying with us for life and the Howard County school system might offer a Jell-O free education. During my time substitute teaching, the kids of the Howard County school system were very agreeable. I welcomed a return to my childhood playground.

My wife's main apprehension was the size of the small rancher. But after I pitched the idea of a new addition with walk-in closets, Krista approved. It was official. We were moving into my childhood home and my mother was moving out. She planned to move back to her childhood home as well. Unfortunately, the time had come for someone to take care of my grandmother. She had recently developed Alzheimer's and had started talking about her days as a child. My mother volunteered to take care of her. It seemed like we were all going back in time.

We completed settlement on the house even before Krista's delivery date. At the end of April our daughter, Marianna Elisabeth Hoffman, was born and Elo and I began moving items from our Violetville home to Columbia. We moved everything one room at a time with plans to move Krista and Marianna last. My mother had already moved back to her childhood home and Elo was using our new home as a bachelor pad while we transitioned.

Elo assisted the foster agency with the inspection of our new residence. Krista and I were more concerned about the complexities of raising our newborn daughter. We were clueless and left to our own devices. The move could not have come at a better time. Just before we moved out of Violetville, the actions of a neighbor ushered us out in style.

****

"Matt, we have a problem."

Caught unaware, I replied, "What?" I was exhausted from the long night at work.

In a flat tone Krista stated, "Somebody reported us to Child Protective Services."

"What? ...Why?"

"It's because Jared was standing at the bus stop in the rain."

Obviously, children today should not get wet. If they do, you should immediately report this to Child Protective Services. As Krista's delivery date approached, she was no longer capable of bus duty. An anonymous report, filed weeks before, was now under investigation as we continued to pack and move. Yet the real problem was not rain, or us, but the fact that Little J's bus driver was about as dependable as Otto from *The Simpsons.*

Jared, left standing at the bus stop, often waited for a half hour or longer for his bus to arrive. Heaven forbid it should rain on one of those days. We had worked out a simple system to remedy the problem with the school bus driver. If Jared was still standing on the corner when I arrived home from my nightshift, I drove him to school. It worked out much better than Baltimore County's attempt at transportation; on several occasions they picked him up and dropped him off at the *wrong school!*

We did not have too many worries concerning the safety of his bus stop. Jared was almost ten years old and stood alongside the kids of Overly Manor Elementary. Our bus stop was on a dead end road situated between the Baltimore County Police Station and the Violetville Fire Station. It could not have been safer unless Jared had a secret service agent posted on the rooftop to protect him. If I ever had a heart attack, my plan was to stagger out to the bus stop to receive help. The problem is that none of this actually matters when you have a moron for a neighbor.

Discovering that you are the subject of a CPS investigation is scary stuff. Through the neighborhood grapevine, I determined that our anonymous informant was the wife of a neighbor named Cooter. Never mind the fact that her husband was occasionally hauled away on drug charges or that his kids only saw him once a month on visitation day. It is still a horrible crime when my kid gets wet. We could not wait to move. Krista and I sat nervously for our first meeting with an agent from CPS.

"Krista, you have experience with this stuff. What do you think is going to happen?"

"I don't know. I've seen the unit director at work make a CPS report, but I've never been on the receiving end."

"Could they take away our kids, or retract our foster license?"

"I certainly hope not, but I have no idea."

The CPS worker arrived and fortunately, they did none of the above. After ten minutes of questions and answers, the agent understood the circumstances. She processed the required paperwork and reassured us, "The report will come back unsubstantiated."

The report coincidentally came back unsubstantiated. The majority of claims made to CPS are false. This report was just business as usual. Never again should we worry if some nutty neighbor made an unfounded CPS claim. They would probably end up looking like a jackass.

Still, we were relieved but apprehensive. Would we forever remain the evil parents who make their children stand out in the rain? I hoped that false claims end up disregarded and destroyed, but probably not. If making kids stand in the rain is an evil act, then my old football coach should receive the death penalty.

****

As summer arrived, Elo and I were busy moving my mother's possessions off to the dump. We needed to make room for our own pile of junk in the old Hoffman household. He and my friend Mike helped me move the very first eyesore, an old upright piano. It had been the centerpiece of my mother's downstairs 'Club' room since sometime back in the sixties. Around eight teamsters must have moved the heavy instrument down the five steps and into its current resting place. Now it was up to the three of us to carry it out.

Elo was strong for his size and his body was pure muscle. He reminded me of an ant that could lift ten times its own weight. Yet he would sink like a rock to the bottom of a pool. Mike was my best friend from childhood and with nearly 300 lbs of muscle and beer gut, he was the right man for the job. A little bribe of beer and pizza and he would even lift the Acropolis for me.

We worked the ancient instrument around the basement floor and over to the basement steps. Together the three of us lifted the heavy piano a step at a time. Once we had it resting in the backyard we levered it onto the bed of my truck.

I yelled out to the ghost of my dad, "Why did you leave this heavy piece of crap here for me!" Now I knew what my mother was screaming about just after the old man died. My father should have helped my mother to get rid of all this crap years ago!

Mike taunted, "Matthew, Robert left you a wonderful gift to haul.

You should give him thanks and praise."

Elo laughed which resulted in a loss of his strength. This was no time for jokes. We heaved the last bit onto the bed of the truck and stopped to catch our breath. I climbed into the driver's seat, then instructed Mike and Elo to guide me through the yard.

"Make sure I don't hit that tree when I'm backing up," I said. "Remember, I can't see squat with this thing in the bed of my truck."

My two assistants waved me off and then started their usual banter about school. I am sure Mike was attempting to persuade Elo to return to college. The self-proclaimed 'Uncle' Mike enjoyed his role as foster uncle and advisor. As Elo listened to the lesson of the day, I backed up and smacked into the tree. I could have sworn I heard my father's laughter coming from the screened patio.

Chapter 19

New Beginnings

Now that we had moved to Columbia, Elo would need transportation to hold down steady employment. My wife and I purchased a family minivan and decided to give Elo our old Toyota Corolla. I had already begun teaching him how to drive before moving from Violetville. Elo was a cautious driver but instructing him was still the six scariest months of my life.

He did not manage to kill me, but I do believe I received my first gray hair. How do driving instructors make a career of that job? During one lesson, I had to grab hold of the steering wheel in order to avoid a head-on collision. Fortunately, that only happened once. Elo was a reasonable young man and agreed to drive on back roads for his first year behind the wheel. This was a rule that my father laid down for me, and Elo agreed to carry on with the family tradition. He was having a fun time exploring the woods around our new home and running errands in his new car. The dogs always enjoyed tagging along.

For me, moving back to my childhood home was a needed change. The familiarity of my old neighborhood was comforting while I was operating outside of my comfort zone as a new birth father. I spent a lot of time with my infant daughter while Krista worked part time as a psychotherapist. Whenever she had a break, she would run home and feed the baby. It was a crazy routine.

My daughter was too young for activities other than lying on my chest, so I rediscovered television. But when Krista returned home from work, I spent time in the woods clearing the old trails that I walked as a child. Our property backed to a section of shallow forest where I could find the isolation I desired and reflect upon my childhood days. The smells of skunk cabbage and honeysuckle were consoling reminders. It was a wonderful distraction.

In the summer months, Little J made his first neighborhood friend, Harper, who frequented our home like a neighborhood dog that hangs around for scraps. He was the same age as Jared, but stood a foot taller. The kid was big for his age and his personality complimented Jared's. He was a goodhearted misfit in the neighborhood, regularly found roaming door to door for conversation, or perhaps a free cookie. Harper was a much better friend than old Sammie.

I heard neighbors mention Harper when speaking about the kids of the neighborhood. He was the most visible child in our society of latchkey kids and indoor play dates. The young man reminded me of one of my own foster children. He looked familiar to me and I decided to interrogate him about his family history.

I called out to him across the yard, "Hey kid, what's your last name?"

"Uhhh… Zellmeiter," he replied.

I thought so. He was another neighborhood legacy. I was a second-generation Allview Estates prodigy, and he was a third. Many of the children of Allview had moved back or had never even left.

"Is your Dad's name, Jeffrey?"

"Uhhh… Jeff."

The kid liked to start every sentence with the sound *Uhhh*. I remembered his father. He also started every sentence with *Uhhh*. The boy's father was somewhere around the age of my older sisters. I recalled the days when I watched Jeffrey sling a lacrosse ball with the older kid who lived across the street. Harper was the spitting image of his father, Jeffrey.

I questioned him further, "So, do you live around here with your Dad?"

"Uhhh… yea," the young man answered. The boy was not very descriptive.

"Uhhhhhh… *Wheeeeeeere?*"

"We live on the corner of Evergreen."

I thought to myself, *Jeffrey Zellmeiter, how could I forget his name?* My sister Cindy occasionally told a story of childhood trauma related to Jeffrey. One day he held her to the ground and dropped a wad of spit directly into her mouth. It was a technique straight out of Bully101 and now his son was going to be Jared's new companion. What were the chances? At least he was big enough to protect my scrawny little foster son. The relationship might wind up beneficial for Little J, the kid I sometimes referred to as my foster chicken.

I inquired further, "How is school at Appleton Elementary? Jared will be starting third grade this year." I was interested in hearing Harper's opinion of my old school. Perhaps this young man had spent some time getting to know the staff, principal included.

"Uhhh… I am supposed to be going there, but I am going to go to a new school because... uhhh... I was fighting. I have got something called O.D.D. It has something to do with how I get real angry."

"I'm familiar with it. I've already met a few others in the same boat." My intuition told me that I would be seeing a lot more of Harper. As the boy stood sweating, I smelled a hint of beef jerky rising from his person.

Jared asked, "Can Harper and I get a snack out of the snack drawer?"

Harper's eyes lit up with a look that emanated, *'What is this wonderful thing called a snack drawer?'*

"Go ahead," I approved, and the two boys went inside to help themselves. I realized my grocery bill was about to increase tenfold.

****

Life was improving for everyone. My wife suppressed her grief while being preoccupied with the duties of motherhood. There is nothing quite like the distraction of a newborn baby to occupy your time. Jared was making new friends and he was enamored with his new elementary school. The staff seemed more attentive and the students were kinder than those at Charlesbrook had been. At least Jared never came home covered in Jell-O.

Elo found work at an animal boarding facility. It was a dream job for him except for the poop scooping part of the work duties. The animal shelter was a short distance from our home and the distance was perfect for a practicing new driver. It only required him to drive along the slow moving back roads of Columbia. He loved working with the dogs and quickly made friends with around fifty new canines. Our dogs particularly enjoyed his return from work and would sniff his jeans for a solid ten minutes. I lost myself in my projects, updating the house and designing plans to increase the size of our home. By now, the ripples in our life had faded away so I guess it was time to throw a rock into the family pond.

****

Understandably, foster care kids can come with a lot of emotional baggage, often associated with their birth family. I discovered that Elo's relatives were living nearby in Columbia. His birth brother Wallace even went to the same high school, Oakland Mills, from which I graduated.

So I asked Elo, "What do you think about reconnecting with your birth family?"

"What... when?"

"I don't know... soon." Elo stood hesitant and I continued, "Well, what do you think?"

"I guess." He accepted with hesitation.

I am not sure what motivated me, but I moved forward with my newest plan. Perhaps it was my interest in seeing how Wallace and little sisters Diynah and Carlyn faired in comparison to Elo and his brother Nevar. I wondered who really received the short end of the stick. We had visited Nevar a couple of times over the last year and the foster care system was working out fairly well for him. Nevar was a resilient individual and Elo had done pretty well for himself too, although it did take several rolls of the dice before Elo rolled a seven.

After discovering that Elo's birth mom resided in an area of government Section 8 housing located near my old high school, I became intrigued with the idea of investigating his family. They were now living in the village of Oakland Mills. During my time at Oakland Mills High, I had several classmates who grew up in this same Section 8 housing. Many of those classmates were now very successful, while some were not.

The work of community planner James Rouse created the suburb of Columbia that mixed government-funded housing complexes within neighborhoods of 1970's designer homes. To many, Mr. Rouse is the founding father of Columbia. In 1963, he produced our planned community by buying significant acreage around the postal stop still known as Simpsonville, MD. Simpsonville was once the city address of my current home. Now I was curious to find out how the Columbia experiment had worked out for Elo's birth family.

By incorporating housing from various income levels, Mr. Rouse planned to integrate America on 1,400 acres of Maryland. Part of his plan was to help citizens at the bottom rung of society by sliding them into middle class neighborhoods. From my personal experience, I witnessed mixed results: Some of my former Section 8 classmates became very successful, working as teachers, doctors, or running businesses, while some ended up dead or in jail. Mr. Rouse had taken a different approach to spreading wealth by literally spreading wealthy neighborhoods with government-assisted housing. The plan appeared to have worked for many years, but later had less success with the increase in population density. Eventually, everybody needs some space.

Over the decades, Oakland Mills slid into decay. The surrounding middle class homes were abandoned like their 1970's architecture. The previous residents had moved away from these homes that were located near Section 8 housing. Mr. Rouse had wonderful intentions that generated positive results for a long time, but thirty years later, abuse and neglect had eventually created a few unplanned ghettos. The flight of the upper-middleclass was obvious in the Oakland Mills neighborhoods that were declining and in disrepair. As with the former occupants of the surrounding neighborhood homes, my friends that once lived in these government-assisted houses did not have plans to move back.

Many former residents of Oakland Mills now reside in the newest Columbia village area, River Hill. In my high school days, Oakland Mills won every championship imaginable. The football, soccer, wrestling, basketball, running, and even the "It's Academic" team, all held titles. Now championship trophies reside within the school showcases of more affluent areas, in or surrounding Columbia. There appeared to be a correlation between money and championships, but money from government-funded housing programs did not have the same effect. I hoped the program funding at least helped members of Elo's biological family.

****

On a beautiful sunny afternoon, Elo and I climbed into my truck on a mission to locate the members of his biological family. Just five minutes later, we had entered the village of Oakland Mills. The neatly cropped bushes camouflaged drug needles and empty liquor bottles, the new signs of change. The smell of cheap wine, cigarette butts, and almost-empty liquor bottles filled the air as I slowed down to investigate an empty parking lot. In the location where I had once pumped my first tank of gas, only a sign remained. It was not an old gasoline advertisement. It was an arrow, pointing towards some nearby office space. Below the arrow were the words *Methadone Clinic.*

What had happened here? This was not the same neighborhood of my happy childhood. Fifteen years later and it had fallen apart, or was it I that had always worn rose-colored glasses? Is this the product of government-funded housing, or the product of poor choices? How had Mr. Rouse's approach worked out for Wallace, Diynah, and Carlyn? I was afraid that I already knew.

As we pulled past the Oakland Mills shopping center, I muttered aloud, "Oh man, I hope it works out."

Elo responded, "You hope *what* works out?"

I paused for a moment. "Nothing… we're here."

Elo and I pulled into a small apartment complex that sat behind the shopping center. The center now showed evidence of social decay, no longer the same place I bought my weekly candy bar after Sunday morning sermons in the neighboring Interfaith Center. There was trash lying about and the cracked window of the liquor store indicated that the place had obviously seen its share of crime. A guard stood outside of the grocery store and a temporary police station had been set up in the center's parking lot. McGruff the Crime Dog frequented events at the shopping center. Perhaps Jared would like to meet him.

Like the ghost of Mr. Rouse, I still had hope for the renewal of Oakland Mills. This area was dear to my heart. I would spend my milk money at the local shopping center, and order my pizza there too. The last two grocery chains gave up on the shopping center a long time ago and now Food Lion was the supermarket of choice.

We passed the trailhead to a Columbia bike path, found the correct building number, and parked the truck. Elo was wearing his usual expression of apprehension. I had become very familiar with his "game face." He was wearing it the evening he arrived at my home in Violetville, and the day I first threw him into the Florida hotel pool. I even saw it the first time he turned the keys of his Toyota Corolla.

Together, we walked through the entrance of the building. Apartment number *307* was on the third floor so we headed to the top of the staircase and found the doorway. The hallway smelled like cigarette smoke and the brown paint on the door was dull and faded. Elo stood behind me as I proceeded to knock. There was no answer, so I knocked again.

We waited for a few moments before I commented, "Maybe they're not home. Let me try again."

I knocked harder and louder on the third try but no one opened the door. The door behind us swung open and an elderly woman stood in the doorway. I now knew where the stench of burned tobacco was coming from.

In a raspy voice she said, "Ain't nobody living in there. They moved out about two days ago."

I asked, "Was it a woman named Shirley, living with three kids?"

She replied, "Yep. What? Are you a social worker?"

People always assumed that I was Elo's social worker. Perhaps it was the casual business attire, or maybe working the nightshift gave me the tired look of a social worker with too many kids on my caseload. Most likely, it was the fact that I was a thirty-year-old Caucasian walking around with a twenty-year-old African American in tow.

Together, we often experienced racial profiling. I would not dare take Elo to lunch in Washington's Dupont Circle. Someone might mistake me for his sugar daddy. Sometimes when he stood next to me, strangers called me "officer", and it was not as if he was wearing handcuffs. To some he must have looked like a hardened street tough, but to me he looked like Bambi. Either way I just laughed off the remarks.

To answer the woman's question I replied, "No!" She nodded and closed the door of her apartment. I would have asked more questions, but she obviously was not interested in an interrogation. I turned to Elo and said, "Looks like we just missed them."

Elo had a crooked smile and almost looked relieved. According to my research, they had been living there for several years, but it was not our destiny to reunite with Elo's birth family today. We clopped down the steps and onto the parking lot.

I said, "Well… we'll find out where they moved to."

Elo replied, "If you say so."

****

The winter holidays approached and we made the best of the festive season in our new home. We invited our extended families over to see our new environment. This was Marianna's first Christmas, and she brought joy to us all. She was now eight months old, crawling around at lightning speed. Elo would hold her on his lap for hours in the reclining chair, giving me a needed break. When Marianna was ready to play, Jared, her primary playmate, was always on hand. Little J literally saved my back. He would get out the toys, play with the toys, and clean up the toys.

Marianna and Jared developed a loving bond. She particularly liked to climb up onto his back as if she was riding a camel. He would lower his back down so that she could fit into the groves of his tiny physique. 'Jaaaaa' was one of her very first words. The two were like, 'peas and carrots.'

Uncle Jim and family came to visit us during the holidays. They wanted to see Little J in his new home as well as meet his new little sister, Marianna. It was a pleasant visit for Jared. He enjoyed wrestling on our living room floor with Uncle Jim while Aunt Pat, Aunt Becky, and Aunt Heather played with Marianna. Marianna was a very happy toddler and her laugh was infectious.

Uncle Jim and Aunt Pat expressed their desire to have a toddler of their own and admitted that they were currently working in that direction. I hoped that their plans worked out for them. They were in their early forties and time was no longer on their side.

Uncle Jim updated us on the status of Jared's birth mom. Things were not going as well for her or for other members of the extended family. More than one of the siblings had difficulty with addiction, and there was some sort of trouble with Jared's half sister, Stephanie. Things had been looking up for our family, but for some reason I was afraid that once again it was time for the pendulum to swing.

Chapter 20

Mental Block

Jared stood alongside the edge of my bed one night, shaking me awake and holding his stomach as he grimaced in pain. He released a slow moan like the sound of a pissed off cat and his breath smelled like sewer sludge. This could not be good. In the past three years, I had not seen him sick, not even once. This kid had the immune system of a cockroach and the health records to prove it. Something was wrong.

I took Jared upstairs to wake up Krista who was sleeping in the master bedroom with her roommate Marianna. I gently nudged my wife and whispered her name as I tried not to wake the baby. In between nighttime feedings, the two of them were trying to get as much sleep as possible.

She shot up with a squinty eye and frantically blurted out, *"What is it? What's wrong?"*

She knew well enough that there must be a problem if I woke her up in the middle of the night. I usually do not budge from my basement sarcophagus before dawn on my free-from-work nights. To catch up on lost sleep I claimed the dark underground bedroom as my crypt. Down there, I could not tell if it was day or night, and slept well in the bedroom that once belonged to my eldest sister Valerie.

I said, "Something's wrong with Jared. His stomach hurts badly and he is in a lot of pain."

Jared stood there bent over, moaning in agony.

Krista spoke up. "When I was his age my appendix burst. This could be serious. I think you should take him to the emergency room."

She was right; there was no way around it. If he was sick enough to get me out of bed, then he was sick enough to go to the emergency room. I quickly got dressed and grabbed our coats. I helped him into the truck and we headed for the nearby Howard County General Hospital emergency room.

It was two in the morning on a weekday and the emergency room was empty. It was not long before Jared and I were ushered into a back room. A nurse entered and took his preliminary readings. He was not feverish or ill other than his reports of abdominal discomfort as he sat bent over in pain. About ten minutes later, a doctor entered the room and began to perform some tests by prodding and poking at Little J.

He checked all the areas of his stomach and around both of his sides. "It doesn't look like a problem with his appendix," the doctor said. "He would have more pain on the right side of his tummy."

"What do you think it might be? I mean… this kid never gets sick. If he's in this much pain, something's *got* to be wrong."

"I have my suspicions, but we'll do an x-ray to be sure… Tell me. Does he eat a lot of cheese or dairy products?"

"Nnnn…oooooo." I had a clue as to where the doctor was going.

Maybe Jared was sitting in a twenty-car pileup along Hershey Highway and now he needed emergency services to clear the scene. The doctor left the room and the nurse soon returned. She placed him into a wheelchair and rolled him down the hallway towards a sign labeled radiology. Per the radiologist's request, I waited outside in the hall and sat down.

About fifteen minutes later Jared and the radiologist appeared in the hallway. The nurse returned and looked on as the radiologist held up an x-ray paper. He handed the sheet to the nurse and she walked us back to our previous location in the emergency room area of the hospital. The room was brightly lit, neatly arranged, and clean. Soon we would know the cause of Jared's problem.

The ER was no longer empty, and Little J and I listened to the moans of the patients as we sat waiting. Five minutes later, the doctor returned. With the nurse at his side, he posted the x-ray onto the illuminated board sitting on the wall of the room.

Then he spoke while pointing at the chart. "See that? Yep! It's just as I presumed. He's backed-up further than the Holland Tunnel on a Friday night. Nurse Baker, you know what to do."

I turned to the doctor, "Any advice?"

"Less dairy, more fiber, more vegetables, more fluids, and *more* exercise," he answered. "I have noticed that young men his age are having problems with constipation. It often stems from too much television and too much time in front of a video game console."

The doctor had described Jared to a "T." Little J's idea of exercise was cleaning the disks in his Playstation CD holder. He was like a drug abuser, and had literally drugged himself into a state of constipation.

The doctor walked off and the nurse followed up with Jared. "Here big guy. Have a seat up here on the table." She patted her hand on the elevated hospital bed that was covered by a protective white paper, causing a little crunch sound to emanate from it.

Jared climbed onto the bed and the nurse spoke to him, "Have you ever heard of an enema?"

"You mean like the N-M-mas at the zoo?"

The nurse shot a look of disbelief so intense she inadvertently turned her head to look away. I thought to myself, *Ha! That was nothing. Wait until he tells her about the N-M-mas living in the closet.*

She answered back, "Noooooooo." The nurse reached into a drawer and pulled out a little green and white box. He was about to find out about enemas the hard way. She opened the box, pulled out a bottle shaped apparatus, and continued. "This is an enema. It is a little bottle of cleaning solution meant to help your tummy. I'll need you to lie on your side and I'll need to insert it into your bottom."

Jared was suddenly aware of the situation at hand and his clueless expression disappeared. Now he exhibited a look of total fear. "Is it going to hurt?"

"It *is* going to feel a little uncomfortable. You will need to relax and let me push some fluid into your bottom. Then, you will need to squeeze your bottom muscles in order to keep the fluid inside so that it can help make you feel better. After a minute, you should be able to go to the bathroom. You will feel *much* better after that."

He answered with a nervous "Okay." He slid down onto his side and the nurse stood behind him. I circled around to the front and grabbed a chair for the opening of the big event. I wondered if the ER was selling popcorn and Goobers out in the lobby. Jared arrived with his own supply of Raisinets, soon to be released.

He looked scared so I reassured him, "It's not going to be *too* bad and it does not hurt *that* much. It just feels a bit *weird.*"

In reality, what did I know? I had not faced constipation since I was a kid and I am not even so sure I faced constipation then. All I know is that at age five my mother used some old school apparatus, similar to equipment in the *Matrix* films, to give me an internal cleansing. After setting a warm bottle of fluid on my stomach, a hose attached to that warm bottle ended up in my backside. Unlike the *Matrix*-tool, this equipment did not transport me into a virtual Kung Fu dojo.

I offered Jared advice stemming from my dojo flashback. "Once the enema is in there, make sure you squeeze your butt tightly. You want to keep the fluid in there so it works on the first attempt. If you don't, the nurse will have to give you another enema." His look of apprehension could have turned Medusa to stone.

The nurse turned to me, "Hey Dad. *You* should pay attention, just in case *you* need to insert a second enema." Now I turned to stone.

Where was the ghost of my father to advise us both now? Was he laughing hysterically from heaven or receiving his own version of an enema down in hell? I sat there thinking to myself... 'Patience Matthew... patience.' At this rate, my enema in hell was not too far off. The nurse gently lowered the topside of Jared's dinosaur pajamas and inserted the long, thin end of colon flush into the bottom of his tank.

Just like the scene from the movie *Deliverance*, Little J let out the long, drawn-out squeal of a pig, *"Wwwwwwwwweeeeeeeeeeyyyyyyy!"*

His eyes nearly popped out of his head. Unable to contain myself I broke out into laughter. The sound of my uncontrolled hysterics was pouring through every corner of my mouth, ears, and nose. His expression was priceless and the sound effect was pure comedy at its best.

The nurse looked up at me with utter disdain and snapped, *"Sir.... please."*

"I'm sorry. I am sorry. I just can't help it." It was around three o'clock in the morning and the uncontrolled hysterics that accompany exhaustion had taken over every part of me. I tried to compose myself although remnants of laughter remained around the corners of my mouth.

The nurse kept a straight face and continued to encourage Jared. She had inserted so many plastic water bottles into so many bottoms that she had lost all appreciation for the humor of her task. The nurse counted out the time required before Jared could dash to the bathroom and release his fury. She rolled out a series of numbers, "Thirty-seven... thirty-eight... thirty-nine. You're doing great, you're almost there."

Jared lay on his side with a grimace as he counted along and tried to increase the pace of her count. "Forty-one, fifty, fifty-seven... Can I go yet? I feel something coming!"

The nurse replied. "Just a little bit longer, hang in there." She kept counting.

I tried to count along with her, but I felt the taunting tickle of unbridled hysterics so I decided to keep my big mouth shut. Eventually the nurse let him loose. Little J sprinted across the hallway and into the open bathroom door. I walked over and closed the door behind him just as his butt hit the porcelain. The sounds of his expulsion nearly shook the door.

He let out a huge sigh of relief, "Oooooooo... Aaaaaaahhhh."

It sounded like he was watching fireworks from behind the bathroom door. I could not contain my laughter any longer and nearly fell to the floor as tears began rolling down my face.

Little J called out from behind the door, "Oh, that feels sooooooo gooooooooood!" and then he began laughing as well.

Fatherhood had now taken on new meaning for me.

****

A month passed and I had managed to track down Elo's biological family. His mother Shirley had relocated to another area of Section 8 housing just across the street from a bowling alley on Baltimore Pike. Elo and I hopped into my truck for our second attempt to visit with his birth mom. We found the apartment complex with relative ease and walked up to the entrance of the building. The new apartment was located on the second floor and we stood just outside of the door. Elo knocked below the numbers on the door.

Moments later, an attractive, petite, African American woman opened the door and softly said, "Eloise, come in."

There was no explosion of emotion or even change of inflection in the woman's voice. I did not know what to expect, but certainly not this. It was as if she had just seen Elo yesterday and there was nothing particularly special about a surprise visit from her long-lost son. Everything was unusual. An old man was sitting silently, smiling from a couch on the left side of the room, and the sound of a teenage girl emanated from a back bedroom. The apartment reeked of warm trash. I followed Elo and his birth mother into the center of the apartment.

She casually walked deeper into the apartment towards the kitchen and then called back to Elo. In a flat monotone voice she said, "I'm going to make you a peanut butter and jelly sandwich." Then she started pulling out bread and materials from the refrigerator.

I waved to her and introduced myself. "Hi. My name is Matt. I'm Elo's foster dad." Her body language and mannerisms were subdued. I could see the same glazed-over look that I had previously seen in the eyes of her third son, Nevar.

"Hi," Shirley responded as she continued making the peanut butter and jelly sandwich.

Elo stood in the dining area on the other side of a kitchen countertop. There were no table and chairs in the small apartment, only a generic overhead chandelier hanging where a table and chairs would normally belong. The dining room flowed into the living room, where there was an old couch and a mattress lying on the floor. An old bike was lying next to the mattress. Pizza boxes and other garbage sat around the unkempt apartment. It looked as if they had been living there for quite some time but in actuality, it could not have been more than a month. Elo stood silently taking in the scene, as did I. The atmosphere was awkward to say the least.

Elo finally spoke up. "So how is Wallace?" He attempted to start a conversation by asking about his younger brother. Just then, a teenage girl appeared from the back bedroom. It was Elo's younger sister. She had come out to see who was speaking in the living room and Elo casually greeted her, "Hi Diynah." She looked at him with curiosity.

"That's your brother, Eloise," Shirley muttered.

"I know that!" the girl replied. Diynah was more focused and expressive than Elo's birth mom, but I still did not witness any heartfelt display of emotion. She had the devilish grin of someone with ulterior motives. She looked at Elo, scanning him over from head to toe.

The way Diynah inspected Elo reminded me of the creature from the movie *Alien*. I half expected a little mouth to come jetting out of her own mouth and smack Elo in the forehead. As always, he was wearing his poker face. Shirley was still working on Elo's sandwich and did not answer the question about Wallace. There was no sign of Diynah's twin sister Carlyn.

I stood behind Elo and then moved towards the man sitting over on the couch in order to introduce myself, "Hi, I'm Matt. I'm Elo's foster dad."

The man looked at me with an odd smile. He said nothing.

Shirley answered for him. "That's Charlie. He's a friend of mine."

"Hi Charlie," I continued. Still wearing the same odd expression, he responded with a nod. I felt like I was in a scene from a Tim Burton film. When would the Oompa Loompas show up and carry me off? Elo appeared nervous, yet relaxed. He had created an odd combination of mannerism and expression, mastered over years of dealing with uncomfortable situations. As I often do, I decided to speak up for Elo and me.

I turned towards Shirley and said, "Elo and I live in the area and looked you up. We thought we would stop by to say hello."

"Umm, hmmmm," she responded.

"I was wondering. Where exactly are you from? Elo's early paperwork shows that you once lived on Monument Street."

She replied with a soft Southern accent. "I was a little girl from the Eastern Shore before I ended up in the city," she said. "I used to play outside of our farmhouse. It was my home. There used to be honeysuckle growing along the side of an old garage. We used to pick them before we had to pull them all down. That was our job you know. We were always busy cleaning up the backside of the garage. I am going to go back there someday. Eloise, here's your sandwich." She pushed the peanut butter and jelly creation across the kitchen countertop towards Elo.

The room was silent as Elo took several bites of the sandwich. I was completely out of my element, standing somewhere in the middle of the twilight zone.

I nudged Elo and prompted him with, "You got any questions for your mom... or for your sister?"

"Nope," he simply replied.

"Well then I think we ought to get going. I've got a lot to do today." I really did not have that much to do, but I was looking for any sort of exit strategy. "Okay, we should be going. Nice meeting you," I continued as I waved goodbye and motioned towards the door.

Elo placed what was left of his sandwich on the countertop. Then he followed me towards the door.

"He's at work today," Shirley said. "He works at the food store over in Long Reach." It seems that she was now answering the earlier question pertaining to Elo's brother Wallace. "Goodbye," she continued, and waved as we moved towards the door.

Charlie still sat on the couch watching us with the same odd grin. Diynah still stood in the same spot where she first appeared, watching Elo as we prepared to exit.

I called back to Shirley, "Perhaps we'll stop by to say hello another day."

"Okay," she simply replied. It appeared as if Elo's birth family were not big talkers, nor big on emotion. Now I know where he inherited his quiet demeanor and predilection for short answers. I felt a huge weight lift from my shoulders as I stepped into the hall and the apartment door closed behind us. The outside air felt refreshing and smelled sweet, the sounds of rustling leaves a welcome clamor of natural symphony.

I turned to Elo, "That was strange."

"Yep," he replied with his standard one word answer.

"Are they always like that?"

"Pretty much," he shot back. The length of his answer had doubled. Elo was making progress in regards to his descriptiveness.

"Wow!" I replied, feeling almost speechless. I had lost my ability to elaborate. Perhaps some strange chemical had been hovering in the apartment. We were both in there around fifteen minutes and only a handful of sentences had actually been spoken.

Elo spoke as we walked towards the truck sitting in the nearby parking lot. "I told you about them. They are a little crazy. See why I'm not in any big hurry to reconnect?"

"No doubt," I said and I climbed into the truck. I took some time to reflect. After this recent experience, I realized that Elo and Nevar had received 'the good end of the stick' by being in foster care. Wallace, Diynah, and Carlyn did not appear to be the lucky winners I had originally thought that they were. Their lives were influenced by mental disorders, inadequate housing, and possible drug use.

Even if foster care had been the better option, I sensed Elo's disappointment with the visit. His posture was slouched and he could not even maintain the usual smile that often looked etched in torment. As I pulled away from the apartment, Elo rested his head against the passenger window and silently stared at the doorway to the life that was almost his. He had known what he would find yet hoped for something more. In the end, he got just what he expected.

Chapter 21

No News Is Bad News

When Elo and I arrived home from our unusual bio visit, there was a message flashing on our telephone answering machine. It was the voice of Jared's Aunt Pat. We had not heard from her in a while, at least not since the last time we saw her and Uncle Jim back at the end of December. The message requested that I call her back as soon as possible. I could tell by the tone of her voice that she had bad news. Jared was still at school and Elo wandered off to the kitchen to make himself a snack. I sat down and returned the call to Aunt Pat. The call was short and directly to the point. The phone rang and Aunt Pat picked up her end of the line.

"Hello," she answered.

"Hi Pat. This is Matt, Jared's foster dad. I am returning your call. Is everything okay?"

Something seemed wrong considering that it was the first time she ever called during the day. She or Uncle Jim usually only called in the evening hours to coordinate upcoming bio-visits.

"No. I'm afraid I have bad news and I knew that Jared would want to know." I could sense her hesitation. She took a deep sigh, then silence.

With my most sensitive tone I inquired, "Is everything okay with his mother?"

"Yes, Tarra's fine. It's his Uncle Frankie. His wife found him in bed this morning. He died sometime during the night. We believe it was the result of a drug overdose."

Uncle Frankie had fallen back into old habits. He was a second-generation drug addict and ultimately fell victim to the family curse. I only hoped his children would find a kinder fate.

"I'm so sorry. Is there anything I can do?"

"No. The state is helping to fund the burial and there won't be a funeral." I assured her that I would inform Little J. He would be home in about an hour and I could sit down and talk with him then. It was going to be very difficult for him to hear this horrible news about his biological male role model. Unfortunately, Uncle Frankie had made a very bad decision.

The phone rang and this time it was the Baltimore County social worker, Gail Witherspoon. She was calling to work out the details of her next meeting with Little J's birth mom. Birth mom, making strides, was ready for another visit. Over the last two years, I noticed a trend that she seemed to be more dependable in the spring. From spring into summer, she attended almost every bio visit. She held down a job painting houses and usually settled into some sort of temporary housing. Often she stayed at the home where Jared's sister Stephanie resided.

Stephanie was living in the Hammersmith home. Ms. Hammersmith was an older woman who had adopted Stephanie's father, Logan Hammersmith. Along with Jared's birth mom, Logan Hammersmith was also a second or third generation foster child. When Logan was out of prison, he would come home to stay with his adopted mother.

Gail continued speaking to me on the phone. "So, does next Thursday at four o'clock work for you?"

My mind had already drifted off to the subject of Jared's uncle. "Sure." Before she could hang up the phone I interjected, "There is one thing you should know. I'm not sure if you've heard, but Jared's birth uncle, Frank, died last night – possibly from an overdose."

Gail informed me that she had not heard about the incident. As a social worker in Baltimore, she appeared to have developed the thick skin of an ER nurse.

She responded in a tone that held no apparent emotion, "That's very unfortunate. It looks like the drugs finally won."

Gail had access to all of the family's foster records. She well knew who Frankie was, and had a brief history on him. The only thing she did not have access to was the inside information that we received directly from Jared's biological family members.

Uncle Jim and Aunt Pat had dealt with Gail back when Jared first transitioned to their home. They did not have much to say about Gail except that they did not appreciate the unwelcomed pressure she applied with regards to adopting Little J. A main goal of DSS is to place children in foster care with a biological relative. The overwhelmed couple was not ready for adoption. Pressure from DSS can be very intimidating.

"That brings me to something else," Gail continued. "A member of the bio family has run into a problem and will be entering a foster home. We will talk about it more at our next visit. See you then."

The phone conversation ended and she hung up the receiver. We had not heard any other bad news from Uncle Jim or from Aunt Pat. In fact, we had not heard any other news pertaining to the biological family at all. I always thought "no news was good news" but apparently not in this case.

****

I sat where my father used to sit, on the screened-in porch of our home, and listened to the sound of Jared's bus rolling down the hill. The smell of bus fumes and the sounds of children saying goodbye to one another carried to my spot. Soon Jared darted past me and disappeared into the kitchen. It was amusing to watch him run home from the bus stop. You would think his pants were on fire and that he was running to the kitchen sink to put them out. His backpack always overfilled with books and strapped tightly over his shoulders, forced him to hunch forward as he ran.

Jared's afterschool run always reminded me of the days that I used to run home from that very same bus stop. Except I was not running for something, I was running from something. Around third grade, I had become the target of the neighborhood bully and each afternoon endured a ceremonial 'running of the nerd.' I will never forget the day my mother gave me some good advice. As I ran in a straight line for the front door, I heard my mother holler out, *'Drop the bag!'*

She was right! Why had I not thought of it before? I could run twice as fast without extra weight holding me back. Besides, what would a bully want with my books? I doubt he spent too much time reading in between noogies and arm twists. My mother had the perfect idea. I could easily escape the bully and he would eventually get bored and go home. Then I could retrieve my bag. I followed my mother's advice, dropped the bag, and headed for the door. The bully was left behind in my dust.

When I arrived at the door, my mother asked, "What are you doing?"

"Running?"

"You were supposed to drop the bag so that you could turn around and fight. You can't throw a good punch wearing a bag of books." What was she trying to tell me? Did she really want me to take on the neighborhood bully? She was the one who turned me into the Momma's boy I am today. Now she wanted me to forget all my years of training and go into warrior mode? I exclaimed, *"No way!"*

My mother had not prepared me for the streets. I waited until the bully was gone, got my bag, and lived safely ever after. The fact is, I went into Mafia mode. I had my sister's boyfriend, Dennis, put in a few 'good' words for me. The bully never bothered me again.

For Jared it was different. The moment he got off the bus, he was ready to knock out his homework, not because he was responsible, but because his homework had to be completed for him to gain access to his drug, the

Playstation2. At least he had learned how to pause his games long enough to use the bathroom. He had learned something from his 'Deliverance' night at the emergency room. Even so, I was still concerned about the time he dedicated to video games.

Jared headed for the kitchen snack drawer to grab his afternoon treat. I called out to him, "Jared," but he did not answer. It took a minimum of two calls to get his attention. In a louder voice, I tried again. *"Jared!"*

"Yeeeeeeeeeeees?"

"Come out here, I need to talk to you." He stepped from the kitchen with his chosen snack in hand. I continued, "Have a seat," and patted the seat next to me on the patio furniture. He looked at me with curiosity as he fumbled with a Little Debbie snack cake. I took a deep breath and said, "Jared. I have bad news. You know how some of your relatives, sometimes, make bad decisions?"

"Yeeeeeeeeees."

"Well, I'm afraid that your Uncle Frankie started doing drugs again… and last night… he did too many of them. Do you know what happens if you do too many drugs?"

"You get sick?"

Reluctantly I continued. "Yes, or sometimes you can get so sick that you die."

Little J broke down into tears. I attempted to set my hand on his shoulder to give him some sign of physical comfort but he pulled away. His head dropped and tears rolled down his face. He hid his face in the cushion of the chair, which muffled the sound of his cries.

He whimpered, "Is he in heaven?"

"Yes, I'm sure he's in a much better place than here." I continued to comfort him and took the opportunity to talk more about the effects of drugs. If nothing else, I wanted him to learn a lesson from this horrible tragedy. As with mine, his mother had not prepared him for the streets.

We spoke for a long time about making good decisions. Jared had come quite a way since walking out of St. Xavier's Infant Asylum. He was making good decisions of his own and I wanted him to know that Uncle Frankie's fate did not have to be his own.

His video game play was my biggest concern. It was a sign of Little J's addictive personality. When he played the game, it was almost as if he was spaced-out, high on drugs. I looked him in the eye and said, "You can *never… ever…* even *think* about trying drugs!" He wiped the tears from his eyes and confidently shook his head yes. Little J understood exactly what I was talking about.

****

Thursday arrived – as did Gail Witherspoon, the DSS worker. She was more punctual than a Swiss cuckoo clock and the frequency of her never-ending social worker visits was just as cuckoo. Being the most organized and efficient social worker in all of DSS, Gail was an exemplary state social worker. She understood the overall plan of social services, with 'stepping down' and 'place matters' incorporated into her professional belief system.

It had been over a year and Jared had settled into his new school. His birth mom had been taking strides to improve her own situation, but her efforts pointed in a direction other than Jared. She was making visits with Jared, but seemed happy with the overall status of his current placement in foster care. We were happy with it too, so we did not ask why. Little J had become an integral part of our lives and a wonderful big brother to our daughter Marianna. As it turns out, birth mom had bigger concerns than Jared, the son of Gerald Mean Jean. She was more worried about the future of her daughter, Stephanie Hammersmith.

Jared actually had two maternal siblings. The youngest, Stephanie, had remained with her mother. The other lived with her paternal grandparents. Birth mom and Stephanie moved from one place to another, staying with various relatives along the way. Sometimes they ran into problems.

Eventually the state removed Stephanie and assigned her to the care of a paternal grandparent. Birth mom had been working hard to stay drug free and was holding down a job in order to regain custody of her daughter. The birth father, Logan, was still in and out of prison. In the meantime, Stephanie lived with his adoptive mother.

Gail sat across from Jared in the living room of our Columbia home. She asked Jared if he would like to join her on an outing to McDonalds. Normally he would have jumped at any opportunity for a Big Mac or a Happy Meal with a prize, but he continually declined her offers. Jared did not completely trust Gail. He particularly did not like the part of the visit where I had to leave the room, leaving him to speak privately with Gail. I believe the alone time is a requirement of DSS in order to ensure that a child is not being coerced into any situation. Without the watchful eye of a foster parent, DSS feels that it can ensure honest answers from a child client. DSS private time is a necessary precaution, but is still very uncomfortable for people that have nothing to hide.

I left the room and gave them time to talk. They spoke about his feelings pertaining to the death of his uncle. I was listening from the lower family room as I tidied up the house. Eavesdropping is a necessary tool of every good parent. Besides, I did not exactly trust Gail either. She had also rubbed us the wrong way when she started pushing adoption. We loved Jared very much but there were still a lot of unanswered questions in his life. Once Gail's private time with Jared was complete, he went into the backyard to play.

Now, I sat alone with Gail and she started the conversation. "Remember when I mentioned that another biological family member was having difficulty?"

"Yes." I did not have a clue as to which family member she was referring. Uncle Frankie's kids could not have already moved under the care of the state and Jared's siblings had been stable for several years ... that is, except for Stephanie.

"As it turns out, the state has taken Jared's sister Stephanie into care. She was previously staying with a paternal grandparent, but since that time the birth mom and Stephanie have introduced several allegations of neglect pertaining to the current placement."

I could not be sure the accusations of neglect were legitimate. Jared's birth mom would have every reason to invent some but it seemed unlikely. Even though I thought birth mom was friendly and nonthreatening, I really did not know her that well. Besides, if she was using a drug, how reliable could she be? Perhaps the allegations were false. I would never really know. All I know is what DSS reported, and if there is an ongoing investigation of neglect towards a child, he or she might transition from that home. DSS might decide that it is better to return Stephanie to her birth mom than leave her in the care of a neglectful, non-biological grandparent. We did not know what to expect.

"So, no more visits with his birth sister?"

"Actually, it's just the opposite. We were wondering if you and your wife would be willing to take Stephanie into your home."

This was *a lot* to consider.

Chapter 22

Making Decisions

It was a late Saturday afternoon and I had just awoken from my daytime slumber. Jared was in the family room entertaining Marianna while Elo slept in the family room recliner, my daughter hanging from the arm of the chair. I heard the distinct sound of "Elmo's" voice as I walked into the kitchen and found my wife performing housework. Yesterday I had promised Elo that we would take another stab at visiting his bio family. Over the past month, he had become more interested in reconnecting with them. After all, they were only ten minutes away. He had a car and the desire to nurture a relationship with them after fifteen years of separation.

I called down to him from the kitchen. "Hey, Elo. Are you ready to head over to your mom's place?"

His eyes slowly opened. He always managed to sleep fairly well in the family room recliner even though there was a lot of action. Marianna's noisy baby toys laid spread across the floor. Jared was sitting watching the exciting adventures of Sesame Street. There is something hypnotic about Elmo's mesmerizing voice.

I could not help but imitate the characters of Sesame Street. Wry at heart, I always enjoyed Sesame Street and catching episodes where Oscar sang his song about trash. It always reminded me of my friend 'Uncle' Mike and his habit of pointing out scantily dressed women. It brought new meaning to the lyrics, 'I... love... trash... anything dirty and dingy and dusty!' Elo stretched and slowly arose from the chair as Marianna toddled over to say hello. I picked her up for a moment and gave her the brief entertainment that she required. She was almost two years old, appropriately wearing a shirt with the words, 'The world really *does* revolve around me.'

Elo lumbered out of the chair as I set Marianna down on the floor next to Jared and his cousins Ernie and Bert. One of my daughter's favorite songs was just starting up on the video as Bert began to sing, *Dance Myself to Sleep*. She would try to sing along. Elo and I headed up the stairs and passed Krista who was dusting in the living room.

As I walked by, I informed her, "We're heading over to visit with Elo's birth family. We'll be back in a little bit."

"Okay, but remember it's almost dinner time and we are all getting hungry."

"I'll bring something back." Elo and I climbed into the truck and pulled out of the driveway. Ten minutes later, we had arrived at the parking lot of his mother's apartment building. We began walking towards the entrance.

"I think that's Wallace." Elo pointed to a young man who was looking under the hood of an old beat up Pontiac sedan.

"Well, do you want to go over and say hello?"

"No. Let's just go into the apartment first." We entered the vestibule and walked over to the door. Elo knocked on the door, which soon opened. His mother stood in the doorway.

"Eloise. Come in."

He entered and I followed him into the living room. The room was dim and smelt somewhat like bug spray. Charlie was no longer sitting on the couch. Perhaps he was not a regular in the apartment. The bicycle and other items were still lying around in the same places they had been the last time we visited. Once again, Diynah came out from the hallway, or maybe it was Carlyn. Only one sister was present and she stood watching over us as we stood in the living room.

Elo greeted his little sister. "Hi Diynah."

She smiled a mischievous grin and replied, "I'm Carlyn."

Elo attempted to make additional conversation with her. "So how is school?"

She hesitated so I interjected, "Are you at Howard High down the road?"

"No. I got kicked out for fighting. Now I am at The Forest School. I'm not staying there much longer."

"Oh, so you're going back to Howard?"

"No. I'm quitting school."

Just then, the apartment door opened and Wallace walked into the room. He walked past Elo and towards his mother, who was now standing in the kitchen. The young man laid his keys onto the countertop and looked at us from across the room. He was an inch taller than Elo but built more like Nevar than his older brother.

Elo said, "Hello Wallace."

"What's up?" The two boys were looking each other over. I

immediately felt the level of tension begin to rise within the room.

"It's time for you to see a dentist," Elo said, before letting out a low snicker. This was not going very well. There was obviously some animosity between the two boys. Wallace did not respond to his brother's rude comment. He did have extremely poor oral hygiene and a pair of crooked front teeth that were noticeably misplaced. Evidently their mother had not taken Wallace, Diynah, or Carlyn for regular dental checkups. They surely had full medical coverage under Medical Assistance and the government health care plan includes orthodontists. I am guessing they never made the effort to use the coverage. In foster care, Elo had not missed a dental appointment in sixteen years.

I jumped in to break up the tension. "Wallace, did you go to Oakland Mills High?" I thought we could talk about the staff members of my old high school.

He looked over at me and answered, "Yea, but I dropped out of there." It sounded as if neither child had an appreciation for a High School Diploma. Wallace turned to his mother. "The car is working but I've got to run up and get some parts at Western Auto."

She answered back. "O… kay." Her speech came out slow with pauses between each syllable. Wallace grabbed his keys from the countertop and headed towards the door. He did not look back or even say goodbye. Elo talked with his sister and his mother for a short while before we decided to depart and walked back to the truck.

I turned to Elo and asked, "What was that all about? You know the thing with Wallace?"

"Nothing. He's just a loser." I think Elo had some unresolved issues with his little brother. I wondered if Elo loathed his position as the "chosen one" in the moment of "Sophie's Choice?" He was not yet mature enough to acknowledge any resentment and I would never know exactly what he was thinking.

"So, what did you think of your visit?"

"Matt, if I have another one I'll do it myself. You don't need to come along next time."

"Are you sure?"

"Yea, I've spent a lot of time wondering about my bio family. Now that I've seen them, I'm not so sure I want to see them again. It may be a waste of my time. So, if I come back, I've decided that I'll come back on my own." The conversation ended with Elo's decision.

****

Back home there were other decisions to be determined. I brought Ledos Pizza for the family to devour and my gang of hungry raptors cleared it from the table in a matter of moments. Krista had finished cleaning the house and relayed the fact that the two of us had a lot to discuss. I was weary of her requests to speak with me in private. They usually pertained to something I had done wrong, but we did need to talk. A response to Gail's request to foster Stephanie would take some time to discuss, mull over, and come up with an answer.

After dinner, Elo, Jared, and Marianna went downstairs to the family room to watch television, play with toys, and surf the internet. Krista and I headed upstairs for one of our many pow-wow discussions. In the distance, I could hear the kids fighting for control over the computer.

"Here's the scoop," I began. "Jared's worker Gail proposes that we foster his sister Stephanie."

"That's interesting." Krista sat on our king-sized bed and pondered this new bit of information. "What do you think?"

"I'm not sure. It is a lot to think over. The worker said that she has to transition from her current placement due to an accusation of neglect. An investigation is ongoing, but in the meantime, she needs to transition from the home. This is going to happen fast so we need to get back with Gail before the end of the week."

"I don't know. There is an awful lot going on right now. I'm not sure if I can support the needs of a little girl. We already have our hands full with our own little girl."

I agreed. "Plus I have some other concerns. If the allegations are legitimate, we could have a messed up little girl on our hands. That really worries me. We have a toddler in the house and there's no telling what frame of mind this girl is in."

My wife processed this point. "Yes. You're right. We don't have any additional support since my mother passed away. It's just us. I don't have it in me right now to be the mentor to a little girl. She's going to need a female to relate to. Sorry Matt, but you just won't be able to handle the needs of this little girl alone."

I was not arguing with that statement. I was in my early thirties and still trying to figure out how these creatures known as women survive without the "Y" chromosome. Men were from Mars, women were from Venus, and little girls were from a completely different galaxy. I was still learning the complexities of my own daughter and not ready to attempt raising an eight-year-old female. It was a lose/lose situation for everybody. If the little girl's allegations were false, then we could be her next scapegoat. If the little girl's allegations were true, then she might end up one messed up teenage girl. I did not want to be the victim of any allegations and I had other kids depending on me. I was not willing to take a chance on Stephanie.

There were other factors to consider as well. Thus far, Jared's mom had not been aggressively trying to regain custody of him. She was happy with his placement and so were we, but Stephanie was a different story. Birth mom had never relinquished custody of her youngest daughter. Her plan was to keep Stephanie and reunite with Logan Hammersmith once he was free from prison. In her mind, they would eventually become one happy little family. Maybe she would also work to regain custody of Jared, but considering the past three years, I thought there was a better chance of Mel Brooks playing the part of the Pope in a Mel Gibson production.

"There is something else to think about," I said.

"What?"

"Birth mom has a close relationship with her daughter Stephanie, and always has. If Stephanie comes to live with us, then Jared's mom will follow through with a commitment to both kids. DSS knows this. They will send both kids back with birth mom, and say it's *in the best interest of the child*. They will say it is best to keep the two siblings together and they will be content on the day that birth mom takes over all legal and financial responsibility for both kids. Jared will be out on the streets and the state treasurer will be smiling all the way to the bank.

"Birth mom is happy with Jared here, we are happy with Jared here, and Jared is happy with Jared here. If we take Stephanie, they'll probably both go back to life with birth mom. They'll end up somewhere in downtown Baltimore and that is not in the best interests of the children. Jared cannot handle the harsh reality of life downtown. He is accustomed to good suburban living and not prepared for life on the streets. The kid is soft and he will end up screwed."

"You're right. That's four good reasons to consider saying no, yet my heart wants me to say yes."

"I know. I feel terrible saying no. She's such a cute, sweet, little girl. I hope she ends up with good foster parents who will work out for her temporarily. If she stayed with us even one week, you know we'd want to keep her for life, and I don't think that's going to happen."

"Then *no* should be our final answer. Considering our lack of support, my mom's recent death, adjusting to our new neighborhood, the unpredictability of Stephanie's situation, the possibility of losing Jared, and safety issues concerning a toddler, the answer should be no. Let's sleep on it, and reconfirm tomorrow."

It was the hardest decision we ever made as foster parents. It is easy to turn down a kid that comes with a rap sheet of knife juggling and fire starting, but turning down this little girl was tough. We slept on the decision until the end of the week. I reluctantly called Gail and told her that our final decision was *no*.

Chapter 23

Adoptive Poker

April came, as did Elo's and Marianna's birthdays. Coincidentally, my foster firstborn, and my biological firstborn, were both born on the exact same calendar date, exactly twenty years apart, almost to the hour.

The month before my wife went into labor Elo had said to me, "I know it. I know she's going to be born on my birthday."

My wife gave birth to our daughter a couple of days before her actual due date, exactly twenty years to the day Elo entered the world.

Elo had become more independent on his road to adulthood and a better driver on the road to work. Fortunately, he drove like an old man. He was patient and cautious, everything that I was not. At this point in his life, he had decided to forgo further reunions with his birth family and redirected his efforts to reconnect with a former foster dad, Mr. Freeman. I taught Elo the back roads for his commute back and forth from Columbia to his old foster dad's house, which was located in Montgomery County. From there Elo was in charge of his own destiny.

My foster son began spending time with Mr. Freeman and his new immediate family. He eventually started spending the night at the Freeman home on occasion. Mr. Freeman welcomed his old foster son and the two took time to reconnect. Elo enjoyed the opportunity to reacquaint himself with his former role model as well as to reinsert himself back into the black community. It was a positive experience for him as he matured into adulthood. Over the summer, he went back and forth between our family and the Freeman home.

In the meantime, the bonds between Jared and Marianna continued to grow. Little J had become very protective of his little sister and always kept her company. It often meant playing with baby toys or watching episodes of

Barney, but Jared did not seem to mind. The DSS social worker, Gail, was astutely aware of the growing bond as she followed through with her duty as an employee of the state. She was a tenacious member of her department and understood the overall progression of foster care.

Gail followed this progression based upon the three goals of foster care. Goal number one was to return the kids to their bio-family or move them to 'Step Zero.' It may or may not be the best thing for them, but it certainly is the best thing for the state budget. As long as no one ends up in jail, everyone theoretically ends up happy.

Progression number one or goal number two is to persuade the current foster home to move towards adoption. It may not have been the family's original plan, but it may be the best option for the child. This also reduces the costs of the state budget pertaining to foster care. Adoption stipends are usually less costly to the budget than foster care stipends.

Progression number two or goal number three is to move the child to another home for adoption. If the current foster family is not ready to adopt, then moving the child, or a suggestion to move the child, is the next option. This may include moving the child to another home willing to adopt the child and/or pressuring the current foster parents into adoption. In this scenario, the current foster parents were Krista and I.

Gail arrived for her monthly visit and sat down in our formal living room. The room mainly used for our many social worker visits sat decorated with nondescript forest paintings of the seasons. Gail positioned herself on the Victorian couch, just below the painting of winter and started by taking time to consult with Jared. During that time, she discussed the prospect of adoption with him and now it was our turn to discuss the options.

My wife and I sat in the living room with Gail after Jared had gone off to play.

She said, "Jared's long term goal has changed. DSS has decided to terminate his mother's parental rights and we'd like your help."

Help sounds like a simple request.

She continued, "In order to terminate parental rights without a drawn out battle, the birth mom has agreed to terminate rights if you two are the adoptive parents."

Krista and I glanced at each other with a look of understanding.

I replied, "Well, we certainly have considered it as an option."

Over the bio visits, birth mom had given me more than enough signs to communicate her appreciation of Little J's upbringing. He had been doing very well in every aspect of his life and she would often compliment us upon his progress.

Krista chimed in. "Frankly, we didn't really intend to become adoptive parents. We originally signed up to *give back* and perform the service of foster care."

We were both rather unsure of the prospect of adoption. It was obvious that Jared's reunification with his birth mom was unlikely, but how would Jared react? Over the past few years, we had always told him the same explanation pertaining to adoption. When the subject arose, we simply stated, 'Your mom is working to get her life together. For now, you'll stay with us for as long as that takes.' It now looked like, 'as long as that takes,' was going to be a lot longer than we originally expected.

I turned to Gail and said, "It's definitely something we have to think about. Now that we know this plan, we will talk it over, and figure it out. We'll need to talk to Jared as well."

Gail replied, "Oh, I already talked to him about it. He wants you to adopt him. Take some time to think it over and let me know. I will need to start processing his paperwork as soon as possible. Either way, it is going to be a move towards adoption, whether it is with you, or somebody else. Our goal is to find a permanent placement for Jared."

"*What?* Do you mean you're going to move him if we're not ready to adopt?"

Krista commented, "Isn't there such a thing as long term foster care?"

In a business like tone, Gail replied, "The state is moving away from any long term foster arrangements. We feel that adoption equals permanency and permanency is what we consider to be *in the best interest of the child.*"

"So, if we're not ready to adopt, then moving him to a family of strangers is *in the best interest of the child?*"

She replied, "In the long run, yes."

In reality, adoption is in the best interest of the state budget. For starters, they wanted us to commit to adoption in order to make the termination-of-rights process simple and cheap. If you can get a pair of adoptive parents to participate in relinquishing the biological parental rights, then you can save a lot on court costs. It is actually doing the taxpayer a favor.

Once an adoptive resource has committed, DSS wants to negotiate the terms. From my experience, the terms might depend upon how easily they can twist your arm. For us, nothing was straightforward and our DSS social worker gave us very little information. The preliminary terms for Jared's adoption was not documented anywhere. In our case, no one provided information until the very last week before the adoption court hearing.

Our first concern was the cost of not-so-distant college tuition payments. We had just finished paying off Krista's student loans and now we had to consider a future riddled with bills associated with Jared's college education.

Krista answered, "Matt and I will talk it over. Can we discuss this again at next month's meeting?"

"Not a problem," Gail replied. The visit ended and the social worker left. Once again, my wife and I had *a lot* to think about and we were not going to reach a decision concerning adoption in only one month.

****

Another summer passed and we enjoyed the warm weather as a family. Once again, we spent a week at Lake Raystown right before the start of the school year and were now transitioning into the fall school schedule. Jared was in his final year at Appleton Elementary and was on track to reach his curriculum goal of fifth grade completion. He had been playing grade-level-catch-up ever since missing kindergarten and much of the first grade. Appleton Elementary and their team of special education personnel did an excellent job to get him back on track.

Elo was spending much of his time at the Freeman home after acquiring a position working at a nearby Taco Bell. He would stay at our home and leave when he pleased. We gave him as much freedom as possible while he traveled on his journey into adulthood. Life was going well for him.

In the meantime, my wife and I worked to maintain the requirements of foster care. When you have children in your home, the requirement list expands with the size of your family. Not only do you need physicals for yourselves, you need to have the physical and dental documentation for every child in your home. When we first signed up four years earlier, we were only required to provide our own documentation. Now we needed the same for ourselves and our dogs, as well as Elo, Jared, and Marianna. Add that to Jared's bi-weekly therapy appointments combined with Marianna's play dates, and our plates were full.

Whenever an unfortunate incident occurs to a child locally, the foster parent requirements sometimes happen to increase. If new information pertaining to booster seats appeared in the news, 'recommendation notices' would suggest that we run out and upgrade our booster seats. Currently, the national economy had peaked with an inflated housing market and the fictitious property values were turning everyone into fictitious millionaires. With the good economy, no *new* foster care requirements appeared due to a downturn in the economy. In other words, the push to *Step Down* or move kids into to less costly placements was currently on hold. Still, the business of foster parent training kept us occupied at all times. As the year closed, we squeezed in our annual training hours while taking turns watching the kids.

Dealing with the adoption side of foster care had now become our first priority. As the holidays approached, we mulled over the decision to adopt Jared. We did not want to rush into anything but DSS wanted an answer. So far, we had called the DSS on their adoptive bluff. We had not given them any definitive answers concerning Jared, yet they had not located another 'adoptive resource' for Little J. If they had, we would have signed up to adopt immediately and even joined the Fran Drescher Karaoke Club if it meant securing Jared with a place in our lives. Instead, I suggested that we hold off and find out what approach DSS was going to take.

My first goal was to guarantee that Jared would receive a college tuition waiver. I did not want to deal with grants or loans. The thirty-some pages of legal documentation that comes with the Maryland tuition application would never again haunt my future. Elo had his opportunity for a tuition-free college experience and I wanted Jared to have the same.

The adoption stipend was another issue. I was not going to take zero for an answer so we waited for the DSS worker Gail to offer her suggestions. The standard Maryland adoption stipend would be just fine. I wanted *some* assistance with feeding our teenage eating machine. Elo could consume an entire refrigerator in a matter of hours and Jared was well on his way to overtaking Elo's appetite. I believe DSS would have preferred if we jumped at the prospect of adoption and signed away on the dotted line. I am sure many adoptive parents have done just that. I imagine the workers with a promising future in DSS are well versed in the art of coercion.

Gail arrived promptly for our first social worker visit in the calendar year 2006. We were prepared to negotiate. The usual visitation routine took place. She huddled with Jared before he went off to play his drug in the downstairs playroom. The social worker sat across from my wife and me as we discussed the options of adoption.

Gail started the conversation. "We are prepared on our end to proceed with adoption for Jared. He has officially moved from a foster status to an adoption status. Once we find the suitable adoption placement he will be assigned a new worker."

Gail was still playing hardball. The only good news was that we would finally deal with a different worker. Gail was a decisive and efficient caseworker, but she was a bit too aggressive for our taste.

"So you're no longer going to be Jared's worker?"

"That's correct. In fact, even if Jared wasn't changing to adoption, I would be moving on."

"So you're leaving DSS?"

"No. I've been promoted." Years of due diligence, Place Matters, and Stepping Down had worked to her advantage. I could not argue with the fact that she was a smart cookie and one hell of a poker player.

"We have come to a decision concerning Jared, but we need to consider a few factors. Our main concerns are healthcare, college tuition, and the adoption stipend. If we suffer financially due to any of the above, it would not be *in the best interest of the child.*"

Krista added, "Simply put, we are not willing to completely forgo assistance from the state. We didn't actually give birth to Jared and we see a lot of potential costs to providing him with a secure future." My wife should have been a lawyer.

Gail continued, "The adoption stipend the state offers is significantly lower than the amount you receive as therapeutic foster parents, probably around half as much."

"That's fine," I replied. "We just don't want to be left out in the cold.

This whole parenting thing is expensive. Clothes, school supplies, food… the kid can eat his own weight in less than three days and he is used to the upscale Howard County lifestyle. This kid prefers sushi over McDoubles."

Gail continued, "I understand. I'll work on that for you and we'll make sure that you're in line for the adoption stipend. The healthcare also comes standard, no matter what the situation, unless you opt out."

"No. We'll opt in." I would be happy with the least amount of financial responsibility possible. If I lost my job, Jared would still have health insurance. Even though the kid never got sick, you never know. I continued laying out my guidelines to Gail. "One more thing… he needs to have college paid for. That is a must-have. I'm happy to say his grades are going well and I've not saved for anyone's college education. Will the state at least cover in-state fees?"

Gail looked us in the eye and responded, "Yes." It was decided. We were about to experience the evolution of foster parenting, adoptive parenting. The social worker continued. "Fine, then it's settled. You'll receive a call from his new adoption worker sometime in the next few weeks. Her name is Kathryn." Gail said goodbye and our round of adoptive poker was complete.

Part IV – Challenges

Chapter 24

God's Way Of Remaining Anonymous

'Why did I choose to become a foster parent? Was it my destiny to become an adoptive parent? Was anything actually, meant to be?' Faith is a dish best served warm, and it was time to heat up the stove. Pertaining to life and to the choices I made, I have constantly searched for reasons and justification behind my decisions. *'Why did I choose to stay in Maryland? Why did I marry this particular woman? Was I making good decisions? Where is the science to support the twists and turns of my life?'*

There is no proven scientific formula for making decisions. You can weigh the positives over the negatives, you can roll the dice, or you can look for signs. I was a foster parent because my wife led me down a path towards foster care. Before I had only toyed with the thought of donating time to the community as a volunteer with a program called BBBSCM or Big Brothers, Big Sisters, of Central Maryland. The closest I had ever come to performing philanthropy was taking my nephews and nieces on tube rides down the Potomac River.

'Why did I stay in Maryland?' I always wanted to move away, to travel, and seek a new environment. I have desired to live in faraway places, to experience new cultures, new climates, and new possibilities. Yet I live in my childhood home. The answer goes back to my wife. I pushed her to move to Arizona. I pushed her to move to Texas. I even pushed her to move to nearby West Virginia, but my wife convinced me to stay in Maryland, so I figure the answers to 'Why,' must be tied to my relationship with her. The answers to the many questions, including 'Why foster care?' certainly did not lie within me.

I met my wife through a series of unordinary coincidences. Coincidence number one: Andy, a friend of mine, and I unknowingly went to the same TGI Fridays on the same Friday night. Coincidence number two: He and I were both at TGI Friday's for work parties, separate work parties. Coincidence number three: I had previously introduced Andy to his wife just a few months earlier. Hmmm, the coincidences were adding up.

Andy spotted me across the restaurant and ushered me away from my table. He asked if I would join him at his work party once mine had ended. I agreed and later excused myself to join Andy and his associates. The persons attending Andy's work party were standing along the bar of the restaurant. I walked over and Andy made introductions. Of course, I had no idea that Andy had just introduced me to the woman who would become my wife.

The moment I met Krista, I knew that I was going to marry her. I am not even sure why, I just knew. It sounds cliché but it is the truth. It is as if I did not even make the choice. Oddly, she made the initial effort to date me.

At the end of the evening, she approached and asked for my phone number. "Do you play tennis?" she asked.

"Sure," I replied.

She continued, "Then what's your phone number?" Honestly, it took me by surprise. I had been single for less than a year and I was not exactly 'Rico Suave.' She wrote down my phone number and said, "I'll call you." I did not even know what to say.

The following Saturday the phone rang. On the line was the young woman I had met at TGI Fridays. After I answered the phone, Krista asked me out on a date. The rest is history, but the coincidences kept coming. On our second date we discovered yet another. Accompanied by my lifelong friend Mike we headed off to join his family at the yearly Clarksville Church Picnic.

As we left for the picnic, Mike blurted out a rhetorical question. "Taking a girl to a Catholic picnic. Oh... what would Robert and Beverly think?" He was referring to the Protestant opinions of my parents.

Krista turned to Mike with a confused expression. "How do you know my parent's names?"

He returned the same look of confusion and replied, "*What... do you mean... by your* parents. Robert and Beverly are Matthew's parents!" Mike was speaking with the inflection that imitated my father's tone. Whenever Beverly gave an order to Robert, such as, *'I want you to clean the windows,'* he would reply, *'What... do you mean... by windows.'*

Krista responded to Mike, "That's a funny coincidence... those are my parent's names as well. Weird, huh?"

I softly replied, "Yes, that is weird."

"That reminds me. Did you have a girl living across the street from your childhood home named, Christy?"

"Yes... she used to babysit me."

"That's what she said. She is a good friend of mine from a church group I attend in the Towson area. What a coincidence. I'm friends with your old babysitter."

"Huh. That is odd. Well… what did she say about me?"

"She said that *you*… are a *brat!*"

****

In the spring of 2006, our family had a new concern. I had received several calls from my mother regarding the health of my grandmother and she wondered when I would be able to join her for a visit to the nursing home. My elderly grandmother, known to us as Mom-Mom, had taken a turn for the worse. Her Alzheimer's condition had progressed and she had broken her hip. Mom-Mom moved into a phase of living known as hospice care.

Krista was all too familiar with Alzheimer's disease. Her own grandmother, also known to her family as Mom-Mom, lived with the same degenerative disease. Krista's grandfather, Pop-Pop, spent his time caring for her Mom-Mom.

I liked Pop-Pop. He had been kind to me over the years. He felt like the grandfather I never had, and I admired him as well. He did not say much about his past life but I paid enough attention to learn some of his history. When he married my wife's grandmother, he married a single mother in a time when marrying single mothers was sometimes controversial. Even so, he married Krista's grandmother and cared for her daughter Beverly as if she was his own biological child. Pop-Pop became Beverly's adoptive father.

From my own experience, that is not always the easiest thing to do. I had only met Krista's grandmother a couple of times when Pop-Pop had brought her to Christmas and Easter dinners. Over the holiday meals, Pop-Pop fed her at the table as Krista's Mom-Mom was in an advanced stage of Alzheimer's disease and no longer capable of feeding herself. The disease had slowly taken over their lives.

Now Alzheimer's was rapidly overtaking the mind of my grandmother as well. Mom-Mom was in the final stage of the disease and my family visited with her regularly. We knew it was only a matter of time before she moved on.

Later that week, I came home from a long graveyard shift to have Krista greet me at the front door. "We need to go see your Mom-Mom today," she said. I tried pushing my way around her but she stood her ground.

"What… why? I am tired as hell and I need to go to bed. Come on… I've been at work all night and I'm exhausted." Half of what I said was true, the other half just wanted to avoid the situation standing in front of me, the impending death of my grandmother.

"First of all, I'm going to tell you something that I didn't tell you before because I didn't feel like hearing you call me names or tell me that I'm crazy. As you know I've told you about the dreams I've had about my mother." Since her mother's passing my wife had pleasant dreams about her mother and some had little messages.

"Yes," I replied.

"The other night I had a dream where my mother told me to go visit Mom-Mom. This morning the hospice home called and told me to give you the same message. I think this is it. This is your last chance to see your grandmother before she passes. I am going to make sure that you go. I know it is hard for you, but I am not going to let your lack of maturity hold you back. Marianna loves your grandmother very much and your grandmother was very good to all of us. So let's get in the car and go!"

I could not argue with that. I simply responded, "Sure." We climbed into the minivan and drove to the nearby hospice home that was an old rancher converted into a nursing facility. It was just fifteen minutes away. When we arrived, I entered and sat down on the living room couch to wait for the staff. The caretakers worked around the clock tending to the needs of declining patients. Krista held tight to Marianna's hand and soon a member of the hospice staff entered the room. She was a young African immigrant that I had met previously on other visits to the home. Her name was Tietha.

"Do you need anything Mr. Hoffman?"

"No thank you."

"Please don't be alarmed when you see your grandmother. Her time has come. She has begun a process of dying known as the death rattle. It will not be much longer, a day at best. Are you ready to see her now?"

I solemnly shook my head to indicate yes. Krista held my hand as I rose from the seat of the couch. Together we walked into the back bedroom where my grandmother laid on an adjustable hospital bed. Krista and Marianna followed behind me into the little room. Tietha entered last. Tietha watched over us for a moment, and then left first.

My grandmother laid unconscious, breathing heavily with the vibrations of a small engine ready to putter out. I could smell the scent of her perfume that had always permeated the soft knit sweaters she wore. Tears welled up in my eyes as I tried to hold myself together. I wanted to be strong and did not want to face this moment. I took Mom-Mom's hand and told her everything that came to mind, "Thank you for being a wonderful grandmother and I love you very much. It's alright to move on and I'll meet you in heaven." More so, I talked about Marianna and the boys. I wanted her to know that I was here for her now just as she had been there for me since the day I was born.

Krista supported me with a few kind words before we returned to the living room. I was physically and emotionally exhausted and needed some sleep so Krista volunteered to stay with my grandmother for a few more hours. She stayed behind and prayed for her. Later, my youngest sister Jenny arrived at the hospice home to take watch over Mom-Mom. After a short nap, I picked up Krista and we returned home.

It was slightly after eleven in the evening when I saw a light come on in the kitchen. Krista had awoken early from her nighttime slumber. She had only been in bed a couple of hours while I was downstairs watching late night television. It was my night off from work and my distorted body clock did not allow me to fall asleep before the early morning hours. She walked down the steps, entered the room, and sat next to me on the couch.

With the sounds of late night television playing in the background, Krista spoke. "Matt, I have to tell you something. Mom-Mom has passed away."

My heart sunk. I responded curiously, "How..." but she had cut me off.

Then she continued, "I awoke to a sound, and then I just knew. I did not know how to describe it. The sound was peaceful and angelic. The moment I heard it, I knew."

I was dumbfounded. Despite my own experiences, my rational mind remained a 'Doubting Thomas.' Quietly, I sat thinking of the impossibility of it all and the coincidence of everything. Then the phone rang. I leaned over and picked up the receiver. It was my sister Jenny.

She said, "Matthew, Mom-Mom has died. I'm just calling to let you know."

Jenny was a nurse and had watched over death's front doorstep for almost two decades. Her tone was compassionate yet firm. As she continued, her words drifted away from the forefront of my mind.

I turned to Krista, "You were right."

****

It was a long night of mourning when my grandmother passed. I called to inform my mother who had spent the day working in my grandmother's garage in order to assist her parish with an upcoming church bizarre. She had visited my grandmother the day before and never received word of my grandmother's final condition before her passing. My mother grieved and felt the unwarranted guilt of a daughter that missed the final moments of her mother's life. I reassured her that we were there to help Mom-Mom with her final transition. After a long night of family grieving, morning came, and again the phone rang.

I answered the phone to hear the voice of Krista's cousin. She sounded upset and asked to talk to my wife. I sat next to her on the couch as Krista's cousin informed us of the passing of her own grandmother, Mom-

Mom. What were the odds? Was this just another monumental coincidence? After more than a decade with Alzheimer's, her grandmother passed away just a few hours after mine.

A few days later, our families had worked out the details of the funerals. They were on the same day and at the same time. My wife mourned for her loss and for the unwarranted guilt of a daughter who may have misinterpreted the last message from her mother. Perhaps she should have gone to visit with her own Mom-Mom the morning she persuaded me to visit mine, or maybe this was her destiny.

On the day of the funerals, the weather seemed surreal. Rain poured down hard ricocheting off the surrounding gravestones and the air smelled of drowning earthworms. The mere volume of water seemed like something meant for a Hollywood set. I went to the ceremony for my grandmother and then immediately drove to meet Krista for hers. Then we drove together to the place where our grandmothers would lay to rest, apart yet together. Two empty graves waited in the very same cemetery.

Our two grandmothers had never known each other in life and had lived on opposite sides of Baltimore City. Yet here they were together, for the first time, with us – only a few hundred yards from one another. As the priest read the sermon for Krista's grandmother, I watched the heavy machinery lower my grandmother into her grave. The sounds of beating rain and the gears of a backhoe etched deeply into my bones. As tears rolled down my face and sadness engulfed every part of my being, I thought to myself, *God has a funny way of remaining anonymous.*

It was a sad time for all, but especially for my mother. She had lost her husband and her mother over a short span of time. Alone and grieving, she did her best to close out the financial affairs of her deceased mom and I did my best to assist. With the help of my uncle, she was once again cleaning out another closet. Her childhood home went up for sale and she prepared to leave that place. Her search for an apartment brought her back to us, and back to Columbia. I continued to look for the signs.

Chapter 25

Elo Light

Three months before Elo's twenty-first birthday he opted to leave the care of the state. He signed the appropriate paperwork, left the foster care system, and moved into the Freeman family home in Montgomery County. When I inquired as to why he deactivated his foster child status just three months prior to his twenty-first birthday, he said that he was finished with being a ward of the state and felt like a free man. I believe he wanted to leave foster care on his own terms and not simply by default. Perhaps pride or something in the back of his mind told him to do it. Whatever the reason, it turned out to be, exactly the right time.

Years earlier, another child was born on the streets of Baltimore City. He was underweight and underdeveloped. Even before his birth, the hospital staff suspected a problem as his mother showed signs of drug abuse. Perhaps the abuse had happened over the years or perhaps it happened during pregnancy. They kept the newborn baby for observation. The infant's family had already been under CPS investigation for neglect and this new baby was the young mother's third child. The mother had a history of mental illness and did not always make a lot of sense. She obviously had her hands full with two boys and caring for one more was not going to make life any easier. In the past, the state had stepped in to help, but the young mother planned to handle the challenges of her motherly duties on her own.

The baby named Nevar went home to Monument Street and did not progress along normal infant milestones. His first birthday arrived and he was nowhere near the early stages of walking. The word "momma" had not yet sounded from the tip of his tongue and Daddy was rarely around. The father had been swept up in the crack cocaine epidemic of the 1980's, and some nights he would come home between drug binges to spend time with his three sons. He spent enough time to borrow the family food stamp card, trade a few lobsters for crack cocaine, and impregnate the young attractive mother one more time.

Mom was having a difficult time caring for three children and now had to prepare for yet another. The only income she received came from neighborly handouts and government assistance. As baby Nevar grew, he was more than she could handle, and Mom was about to deliver a fourth child. The state stepped in to assist. The youngest son with developmental disabilities would need more services than his mother could provide and the oldest of the three boys had proven to be quite a handful as well.

With a new child on the way, the young mother made a decision. She would place her youngest son into the care of the state. Perhaps with assistance he could get the care that he required. Additionally, the behavior of the oldest boy made him difficult to contain. He was full of energy and constantly fighting with the middle son who was just nine months younger. She made a second decision and placed her oldest son into the care of the state as well. After giving birth to twin daughters, she went back to her home on Monument Street and applied for government-assisted housing. Eventually she moved outside of the city, but all she ever wanted was to return to her childhood home, the Eastern Shore farm where she grew up.

The Baltimore City DSS agency searched for a therapeutic foster home that could handle two boys requiring two different kinds of services. They had no such foster home placements available within DSS so they reached out to a local non-profit foster agency to find a spot. The two boys were placed into an available private agency home. They remained together for a year but eventually the older brother transitioned. The developmentally delayed baby remained at this placement as the older brother transitioned to another family better equipped to handle his rambunctious behavior. In two different homes, the boys grew up separately but had occasional sibling visits over the years. The younger of the two boys, Nevar, was a physically healthy but mentally handicapped individual. Eventually, he literally outgrew his placement and became too large and too strong for his single foster mom.

As Nevar entered puberty, additional diagnoses that included Oppositional Defiant Disorder came to the forefront of his rap sheet. He was now tall, strong, mentally disabled, and overly defiant. A Step Two foster home could no longer handle his needs. He advanced into the Step Three lifestyle of a group home. The first institution was located in the eastern outskirts of Baltimore City. After several controversies involving abuse, he transitioned to another institution.

Nevar now found himself living in a southwest neighborhood of Washington D.C. The young man did not know which way was up. He had not seen a biological family member for years or even the foster parent that he called mom. His family consisted only of low-paid institution workers and other patients like himself. Hopped up on a cocktail of anti-psychotic medications he functioned as best as he could but had no control over his life.

This was the young man's reality, clouded under layers of medicinal disillusion. Even the gentlest of humans would defy this existence. When you have nothing, you feel like nothing. Every Christmas present from the state would disappear into the hands of another inmate or even a member of the staff. Holidays came and went with nothing more than a staff-led "party" in the facility cafeteria.

You have no one to love and no one loves you. It is a 'dog eat dog' world. You sleep in a defensive position to protect yourself from your very own roommate. No one is truly your friend and you are afraid that everyone is your enemy. Each day you wake up and you follow the institution's routine as best as you can, but there is never any hope in sight. To some foster children living in residential facilities, this is their existence.

Sometimes the bad can work out for the good. In Nevar's case, the state had begun to shut down numerous institutions in order to cut down on cost. It was a sign of the times – the time for a wave of Stepping Down. As the state ran their audits and checks, the private institutions closed down one by one across the region. When Nevar's institution closed, he transitioned again. DSS looked into his file and made a call to his former foster agency for assistance. They began to search for a home. Nevar's last name was Winford. The placement worker thought to herself, "Hmmm. That sounds familiar. A young man named Winford just discharged from the foster home of Matthew and Krista Hoffman. They have an available spot."

****

Summer arrived and school was out! Jared had successfully completed elementary school and was nervously looking forward to attending Oakland Mills Middle School. Elo was enjoying his time with his old foster dad and his status as a twenty-two-year-old with a license to drink. He worked the fast food circuit and spent his money at the local pool hall. Marianna was enjoying the life of a spoiled three-year-old and was developing well ahead of the standard milestones. My wife had started a successful business working out of our home. I was working nights, sleeping days, and managing our home. It was a busy but simpler time.

Then the phone rang and I answered. "Hello?"

"Hiiii Maaaattt!" the voice said. It was our old friend Arlene, Elo's social worker.

"Hey Arlene, Elo isn't here right now. He's out and about in Montgomery County."

The phone call did not seem out of the ordinary. Arlene had been checking in with us since Elo's brave exodus from foster care. She was by far the most caring social worker I had ever met. Her sweet disposition reminded me of my mother-in-law. It was always good to hear Arlene's voice.

"I'm not calling about Eloise. Oh... but how is he?" Arlene never broke etiquette.

"He's doing well. I am always a little worried about the job thing as he has changed jobs so many times and... he even mentioned the military. That's a scary concept, but it might offer the discipline that he desperately needs."

"Oh my goodness, well... what I'm actually calling about is another fine young man."

"Really, wow. That didn't take long." It had only been a few weeks since Elo's official resignation from foster care. I was just getting used to the idea of having fewer shoes to pick up around the house. Elo had more pairs of shoes than any woman I had ever known. I secretly gave some of the pairs away to the oversized kid in our neighborhood, Harper.

"Iiiiii knoooow. This placement request is veeeeery interesting. If you have not heard, there are several group home facilities closing around the state. This young man resides in one and he is in need of placement. He used to be in our agency and yoooouuu aaaaaaaaalso happen to know him." My thoughts went back to our temporary foster son Vance, but he should have aged out by now.

"Who is it?"

"It is Nevar, Eloise's brother. I know you do not have a lot of experience with the mentally disabled but I think you would do a wonderful job with him. Aaaaaand... he could reconnect with his brother Eloise through you. It would be a win/win situation." Considering her kind demeanor, any request from Arlene was hard to refuse.

"Wow," I cautiously responded. I remembered Nevar and thought about the happy-go-lucky personality that he displayed when he and Arlene stopped in to visit with Elo. "Well, let me talk to Krista." I took down the details of Nevar's diagnosis and the highlights of his history, and our conversation ended. Once again, my wife and I would have to make a decision.

****

Life was going smoothly. We enjoyed long walks in the woods with our dogs and tricycle sessions with our daughter at the dead end of our street. The long summer nights gave us time to catch up on projects and other responsibilities around the house. If there was ever a good time to face the challenges of a mentally disabled teen, now was that time. My wife and I talked it over and agreed to accept Nevar on a temporary basis. We did not know if we were patient enough to care for a person with a mental disability and a dual diagnosis that included psychological issues.

There would be many new responsibilities. Nevar would need a Level

5 school with appropriate services and he would need additional programs to help him transition. He would also need a psychiatrist for therapy as well as for medication management. We had just reduced Jared's psychological appointments to one per month and caring for Nevar would require a new regiment of bi-weekly appointments. Still working nights I volunteered to handle the majority of issues for Nevar as Krista would have her hands full with Marianna during the day. She loved being a mother and never argued over handling Marianna's affairs.

I knew that I would have to take a big role in Nevar's care for more than one reason. A male role model would be required for a male teenager. I was the only one big enough to keep Nevar in line if required. With his rap sheet, we did not know what to expect. I did not want to go back to the days of locking bedroom doors or fearing for my dogs. Baby monitors could serve as a household spy tool in case Nevar was more than we bargained for. I promptly called Arlene and told her that our final decision was… yes.

****

The next day Nevar arrived with a couple of trash bags slung over his shoulder. His arrival was like a flashback to the day Elo first knocked on our front door. This time it was summer, it was a new house, and it was a different Winford. Nevar followed Arlene with a huge grin, hauling the two Hefty bags up the sidewalk towards the front door.

As I held open the door to assist, he uttered a proclamation. "*I told you* I was coming to live with you. *God said so!*"

"Awesome," I replied with a look of curiosity. My parental response wheel had automatically kicked on to reply to Nevar's initial comment, my system fine-tuned from years of responding to Jared. Thinking back, the young man standing before me did actually tell me before that he would one day be living in my home. Nevar entered the living room, dropped his bags, and sat down on the loveseat as Arlene followed behind.

Arlene gave me a hug. "Oh, it's *so* nice to see you Matt!" she said before turning to Nevar. "Well, Nevar. We are here. What do you think?"

He responded, as he sat with a huge smile, "It's just like I remember."

This was another odd statement considering Nevar had never been to our Columbia home.

Just then, the dogs came darting around the corner. They wagged their tails in furious excitement and greeted Nevar as he patted them on their heads, "Hi girls!"

It was obvious that there was an immediate bond. Perhaps they sensed another three-year-session of late night scraps from Elo's younger brother. The dogs missed Elo and his late night cooking routine. It seems they remembered Nevar, and he remembered them from his last visit, two years ago. Jared came up from the downstairs playroom to see what was going on. He managed to put down his video game controller long enough for Nevar's arrival.

I spoke up, "Here Nevar, let me show you to your room."

I grabbed his bags and led him down the hallway to his new bedroom. His bag of shoes had the familiar scent of Elo's foot odor. Jared initially followed behind but then stopped to talk to Arlene in the living room. The bedroom, decorated in androgynous fashion, was ready to house either male or female, as needed.

He checked out the closet and asked, "Where can I hook up my games?"

One of the trash bags had the remnants of two game consoles and some scattered cartridges. I could hear the plastic hardware clicking together as Nevar set the bag down on the hardwood floor. Jared somehow heard the sound as well.

"You've got games?" Jared shouted from the living room.

"Oh, Jared's going to love having you here."

Just then, Jared came around the corner and into the bedroom. Nevar had already begun digging through his bags. He pulled out some video game hardware and the two boys immediately headed for the basement.

"Have fun," I called out as the two disappeared through the kitchen and down the steps. I walked into the living room to follow up with Arlene who had already taken a seat.

Arlene pulled out Nevar's paperwork and medication bottles. "Here are his meds, just follow the instructions and you should be fine. The one prescription tends to make him drool a bit so you'll want to consider a plastic covering for his pillowcase."

Mmmm… drool… my first special needs challenge. I could tell this was going to be a lot of fun.

I replied, "Thanks," and placed the medications onto the kitchen table.

"Oooooo Kay. I think you are all set. You have my phone number so just call me if you need anything. I'll keep it turned on so just let me know how it goes." She got up from the chair, moved towards the kitchen, and called down the stairs, "Byyyyyyye Nevar. Be goo… *ood.*"

"O… Kaaaa… Yaaaaaay," sounded up from the basement.

I could hear Jared already barking orders as the two boys were involved in a video game. Little J was very bossy when it came to his digitalized drug. I let the boys play and I waited for Krista to arrive home. She had been out with Marianna on a neighborhood play date. I hoped we were ready for this new chapter of our life. Perhaps the real question should have been, was Nevar?

****

Nevar was about to receive an initiation by fire into his new life and an introduction to our extended family. A few months earlier, we had purchased a new minivan as the day had finally come when our family had grown large enough to require the stereotypical family conveyance. We packed up the van and headed towards Lake Raystown for our yearly family reunion. Once we arrived at our campsite, we met with my extended family and Nevar cautiously settled in around the campfire. Unlike his big brother, he was not quite as comfortable adjusting to life with his new Caucasian family.

Nevar, used to the culture of the inner city, must have felt as if he was the main guest at a Klan meeting in the woods. He spent most of his time attached to my side. He was a little worried about my redneck bother-in-law who kept smiling at him from across the campfire and gave him the nickname 'Elo Light.'

I told him, "Don't worry about Uncle Dennis. It has been three years now and he has not caught Elo yet. You are fast enough to get away. Besides if he comes after you, you can just challenge him to a dance-off."

Nevar smiled and made a friendly wave in the direction of Uncle Dennis who was grinning at him from across the fire.

Chapter 26

Old Routines And New Directions

While we continued with the everyday tasks of life, my wife and I worked to fulfill the demands of our foster care license. As a part of the process to adopt Jared, we were experiencing a routine that was similar to that of the days when we first applied to be foster parents. I also had to take Jared to court to meet his birth mother and work out the terms of her termination of parental rights. We met in a Baltimore County courthouse and worked out the details of future visitation. With the assistance of Jared's assigned lawyer, we came to an agreement. She relinquished her rights with the understanding that my wife and I would adopt Jared. That was the plan.

The social worker had sat in our living room and informed us that we would receive everything that we required, which would be healthcare, college tuition, and an adoption stipend. Jared and his mother had a heartfelt conversation about this decision and we worked together through the visitation agreement. She would have access to see Jared twice a year, once after the winter holidays and once at the end of summer. As a part of the process, she would need to initiate the visits by contacting me and arranging a time to meet. This placed the responsibility in her hands and kept it out of ours. I did not want her visitation to become a job requirement that me, or my wife, had to perform. If a visit was going to happen then it would happen at birth mom's request and not because we were required to make it happen.

Another home inspection was required for the adoption. All of our regular requirements needed review, and all of our personal information needed updating. The dogs needed their yearly shots and everyone in our home needed current physicals. It was a very busy time. Our new social worker, Kathryn, was coming and going. We were signing forms and completing requirements.

With each visit, I would ask the social worker, "When do we get some sort of documentation concerning the adoption? I want a written guarantee of Jared's current and post-adoption benefits."

She had stated that DSS would have something provided for me before the time of the adoption. Kathryn did not really have answers to my questions and had no clue about Gail Witherspoon's proclamation concerning college benefits. Kathryn just continued working on her compartmentalized portion of the adoption process.

Elo appeared around the house more frequently since Nevar arrived. He had had a recent fall-out with his old foster dad, and after they had reached an impasse, Elo was again leaning on me for guidance and a place to stay. His job with Taco Bell was not everything he had envisioned. He was lost and looking for direction from the reclined position of our family room chair.

I sat down on the nearby couch and called out to him. "Elo!"

His eyes slowly creaked open as he replied, "Huh?"

"What's the plan for today?"

"Nothing." That was the same plan he had yesterday, and the day before that. It was time for me to stoke the fire.

In the voice of a concerned father I decried, "Son, it pains me to see you lying around each day while I go to work. It's just not fair."

"I know. I was thinking of heading over to the recruiting office later today. I need to schedule myself for the written test to apply for the military. I already stopped by the office in Gaithersburg and I need to follow up."

"So, you're back on the military thing?"

"I never stopped."

"Well, I recommend the Navy or the Air Force, but I think the Army and the Marines are the big recruiters right now." Our country was in the middle of a conflict with Iraq and new blood was always in demand.

"I was thinking Marines."

"Why? We are in the middle of *a war!* Marines are the ones that go in first… you know the ones that come out first… often in a body bag."

"I know, but I've always wanted to be a Marine for as long as I can remember. I want to *give back* to my country. My country took care of me and now I'm going to take care of it." Elo was either brave or prideful to a fault. I am not sure which. I was not sure if I should be proud of him or shake his brain cells loose.

"Well, we'll see. I still say pick any of the above before joining the Marines. Do you want me to go up to the recruiting station with you?" It was a sunny day and I wanted to get out of the house.

"Sure."

"Can we leave in about two hours?"

"That sounds good. Let me just jump in the shower." He picked himself up from the chair, grabbed his shoes, and headed downstairs to clean up.

Before I could run to the nearby recruiting office, my wife and I had a final visit with Jared's old social worker, Gail. Kathryn was on summer vacation and Gail would be filling in at the monthly visit. This worked out well because Krista and I planned to put our foot down concerning Jared's adoption benefits. So far, all we had was Gail's word that Jared would receive all of our requested future benefits.

The doorbell rang and Krista answered the door. Gail came in and sat down in the living room across from us. Jared joined us and did his little routine before heading downstairs to play. Then my wife and I sat alone with the social worker.

The adoption date was less than a month away. "When will we receive the paperwork with Jared's benefit information?"

"There really isn't any official paperwork. You just sign at the adoption and the judge approves. It all happens on the court date."

Krista and I looked at one another in disbelief. How could there not be any documentation available for adopting parents?

I was tired of the runaround. "We're not adopting him unless I see written proof that he will receive healthcare, college tuition, and the adoption stipend," I said. I had placed my cards on the table and called her bluff.

She looked surprised and asked, "Even if he already thinks that he's being adopted? You would cancel it?"

"*Yes!* I have no problem explaining to Jared that things are being delayed because the state is not going to provide him with what we expect."

She looked displeased as the distant sounds of Jared's video game carried up from the basement. "Hmm, then there is a problem," she said. "All children adopted through foster care are eligible to receive healthcare after adoption. I can also assure you that you will receive the appropriate adoption stipend. Stipend information is on the paperwork that you sign shortly before adoption. The problem is that a child cannot receive the state college tuition waiver unless adopted after the age of fourteen. Considering that he is twelve, he may only receive grants or loans. Since he will be a former foster child, he should receive plenty of those."

"Some grants? I do not want him to receive some grants. We want him to receive the paid tuition we requested. You know… the one you told us he would receive!"

She responded to me in a professional tone, "I know. I was referring to the grants and loans."

"You knew what we meant. Did you deliberately mislead us?"

"It seems as though *you* misunderstood." She had been playing adoption poker all along and we had finally called her bluff. If we had not called her bluff, we would have walked right into court and been enlightened while standing in front of the judge. That would have really put us on the spot, forcing us to complete the adoption without any tuition waiver.

I answered, "Then I guess we're waiting for a little while longer."

"What?" Gail replied. "What will he think? He will be very disappointed."

"Actually, he won't. He'll be fine just as long as he still gets to have an adoption party. In fact, he will be happy, because now he's going to get *two* adoption parties! He can have one this month and then one next year." I grinned.

Gail was obviously perturbed. She had to show all of her cards and was now flat out of poker chips. Gail abruptly packed up her things and walked out our front door. We now had another year to prepare for the adoption of Little J.

Elo climbed up the stairs and was ready to head to the recruitment office. "What was that all about?"

"Nothing. Are you ready to head to the recruiting office? It's over by the Columbia Mall, right?"

"I'm ready to go, but you don't need to come. I'm going to go up to the Montgomery County recruiting office and I will probably be there a while. There's going to be a lot of forms to fill out and then I'll probably stop by the Freeman's house afterwards."

"Alright then, good luck."

Elo headed out the front door. I did not argue because I had other concerns on my mind. My mother had found an apartment in the nearby neighborhood of King's Contrivance. She would soon be living in a nice first floor apartment, next to a shopping center, and next to her church. I was a big part of her moving plans. With the help of my uncle, my siblings, and other relatives, I spent several weeks slowly moving the remaining contents of her life into her new home. She had downsized for a second time in just a few years and her lifetime of possessions was more than the tiny apartment could hold. With a lot of stacking and packing, we managed to make it all fit.

As usual, things were hectic. My grandmother had passed away and my mother was now settling into her new Columbia home. The good times living with the Freemans had ended and Elo was in the middle of moving towards a career in the military. Jared was now on adoptive hold and we needed to work out the next step for ourselves. Krista was busy with the needs of our active three-year-old daughter and Nevar was adjusting to the rules of his new home. I was just trying to figure out what to do about this whole mess we called our life.

It took three yells before Jared joined me in the living room. I said to him, "I've got news for you J."

"What?" It was obvious that he was intent on returning to the video game console waiting downstairs.

"Your adoption is going to be postponed until after your fourteenth birthday. What do you think of that?"

"Am I still going to have an adoption party?"

"We'll still have the party; the pizza, the ice cream, the works."

"And my friends can sleep over too?"

"No problem," He looked back towards the basement stairs and asked "Is that all you want?"

"Yep," and off he went. Apparently, delaying Jared's adoption was not going to be the traumatic experience that Gail Witherspoon had envisioned.

Chapter 27

Nevar's Honeymoon: A Tale Of Two Chickens

Our first month of adjusting to life with a new foster son was going smoothly. Nevar was in a state commonly known as the honeymoon phase, and the beginning of our relationship with our new special needs teenager was completely free of controversy. Nearing the end of summer, I thought it would be a good idea to start by parenting Nevar with the techniques that my wife and I had used in the past. We introduced him to nature. On the hottest day of the year, we decided to take Nevar and the rest of our family to Cunningham Falls in the Catoctin National Forest.

After a short hour drive, we parked our van near the entrance of the area ranger station and an adjacent building of natural exhibits. Krista and Marianna ducked into the restroom while the boys and I took a tour of the mini museum. The main room, filled with a variety of local wildlife, displayed the decorations of a taxidermist. The small exhibit area of dead animals was silent, abandoned, and smelled of moist earth.

Within the room, there was a stuffed raccoon, a stuffed rabbit, and a stuffed fox. Jared was intrigued with the displays and asked several questions pertaining to taxidermy. Once again, Jeffrey Dahmer popped into my head and I decided to change the subject. I did not want Jared to become obsessed with the stuffing of dead things. A snake exhibit was the perfect distraction for Little J.

While we checked out pictures of the local snakes, Nevar walked around the museum and exclaimed, "Maaaaan, this place is creeeepy. I ain't goin' near those things. They look mean!" At the same time, he was laughing and pointing at the exhibits.

"Don't worry Nevar, they're all dead. There's nothing in here that can hurt you."

He stood looking in the direction of a stuffed raccoon. "Oh... I know. I just don't want no rabies or nothing. One time I was in the woods and I saw one of those things... and I got the hell out of there."

Jared chimed in with his high-pitched youthful voice of wisdom, "Ne...var, the wild am-i-nals are just as scared of you as you are of them."

Nevar replied, "Then this must be *one scared-ass raccoon over here!*"

Nevar was turning out to be a very interesting character and appeared to have a great sense of humor. His humor was extremely complex for someone identified as mentally retarded and he seemed to be in tune with everything going on around him.

I called out to the boys as Krista reappeared from the restroom, "Let's go guys." We headed towards a two-mile walking trail that began at the parking lot. My plan for the day was to get some exercise, visit the park waterfall, and then take a dip in the park's swimming lake. My father used to take my family on similar daytrips to nearby Greenbrier State Park. Cunningham Falls was my version of a reenactment.

As we walked to the trailhead, we stopped and looked uphill where a steep incline rose before us.

Nevar asked, *"We're walking up that?"*

I had not considered the fact that he was not physically ready for a two-mile incline. Even though he looked relatively fit, Nevar had spent the last three years inside of an institution. The boy had received less exercise than a hamster without a wheel in his cage.

"Come on Nevar. You can handle it."

"Oh, I know I can handle it. I just think you white folks are crazy. Ain't *no* black person crazy enough to go roamin' around in the woods."

"Don't worry Nevar. Jared will protect you." Little J looked simply confused. We walked up the trail and took numerous breaks along the path. Krista toted Marianna in a child-carrying backpack and I followed along with a manly grunt. All fifty pounds of Jared led the group while Nevar stayed in the back, huffing and puffing behind me. His cardiovascular system had not seen this much action in a long time.

Forty-five minutes later, everyone was asking, *"How much further?"*

"Patience people... patience!"

Soon we reached the waterfall and decided to climb the rocky embankment leading to the top of the falls. The rushing water of a crisp spring monopolized the natural retreat as rays of sunlight danced through a thick canopy of trees. The branches leaning out over the embankment stretched high atop the falls. I walked over and gave Nevar a hand as he climbed the side of the smooth rock. He required assistance as his balance was either untrained or impaired from the cocktail of psychotropic drugs.

We reached the peak of the falls, took some time to enjoy the scenery, and headed back down towards the base. Laughing and smiling,

Nevar and Jared enjoyed the short climbing adventure before we landed on a beach sitting at the bottom of the embankment. Here a pool of cool water collected from the waterfall that rushed overhead. I coaxed Jared out into the water and Nevar curiously watched from the safety of the sand.

I called out to him, "Come on Nevar. Get in here. The water's fine!"

"Hell no!!"

"Oh come on. I'll help you out." I worked my way across the pool over to the nearby beach where he was standing. I grabbed his hand and starting pulling him toward the falls. He pulled away.

"Maaaaaan, you're crazy! There might be snakes in there."

"Oh... come on Nevar. Everybody knows that snakes prefer white meat."

Jared chimed in, *"They do?!"*

I called out again, "Get in here," and Nevar cautiously followed me into the water. We positioned ourselves under the waterfall. On the hottest day of summer, the cool water felt refreshing as it rushed over the tops of our heads and down our shoulders.

"*Damn*, this feels pretty good," Nevar interjected as he followed me further under the heavy downpour.

"Have you ever stood under a waterfall before?"

"Nnnooo."

"Well, you've got to love it!" As I stretched into the cool water, a nearby photographer took several photos, catching Nevar lost in a state of pure bliss. As I exited the water, I walked over and the man waved to me. He said that he was from the local newspaper, *The Washington Post*.

"Do you mind if I use this young man's picture for the local newspaper?"

"No problem." I replied, then called out to Nevar, "Do you mind if this man puts your picture in the newspaper?"

He pulled his head from the downpour of water and replied softly. "Okay."

The rest of the day was relaxing and amusing at times. We walked down to a nearby lake to take a swim. The water was seasonably warm. Marianna splashed around in the shallows and played in the sand while Jared scuttled about in an attempt to catch minnows. Nevar did not like the feeling of the silt-covered bottom squishing between his toes and quickly evacuated the water, never to return.

As he clamored from the water he hollered, "These fish are trying to eat me!"

Schools of minnows had encompassed the warm lake and were attempting to nibble on strands of leg hair. They were a bit annoying. We stayed a little longer, drying off before hiking back to the car.

Our first adventure with Nevar had been successful. We celebrated the day with dinner at the Mountain Gate Family Restaurant, enjoying a buffet of fried chicken and home baked strawberry pie.

As we devoured the meal, Jared inquired, "Is this chicken white meat or dark meat?"

"Well, it depends on the piece you picked."

He investigated further. "I mean… is this chicken from a black chicken or a white chicken?"

I took a moment to compose myself. "Jared, there aren't races of chickens. Breasts are white meat and pretty much everything else is dark meat. Why do you ask?"

"So… no matter what color the chicken is… black, white, red, yellow… it's all the same inside?"

I enjoyed a small chuckle. Everyone else at the table stared in Jared's direction, speechless. "Yes Jared, just like people."

"Then why do people have races?"

Nevar laughed and then interjected, "To see who runs the fastest!"

Jared continued, "So people are just like chickens?"

Stupefied by the conversation before me, I bluntly replied, "*Some* more than others."

Nevar added, "And I'm the fastest chicken here."

I agreed. "Nevar, in many ways yes, yes you are."

I now knew 'why the chicken had crossed the road.' He was running in the Boston Market Marathon.

****

My second adventure with Nevar did not go as well as the first, nor was it planned. A simple outing to Kentucky Fried Chicken turned into a complete nightmare. While Krista worked in the home office, I took the kids and drove her minivan to the neighborhood KFC. We picked up some food and headed home in the evening rush hour traffic.

The kids were in rare form attempting to dig through the food bags as I instructed them to hold off until reaching home. In the corner of my eye, I could see Marianna fuddling with my gym membership card. It often disappeared from my wallet and I was happy to have it within my sight. The boys were slapping at one another, laughing, reacting. Smells of fried chicken wafted through the van and the sounds of the boys arguing over the food bag overtook the sounds of the radio. Tired and distracted I reached back to snatch the gym card from Marianna's paws when I ran into a bigger problem. *'Boom!'*

As we rounded the corner onto Broken Land Parkway, I swung wide and clipped the curb. I also popped the front tire of the minivan. I yelled *'jeepers'* or something more appropriate as I pulled off to the shoulder of the road. The kids were no longer fooling around in the backseat, but silently stared at me in complete shock. I climbed from the van, walked to the front of the vehicle, and assessed the damage. I thought to myself, *There is no way to change this tire on the side of the road with these kids in the van. It would be easier to walk back home before it gets dark.* If we were lucky, we would be home well before sunset.

Wearing nothing more than gym shorts and a t-shirt, I unloaded the kids from the car, turned to my new teenage assistant, and said, "Hey Buddy. I have to carry Marianna on my shoulders and I do not have any pants pockets. Could you carry my wallet and keys?"

He replied with his usual "Okay" and I handed him my wallet and keys. "Can I carry the KFC chicken bag too?"

"I don't see why not."

"And the biscuits?"

"Sure, why not?" I handed him the bags of food and we began our journey towards home.

With the sun setting, we walked across a parking lot, along a bike path, over a stream, and through the woods. *To grandmother's house we went.* Marianna bounced on my shoulders, happily ducking and weaving around every low hanging branch. Jared and Nevar followed closely behind chatting, chuckling, and poking at one another.

When we arrived at the front door, I turned to Nevar for my keys. "Hey Nevar, hand me the keys."

"What keys?"

"The keys that I had asked you to carry along with my wallet." He started to dig through the pockets of his jeans and his oversized red jacket. My anxiety rose and I began digging through his pockets as well, frisking him as he giggled like a big red Tickle-Me-Elmo doll. My keys and wallet were nowhere on his person. They must have fallen somewhere along the mile hike. Amazingly, he managed not to lose even one single piece of the chicken or any of biscuits that he eagerly requested to carry. I took a deep breath and released a flurry of curses that must have sounded like a family of turkeys having Thanksgiving dinner.

Once I had composed myself, I turned to Jared, bit my lip and flatly stated, "Give me your key."

He looked at me as if I had just asked him for a kidney. He coveted his house key, as well as all of his other possessions. You would think that anyone of his coveted things could open the gates of heaven. Jared was capable of forgetting his own name, but he never lost track of anything, and held onto everything. He pulled the key deep from within his pocket and held it tightly within a closed fist.

I rolled my eyes, let out a sigh, and shoved my open hand outward, waiting for the key. "Jared, when the day comes that you find yourself confused and staring at a bright light… just walk into the light. Drop whatever things you are holding onto and just *go* to the light! I promise! There will be more keys in the light!"

Then, reluctantly, he handed over the key. I took the key and entered the house. Consumed with concern for my own keys, I mindlessly dropped his on the kitchen table.

Krista had just finished working and her clients had left for the night, so I began searching the woods for my wallet and keys. I searched all evening and then the next day. I searched for weeks. I searched everywhere. I checked around the van, through the woods, and across the parking lot. I held onto hope.

Most likely, the keys and wallet washed away in a little stream. A steady run of water flows across the path, in a place where a bridge once stood. We planned to cross that bridge when we came to it, but instead we used stepping-stones. It was time to let go.

I had just learned my first lesson about Nevar and my first lesson about mental disability; things are not always what they seem. I had lost my preconceived perceptions about mental disability along with my wallet and my keys. Nevar's appearance and mannerisms were very deceiving. To me, Nevar was Elo Light… but it was time to change my thinking completely. I was beginning to understand that being labeled retarded does not mean you will think or act the way others expect. It does not mean you are stupid. It does not mean that you do not have a sense of humor, and it does not mean you do not understand the need for a loving relationship.

Nevar apologized with sincerity. "Hey Matt, I'll never lose your keys again."

Disgruntled, I thought, *That's right, because I'll never give you my keys again.* Then I calmly replied, "Don't worry about it buddy. It's my fault." I stood there deflated.

He looked up, smiling with a dopey grin, and then asked, "Can I call you Dad?"

"Sure… why not?"

****

Fathering Nevar was an interesting experience to say the least. My wife and I often became frustrated with the endless number of issues that can affect a person with mental disabilities. Mentally handicapped individuals sometimes have a repetitive nature and these repetitive qualities sometimes got on my nerves. Humor often sustained me and remained my saving grace. Our new foster son had a propensity for repetitive speech much like a young man we once fostered named Nicholas. Nicholas constantly used the phrase 'Hey Buddy.' He said it so many times on one particular weekend that my wife and I almost snapped.

Nevar had met Nicholas over the years in foster care and knew of our history as his respite parents. Nevar also knew that the phrase 'Hey Buddy' could annoy me to no end. Occasionally he imitated the phrase just to mess with me and get under my skin.

"Hey Matt."

"What?"

"Hey Buddy."

"Ha-ha, funny Nevar."

"Hey Buddy."

"Okay Nevar, the joke's over."

"Hey Buddy."

"Does somebody need some chores to do?

"Hey Buddy."

Finally, I'd reply, "Enough already!"

Then Nevar would laugh continuously as he carried on.

Nevar's own repetitive habits were much more sophisticated than Nicholas' repetitive habits. Nevar regularly repeated entire monologues about God and the details of his communications with The Creator. It was like having your own Southern Baptist minister standing over your shoulder. Perhaps I should have feared this direct connection with The Almighty, but Nevar always ended each godly command with a lighthearted laugh. None of the instructions from The Lord ever pertained to violence. Most of his saintly messages were simply orders to forgive. Nevar regularly informed me that God had ordered him to forgive Jared for lying. It all seemed rather harmless.

Nevar spent most of his time at home playing video games or talking on the telephone. He paced around the house while speaking on the cordless cell. The person on the other end of the phone was often a staff member from an old residential treatment facility. Sometimes he spent hours talking to other kids from his former placements or speaking with a former foster brother, sister, or mother, and sometimes I found him talking with a young woman from his old school.

It was fun to eavesdrop on Nevar's conversations, especially when the person on the other end of the phone was patiently accommodating Nevar.

Nevar would proclaim, "Hi, Ms. Stacey! It is me, Nevar!"

"Ooooooooooohhhh… Hello Nevar." *(Sigh)*

"Guess what!"

(Sigh) "What?"

"X, Triangle, Circle, Circle, Square will make Beast perform his best finishing move."

Nevar was speaking about the cheat codes for his video game and I do not think Ms. Stacey was quite as interested in the latest video game playing techniques.

"Really, that's very interesting." *(Sigh)*

"And you can make all the characters look like bobble-heads in Mortal Kombat if you push X, X, X, Triangle, Triangle, Triangle while holding down the left back button."

"Wow Nevar. I really have to get back to work now. I have to pass out medications."

"And The Fantastic Four has a lot of cheat codes too!"

"Okay Nevar. That's great." The conversations would drag out for about ten minutes before the inevitable reply, "I've got to go now Nevar...." *Click.*

I could feel Ms. Stacey's pain, but I could not hang up.

Another activity Nevar enjoyed was watching movies. He particularly enjoyed comedy spoofs such as the *'Scary Movie'* series of films. It was obvious he had spent a large part of his life indoors watching T.V.

One day *Forrest Gump* was on the television and I turned to him and said, "Nevar, you remind me of Private Bubba."

He turned to me with the serious face and replied, *"Dey's uh, shrimp-kabobs, shrimp creole, shrimp gumbo. Pan-fried, deep-fried, stir-fried. There's pineapple shrimp, lemon shrimp, coconut shrimp, pepper shrimp, shrimp soup, shrimp stew, shrimp salad, shrimp and potatoes, shrimp burger, shrimp sandwich. That- that's about it."*

He had repeated the line from the *Forrest Gump* movie verbatim. We had not even reached that particular scene in the film. He was already aware of his similarities to Private Bubba and had done a little practicing on his own. I laughed so hard I nearly broke into tears. He had a good chuckle at the end of his soliloquy as well. The shrimp monologue was a repetitive phrase that never got old.

Having a sense of humor was the key to Nevar's success. His rap sheet was a mile long but his energetic smile told an entirely different story. When it was time to enroll Nevar into school the agency worker Arlene did some preliminary research. She found that Oakland Mills High had a Level 5 program fit for Nevar. They had a program designed specifically for students with disabilities. OMHS is where I graduated high school and I was excited about Nevar's enrollment at my old alma mater, but before I could complete the required enrollment forms, the school staff wanted to hold a meeting with Nevar.

****

I received a call from the special education director at Oakland Mills High School and she informed me that due to my son's rap sheet, the team had some reservations about Nevar's enrollment. They suggested that he could possibility travel to Baltimore City for school and wanted to investigate further before accepting Nevar into the Howard County Public School System. He had been in several fights over his years of institutionalization, but as far as I could tell, he had turned over a new leaf. Nevar knew that living in our home was an once-in-a-lifetime opportunity and he wanted to stay. The label 'mentally retarded' did not mean that he was dumb. I spoke with the school staff and we set up an introductory meeting.

In preparation for Nevar's introductory meeting, I reminded him of the rules of our home. They were a PG version of the rule speech I had previously given his older brother Elo. Nevar had heard the speech once before, but I wanted it fresh in his head before entering the meeting.

He and I discussed the tools to avoid punching or fighting. I suggested punching a pillow if he was mad or going for a walk if he was angry. He listened and agreed that he would never get into a fight again. Through the summer, he had been true to his word.

As we walked through the front entrance of Oakland Mills High, I turned to remind him, "Keep that good looking smile on your face. We want you to make a good impression."

At that moment in time, he did not know that there was still a chance of returning to Baltimore City schools or possibly returning to an institution. Without the help of a Level 5 school, Krista and I could not manage Nevar and the amount of services he required.

He answered, "Oooo… kay" and we walked down the hall.

We stopped at the front office and they directed us to a nearby meeting room where we entered, sat down, and waited. It was a small conference room with white block walls. The room barely held a small conference table surrounded by ten chairs. When I was a student, I had never been in this meeting room. We arrived early and waited until the first member of the special education team arrived.

The first person to enter the room was a short middle-aged man who greeted us kindly. "Hello. It is nice to meet you. You must be Nevar. I'm Mr. Pojalski."

Nevar smiled cautiously and softly replied, "Hi."

With a big smile, the man shook Nevar's hand as several other team members arrived, sat down, and said hello. They each took a seat around the conference table. We made introductions and the team leader began the meeting. The entire team was friendly and the atmosphere was very professional. One member began taking the meeting minutes while the team leader introduced herself as Ms. Buckley and started the organized proceedings of the assessment.

Ms. Buckley spoke. "The reason we're here today is to introduce ourselves to Nevar and discuss his possible enrollment into the Howard County Level 5 program here at Oakland Mills High School. Nevar, do you understand the purpose of this meeting?" The scribe feverishly jotted down the notes.

He sheepishly replied with a grin, "Yep, the meeting's because I've been in fights." The staff looked towards one another and Mr. Pojalski gave a nod of recognition.

"Yes and no. We just wanted to meet you in person and talk over your school history. I see you went to Mt. Turnkey Academy near Washington D.C. and you ran into a few problems while you were there."

"*Yep!* Those people are mean! D.C. is *hard*, but this place is *tight!*"

"I see." Then Ms. Buckley turned towards me. "How has Nevar been over the summer?"

"Great. We've had no trouble at all. He's following directions, never fights, and likes to have a good time. He's good with our dogs, and takes them for walks. He's good with my young son and good with my three-year-old daughter as well."

The staff again looked at one another, but this time each person wore a subdued smile. Mr. Pojalski raised an eyebrow and responded positively as the scribe continued to scribble away. "Excellent."

Ms. Buckley confirmed. "Wonderful. I think Nevar should fit into our program. Mr. Pojalski will work directly with Nevar most of the time. We have a special education area of the building where we teach students like Nevar about life skills and other tools to succeed. We also have great programs like *Best Buddies*, which incorporates other students from outside of special education to work with the kids. If he likes, the program will match Nevar with a Best Buddy student here at Oakland Mills."

"So that's it?"

"That's it. Here is some information and a packet full of forms. Fill them out along with the required documentation and turn them into the main office. We really just wanted to meet with Nevar to get an idea of his attitude towards school, and yes… that's it!"

As we all stood up Nevar interjected, "Yep, I like cooking, and stuff."

Mr. Pojalski patted Nevar on the back, "I was just going mention the kitchen facilities in the special education room. Big guy, you'll get your chance to cook soon enough."

Looking down towards the floor, Nevar answered with a shy smile. "I know."

The meeting ended and I thanked the kind staff members for their time. Nevar was going to get an opportunity in the Howard County Public School System. Summer would soon be over, and classes would start in a couple of weeks. Nevar's honeymoon was officially over and the halls of Oakland Mills High would soon echo with the arrival of a new graduating class.

Chapter 28

Better Than Africa

It was not long before the honeymoon ended and the difficulties of raising a special needs teenager arose. Nevar had integrated into our family with relative ease but we now faced a number of growing concerns. The first issue confronting our integrated family was race. In addition to receiving the benefits of an excellent educational program at Oakland Mills High School, our son was reacquainted with members of his former community.

After landing in our middle class lifestyle of predominantly Caucasian family members, Nevar was showing the signs of an identity crisis. One of the teacher's aides at school knew members of Nevar's birth family and she gave him updates pertaining to his biological relatives. I am not sure that was such a good idea. Numerous OMHS students also encouraged Nevar to accentuate his African-American roots.

We did not have a problem with Nevar's desire to express style as he began 'keeping it real' in the classroom and at home. My wife took him shopping for oversized clothing that would fit various cultural requirements. We tried to help him in fashion so that he would be able to 'represent' with other students. Elo assisted by taking Nevar to a nearby barbershop that specializes in African-American hair and had him 'hooked up' with the latest hairstyle. According to Nevar, it was all very 'tight.'

We did our best to overcome race inside of our home, but we could still feel tension lingering outside the walls. Even though Allview Estates welcomed residents from every background over the years, it remained predominantly white. No neighbor would dare make a comment pertaining to race or one of my family members, but I still sensed a level of apprehension from people in the neighborhood. Perhaps I was just paranoid, or perhaps not, but sometimes I sensed that something unfriendly was in the minds of some neighbors. I do realize that it does not help to have a six-foot tall African American dude with glossy eyes pacing around in your driveway while delivering prophesies from God. I am sure that many of my neighbors actually thought that I was the crazy person.

The second issue we faced dealt with good looks. Yes, good looks can be an issue. At first glance, Nevar does not appear mentally handicapped nor does he act mentally disabled when he is out in the public. He was self-conscious about being labeled 'retarded.'

Combined with the misconceptions of others, Nevar's good looks became problematic. Strangers were confused after conversing with him. Those who did not know Nevar were not usually prepared for his off-the-wall remarks.

A friend of mine once asked Nevar the standard question, "What's up?" and Nevar replied, "Green Lantern could beat Spiderman in a fight." For Nevar, that is what was up.

My friend simply looked over at me with a raised eyebrow and said, "What?"

The oddest part of Nevar's nonsensical statements is that Jared always had to argue with him, but I will come to that in a moment. The illogical verbal banter between my two foster sons was the fifth concern in our long list of ongoing concerns.

Nevar's good looks were getting him into trouble at school. Some of the more aggressive, yet less attractive female students were making sexual advances towards him. I guess they were willing to ignore the side effects of his medication, which included drooling... as well as ignore the mentally disabled blank stare thing. It seems that he was that good looking. These girls even put up with blatant insults when my mentally disabled son would 'excusably' blurt them out.

One time, we were in the Food Lion grocery store and a young woman ran over to us. I watched as I picked through some apples.

The girl handed Nevar a torn piece of paper with a phone number and said, "Call me."

Nevar was blunt. "You're too fat. I'm not calling you!" Then he let loose with boisterous laughter. Sometimes he would come home with a phone number or two in his pocket. I made sure they were all from appropriately-aged girls and then warned him, 'Stay away from women!' Each time my wife and I had an argument I used our disagreement as a tool to convince Nevar to, "Keep it real... real single!"

The third concern, also directly related to Nevar's good looks, had to do with the perception of his psychiatrist. Again, his appearance and public demeanor were misleading. At each psychiatric appointment, the psychiatrist always forgot that Nevar's diagnosis contained mental retardation. I would sit down at the beginning of each meeting and she would ask, "So why is Nevar here today?"

Nevar would then go into a rant about how he did not need meds and eventually went off on a tangent about his direct connection with God.

Then the psychiatrist would ask, "Why is he on medication?"

I would request that she check her file.

The psychiatrist was never prepared and never had a clue about Nevar or his condition. I was beginning to wonder which person in the room had an advanced mental deficiency: Nevar, me... or the psychiatrist! Perhaps she had some information to share with us about her own prophetic message from God... or at least a message from an invisible rabbit.

I looked over at the psychiatrist and asked, "So what medications are popular this month?"

She never laughed, and just stared back looking confused.

One time my wife took Nevar to an appointment and the psychiatrist began to question him about college applications, whether or not he had done well in algebra and his overall educational achievements. Krista sat in disbelief with her mouth hanging wide open. Either way, I did not need a psychiatrist to check calculus homework for my retarded son. What I needed was for her to write his prescriptions. She would sit with a confused look while writing the scripts for his ongoing psychotropic medications. I often reminded her that if the meds ran out, and he went cold turkey, he could possibly have a seizure. I would ask her, "Do you want to be the physician who created a Medicare funded ambulance ride to the E.R.? If not, you had better pay attention and continue to manage his meds."

Add that psychiatrist's name to the long list of people who hate me.

Med management was truly a huge pain in the ass and was the fourth issue that was a major concern. Nevar required a fine-tuned cocktail of medications to keep him in balance. We made it our goal to wean him from as much medication as possible, especially the medications that were making him drool, not just for the obvious reasons, but because I was tired of washing a rotation of pillowcases. With the help of his quack doctor and the city social worker, we successfully reduced his volume of medications. As a result, Nevar became much more lucid and wittingly sharp. His demeanor improved as he became more independent with the reduction of the psychotropic meds.

Another difficult task was transferring Nevar from one physician to another as well as transferring his medical records. While transitioning, Nevar needed to remain on his current regiment of psychotropic medications. The meds were so high power that a new 'receiving physician' did not want to sign off or continue to prescribe the current medication, but there really was no choice. A patient cannot simply stop taking these types of high power medications. Like it says on the side of the bottle, serious side effects may or will occur... perhaps even death! It took a bit of convincing to get a new local physician onboard with the program. We needed to have the new physician receive Nevar's case and accept the task of adjusting him to a better regiment of psychotropic drugs.

For the first two months I had to drive to Washington D.C. in order to receive medication prescriptions from Nevar's 'current attending' physician. This discharging physician no longer wanted to provide our foster son with the cocktail of medications that he himself originally prescribed. I kindly informed the physician, "It's too late buddy! You've been writing these prescriptions to Nevar for years and now you're going to finish the job!" It was the first time I ever confronted a physician and it felt good. This must be what foster care trainer meant by "Advocating for your child." Add another doctor to my growing fan club. It was all in a foster parent's day's work.

****

The concerns of caring for our mentally disabled foster son did not stop with culture, etiquette, school, and medical concerns. The fifth concern was in our home. It was Jared's inability to understand the thought process of a mentally handicapped individual. He and Nevar would argue for hours over the most trivial things such as which video game was the best, which superhero was the strongest, which WWE wrestler was the coolest. The illogical banter carried on continuously.

On several occasions, I tried to explain to Jared why Nevar argued, and the fact that Nevar receives a free pass to win every argument. Jared never understood why it is pointless to argue with a mentally retarded person. I would tell Little J, "Does it really matter whether or not Aquaman can talk to land animals as well as sea animals? Does it really matter if Aquaman can swim faster than a dolphin? Does Aquaman really even exist?"

Jared would stand there perplexed with these questions in hand. He never 'got it.' On the other hand, Nevar understood why it was fruitless to argue with Jared, which, if you have read this far into the book, does not require further explanation.

Personally, I had mastered the art of agreeing with Nevar. If he said, "Matt, the moon is a big round block of cheese."

Then darn it, I replied, "Yes Nevar... the moon *is*... a big round block of cheese."

Of course Jared would chime in, "What kind of cheese?"

"Swiss Jared... Can't you see all the holes?" It was no wonder Jared was failing science. Nevar on the other hand was receiving straight-A's. Perhaps I needed to have Jared transferred into some of Nevar's special education classes. Maybe Jared could also receive A's for baking scones... probably not.

My wife and I addressed Nevar's concerns with long sessions of homeschooled therapy. Nevar's psychiatrist, who doubled as his therapist, was unable to relate to our son. The psychiatrist was a humorless, ex-military, Caucasian, middle-aged female. Evidently, she was unable to relate to our mentally retarded African-American male teen and I would not consider the results of their therapy sessions productive. At least she eventually understood that it was her job to write his prescriptions.

Each session went through the same conversational progression. The psychiatrist started the session looking over her chart, "Hello... ummm... Nay-ver, what can I do for you today?"

"I don't know," he would reply.

"How is school?" The psychiatrist continued looking over her chart, waiting for an answer to her question about school.

Nevar sat smiling for a moment and then eventually replied, "Gooooooooooood."

"Good. Good. I see that you are a senior now. Are you currently taking a physics course in school?"

"Nooooooo, but I want to *fys-ics* computers when I grow up."

"Well that sounds like a good idea."

"Yep... I want to fys-ics computers with Matt... or maybe use my superpowers."

"Excuse me?"

"Why? Did you fart?"

"No! I certainly did not!"

"Okay, because it smells funky in here." Nevar began laughing uncontrollably, holding his hand over his mouth to avoid launching missiles of spittle.

This seemed like a good time for me to interrupt the fun. "Nevar is doing well in his Level 5 classroom. If you check further down your chart, you will see that he is here to receive prescriptions for his psychotropic medications. By the way, his name is pronounced Ne-vaR, not Nay-ver."

The psychiatrist looked down, reviewed her chart, and responded, "Has Nay-ver taken his S.A.T.'s yet?"

Rolling my eyes, I flatly responded, "No."

"Wow, you really need to get on the ball with that. He's going to need those test scores when he graduates next year." Like Jared, the psychiatrist never 'got it.' Turning to Nevar, she continued the conversation in something similar to baby talk.

"Well Nay-ver, before you go, would you like to pick a prize from my prize box?"

With a laugh Nevar replied, "*Hell no!* I don't want your prize box!" then he cocked his head and added inquisitively, "Are you retarded or something?"

****

Nevar has many issues to *resolve*. Actually, Nevar has many issues to *reconcile*. A solid resolution was probably not ever going to happen with Nevar. You do not simply resolve a mental disability. You discuss, you understand, you adapt, you compensate, you persevere, and with luck, you overcome any issues resulting from the mental disability. In fact, anyone could use this recipe to overcome any difficulty in life and this was how we addressed our therapeutic sessions with Nevar.

My wife would remind Nevar of her own shortcomings, as little as they might be. She would talk with him extensively and point out many of the problems and disabilities that we all face. Each one of us had at least one, if not several issues. Marianna was a spoiled whiner, Jared was a little clueless and a complete ADHD freak, and I could not multi-task to save my own skin. Even the dogs were impaired. Sadie had spent the majority of her life under a bed due to an anxiety disorder and who knows what is up with Sassi. She regularly hangs by her teeth on a vine in the woods.

One time Nevar asked me, "Am I retarded?"

I replied, "Yes. You have a mental disability and your brain does not work the same as everybody else. It is not your fault, and it is not something that should make you worry. We all have faults and nobody is perfect. Everybody also has other characteristics that can help overcome deficiencies. You are strong, fast, funny, and good at video games. You don't have any problems whipping Jared's butt in video games do you?"

"No."

"See, your brain works better than his when you're playing video games. So do not worry about it. If someone calls you retarded, just tell them... so what, I'm strong, I'm fast, I'm funny, and I can whip your butt in *Halo2*."

Nevar walked off with a contented smile and immediately challenged Jared to another game of *Call of Duty*.

The homeschooled therapy sessions helped Nevar with other aspects of his life as well. He wanted to know more about his birth family after Elo mentioned them several times. Even though Elo had written them off, Nevar was still curious and very confused about biological relatives. He did not understand why his birth mother had placed him into foster care, nor the reason why I recommended avoiding her. I felt that Nevar could not handle the mixed emotions and bizarre behavior associated with his birth family. I advised him to stay clear of them.

When Nevar was upset, Krista would comfort him. "Nevar, each one of us has a birth family, and they're not always what we want them to be. We are lucky to be able to choose our family and lucky to have you as a part of it. I do not spend a lot of time with my birth family. Jared does not spend a lot of time with his birth family either. Now Matt, his birth family... they speak for themselves, but I'm just glad we are able to be a family together."

Her reassurance helped Nevar, but thoughts of his birth family sat on the back of his mind. Being confused, he sometimes claimed that various foster families were, or were not, his actual birth family. All I really knew was that the kid who once lost my wallet and keys in the woods still liked to call me Dad... and I was fine with that.

The homeschooled therapy sessions with Nevar were endless. He talked all the time and had many questions. The latest topic of concern was foster care and the lives of foster care children here in America. The conversation was like a session of *'Deep Thoughts... with Jack Handy.'*

Nevar, a bit of a complainer, ranted about the inadequacy of his experience in foster care. He exclaimed, "Maaaaan, foster care sucks! They send you house to house, feed you crappy food, and stick you into group homes. I wish I had been born back in Africa."

Even though he was right about U.S. foster care, I imagined that the African foster care experience was not much better.

I laughed and replied, "Have you ever seen the foster care system in Africa? I imagined it had something to do with a lion. Any child 'left to the state,' finds himself left to a 1,000 lb. eating machine. I bet foster care does not even exist in much of Africa. The lucky kids of the Dark Continent wind up in the AFCS or African Feline Care System. I am sure it is not nearly as good as the program here in Baltimore City. Have you ever seen those commercials on TV with kids covered in flies? Did you ever have flies landing on you downtown?"

"Dammmmmn. I don't want to get eaten by no lion, and I don't want no flies around me either!" He ended his last statement with an energetic laugh.

"In fact, I don't think I've even heard of a program for the mentally disabled in Africa. To be honest with you, the mentally disabled in Baltimore probably have a better rate of survival. You think D.C. is hard, wait until you try life on the Serengeti. Bad food will be the least of your problems; your real problem will be not being the food! If you like, I can take you to the zoo, or we could put a lion in the woods behind our house. Then we could try to reenact the African foster care experience right here at home."

"Hell no!!"

Nevar got the point, but I understood his concerns. The American foster care system was still a long way from perfection.

Jared chimed in, "If we put a lion in the woods, then what would he eat?" Jared still did not 'get it.'

Chapter 29

Going To War

Elo returned home from another visit with his old foster dad and had some news to tell the family. He had officially registered as a recruit of the United States Army. His select option for the Marines had not worked out for him and I was happy to hear that. I did not want him to receive an express pass to the front lines of the Iraqi conflict.

Elo entered the family room and made his announcement, "It's official. I signed up with the Army. I've completed the written and physical tests and should be ready to go in about a month."

Eloiro Jax Winford was once again the property of the United States of America. He had gone from being a ward of the state, to being a ward of the Feds, caught up in the American cycle of work and debt just like the rest of us. In fact, he was now a property of the cycle to boot. I was happy for him and hopeful that one day he would benefit from discipline provided by the army. Perhaps he could expand his knowledge of the world through a foreign assignment. There was more to life than just Baltimore City and Disney World, but I hoped that he could avoid the Middle East.

The story sounded all too familiar. Abandoned to the streets of Chicago, my father joined the military at age sixteen. After lying on his naval application, he served during the Korean War, stationed on a boat in the Mediterranean Sea. The only hazards he faced were the STD-carrying women of the docks. I hoped Elo's fate would be the same.

Elo gave me of the details his military contract and chosen field, auto mechanics. It sounded better than infantry did. He had always taken an interest in auto repair, but somehow his own Toyota Corolla was on its last legs. In a few months, Elo would ship out to Fort Bragg, North Carolina and to the boot camp that awaited him. I was concerned about him and the dangers of combat, but the green zone in Baghdad still sounded better than some parts of Baltimore.

****

Fall went by and Jared's latest status – 'adoption on hold' – fared well. In fact, he was looking forward to the next round of adoption celebrations. The last shindig involved pizza, some ice cream, and an all-night video-game sleepover with his friends. Then the next day the boys played war games in the woods. Together, Nevar and Jared enjoyed sleepovers and dueling joysticks with their neighborhood friends, Harper and Bryan. Like Harper, Bryan was another misfit legacy of Allview Estates and another oversized middle school kid turned companion.

The four boys enjoyed playing imaginary battle games along the riverbeds behind our house. Then, Jared and Bryan would pair up to go play video games or Legos while Harper and Nevar would go off on some outdoor adventure. Harper and Nevar had become an inseparable pair and the two spent mild autumn afternoons walking to various village centers, shopping for everything from Big Macs to dollar trinkets. Nevar valued his new friendship with Harper.

"Matt! Did you know that Harper can lift his bike over his head?"

"No Nevar. I did not know that." Jokingly I inquired, "Is this true Harper?"

"Uhhhhh… yep."

Nevar continued, "And Harper can throw a football forty yards."

Sarcastically, I inquired with intent interest, "Is this true Harper?"

"Uhhhhhh… yep."

"And he beat the game *Lost Planet* in one day!"

"Wow guys. You two should take a walk to Heinkels and celebrate with some Roma pizza. Here's a ten dollar bill."

In unison, Harper and Nevar excitedly replied, "Okay!" and they took off with the money. It was nice to see Nevar developing true bonds of friendship, which he had never experienced behind the walls of an institution.

****

As the holidays approached, it was time for Elo's induction into the military. He had spent much of the fall visiting friends and making the most of his free time before his impending departure. I took him out for a final farewell at the neighborhood bar, Nottingham's. On that night, he was the responsible member of the party. In preparation for his trip to Fort Bragg, he decided to forgo alcohol and drove me through the late night Taco Bell window. Over a few pints of beer, I had a good time announcing Elo's last night as a civilian. I filled the role of irresponsible citizen as he transitioned to his new role as a responsible enlisted man. Too bad his responsible demeanor did not carry into the next day.

The next morning I awoke to the sound of a ringing telephone. I picked up the receiver and it was Elo's recruiter on the line.

"Hello. Mr. Hoffman. This is Sergeant Fipps. Is Eloiro en route? The transportation shuttle is waiting for his arrival."

"Uhhh, I'm not sure." I put the phone on mute and stumbled downstairs to find Elo sleeping in the recliner. In a tired voice I called out, "Elo! Wake up! You're supposed to be at the recruiting office. They're waiting for you. Sergeant somebody is on the phone." The boy's eyes creaked open.

He muttered, "Tell him I'm on the way." He arched his back and straightened his arms upwards into a slow lazy stretch.

"They're waiting for you... now!"

Casually he replied, "I know. They're always waiting for me. Don't listen to the Sergeant. It's a load of crap. They'll wait for me." I had my doubts. I did not find this scenario to be a good start to a military career. He had not even left the house yet and he was already AWOL.

"Okay. I'll tell him you are on your way. Now get your butt up and get moving. I'll be in the car in ten minutes!"

He let out a long, lazy yawn and began to move from the chair as he answered, "Okay."

I took the phone off mute and informed the Sergeant that Elo would arrive soon. "He's on his way," I blurted. Ten minutes later I was dressed and waiting in the kitchen. I hollered down the steps, "Elo! Let's go!" There was no answer. In a louder tone I called down the steps again, *Elo! Let's go!*

Jared responded, "He's in the shower."

I stood for a moment, shaking my head in disbelief. Elo was going to miss his flight to North Carolina. According to the Sergeant, today was 'the big day' and he was already 'Missing in Action.' I walked downstairs and banged on the bathroom door.

The water shut off and I yelled into the door, "Let's *go!* Where is your stuff? I'll load it into my car."

"Okay. My stuff is all together by the basement door."

I walked through the basement and picked up two huge overstuffed duffle bags sitting by the back door. A football sat on top. I put it under my arm, carrying the football and the bags out to the driveway. After opening the trunk of my car, I lifted his belongings into the storage compartment. I could only imagine how many pairs of shoes were inside the bags, perhaps one entire bag designated for his 'kicks' alone, and what was up with this football? I threw the football into the backseat of the car and thought to myself, *What... does he think he's going away to summer camp?*

I walked back inside and called downstairs to Elo.

He replied, *"Coming!"*

I could see down the stairwell into the basement where he knelt, tying the laces of his shoes, so I went back outside to warm up the car. Moments later Elo appeared. He climbed into the car, sitting next to me in the front seat, and we were off to the Montgomery County recruiting office.

It was a clear sunny day as we drove along the back roads, a great day for football. Elo reached back and grabbed the football sitting in the backseat. He held the football in his hands, gently tossing it a few inches into the air. The ball spun repetitively and then slapped down into his hands. With the windows open, I could smell the fresh manure of a nearby farm.

"Do you plan to walk into the recruiting office carrying a football?"

"Sure." He thought nothing of it.

"Are you sure that's a good idea? I cannot imagine what your drill instructor is going to say when you walk into boot camp with a football in your hands but I am sure it is not going to be… '*Go out for a pass!*'"

"We'll probably have some free time for a little football."

I gave him a smile etched with wisdom, "Whatever you say Elo… whatever you say." I was through instructing Elo. Now it was time for Uncle Sam and Sergeant Ass Kicker to take over.

"Did you ever stop by and talk with your bio family again?"

"One time I stopped by, but Wallace and I got into a fight."

"You got into a fist fight?"

"Yep."

I just could not fathom the deep seeded animosity the two brothers held for one another. They had only met a handful of times yet they wanted to tear at each other's throat.

Elo continued, "I stopped by recently, one last time. I wanted to tell my mother that I was leaving for the Army, but when I got to the apartment, they had already moved, vanished into thin air."

I sat listening, imagining that the Section 8 visa had once again expired.

Along the ride, Elo and I continued talking and had the closest thing either of us wanted to a heart-to-heart conversation. I gave him the advice that my father would have given me, "Make sure you wear a condom, keep an eye on the other guy in the foxhole, and don't ask don't tell." That should be easy for Elo. He was not big on asking or telling.

Soon we arrived at the recruiting office and climbed out of the car. I opened the trunk and Elo and I each grabbed a duffle bag. He flipped the football into his free hand as we walked though the main entrance of the building, down the hallway, and into an area with a sign that read…*United States Army Recruitment.* The recruiting sergeant was standing just inside of the office.

He spoke, or more like shouted, at Elo, "Welcome Private Winford! I'm glad you've decided to join us!" He looked down at the football and then looked up at Elo, "*What… is… that?*"

Elo casually answered, "A football."

The sergeant laughed, *"What? You think you're going to Summer Camp?"*

I tapped Elo on the shoulder and motioned for him to toss me the football. It rolled off his fingertips and landed in the palm of my hand. Elo turned to an area where other recruits were sitting with luggage and fell in behind them. Each recruit sat pensive, trying not to laugh at the Sergeant's comments about Elo and his football. I do not think any of them was willing to go out for a pass.

The only thing Elo threw was a departing wave and then he confidently said, "Later Matt."

I responded with a smile and then a nod, "Later Elo... and good luck!"

The sergeant turned towards me, *"You,* looking to join up?"

I tried not to let out a laugh, "No sir! I'm too old."

"Nonsense!" he shot back. "You're fine. We could use a recruit like you." The short, stocky man was very persistent.

I considered the prospect for a moment. *Fighting a war in Iraq, hmmm... sounds easier than dealing with all these kids.*

"Sorry, but my wife would kill me." I thought to myself, *Better her, than some stranger wearing a turban.*

"She'll love the benefits."

He was right about that. She would get a long vacation free from my dictatorship, and even a $100,000 bonus if I came to an untimely demise. That money could pay for many a Broadway ticket in New York.

"Sorry, but I'll have to decline. I have a bunch of kids to deal with at home. Maybe one day you'll meet one of them."

I waved goodbye to Elo and I headed for the door. What the sergeant did not understand is that I had already signed up for a different war. I was the Captain Kangaroo of lost children, directing them to consider every option before going into battle. This war included an endless number of foster children, some transitioning to the front lines, stepping down into a final placement that would matter.

A few months later, I did some research and discovered that Elo's birth mom Shirley had acquired a new address in an area of southwest Baltimore City called Liberty Heights. She was going in reverse. Once a little girl from a farm on the Eastern Shore, she had gone from Baltimore City to Columbia and then back again. I just hoped that one day she might find herself assigned to the honeysuckles of the Eastern Shore. Her son Elo would be busy attending to other flowers.

****

The holidays passed and we were entering into the next phase of our lives. Elo was off to boot camp and Jared and Nevar were halfway through the first year of class at their new schools. Jared was learning the social changes of a middle school lifestyle and Nevar was enjoying the benefits of a Howard County special needs program. Jared would wake up early and get himself moving for school while Nevar was a morning monster. Nevar had difficulty getting started in the mornings. His regimented cocktail of psychotropic drugs made him sluggish at the beginning of the day but by afternoon, his personality would flourish.

The program at Oakland Mills High School was doing wonders for Nevar. He complained about school as much as any kid but he made sure that he never missed the bus. Secretly, he loved his time at Oakland Mills. He talked about the program activities and spent time with the *Best Buddies* program. Near the end of the year, he particularly enjoyed the school field day, complete with a cream pie throw and a dunking booth. The general population of students at OMHS treated him wonderfully as well. When I picked him up from school for doctor appointments, the students gave Nevar 'high fives' and enthusiastically greeted him in the hallway.

Krista and I witnessed drastic improvements in Nevar as he attended Oakland Mills High School. It was a shame that he would only get to enjoy this wonderful experience for a year. He was turning twenty-one in late spring and it would be time for him to transition, but I was glad that he could end his schooldays on a positive note.

****

Sometimes, Nevar appeared as though he had outgrown his mental disability, but my wife and I would quickly be returned to reality once he informed us of his latest existential conversation with God. Eerily, some of his messages were right on the money. Since Elo's departure, he was making all sorts of predictions.

As we watched television in the family room Nevar casually informed me, "I'm worried about my brother, but The Lord told he me was going to be okay. So I'll try not to worry too much."

"Really, what did The Lord tell you?"

"In my dream last night he told me to forgive Eloise for leaving. He told me to forgive Jared for being selfish, and he told me to forgive Krista for telling me what to do."

"Well, what about Elo... what else did The Lord say about him?"

"He told me that Eloise was going to help people and become a fireman."

In reality, Elo had elected an automotive track and was currently enjoying the rigors of boot camp. He had not yet received any particular military duties.

"Elo's in the army, but I don't think he'll be fighting fires. He'll probably just work on jeeps or trucks… or something like that."

"*Yep*, but he's not going to work on trucks. He's *going* to help prevent forest fires."

"Like Smokey the Bear?"

"What? No… not like a bear, like a fireman."

Nevar was too young to remember the old Smokey Bear commercials that ran into the 80's. My sarcastic joke flew right over his head.

"Ooooo… kaaaay," I replied. "Like a fireman. So Nevar, why is it that you never tell me what God says about me?"

"I don't know."

Laughing, I commented, "Well Nevar, tell me. What *does* God say about me?"

"He says you're going to make a grandma's hat-proud?"

"I'm going to make *a what?*"

"You're going to make a grandma's *hat-proud.*"

"What does that mean?" I curiously waited for an explanation.

"I don't know… that's just what God told me. You've got to ask him."

"Do you mean Grandma *Hat-tie* proud?"

Nevar looked at me inquisitively, "Had-he proud what?"

I stood there shocked and dumfounded. I smiled nervously, took a moment to think about Nevar's odd comment, and then replied, "Okay. Good enough."

Just then, our phone rang once, and only once. The light on the machine illuminated, indicating a voicemail. I immediately checked the machine. The only message was a coworker with an unrelated question pertaining to work. Oddly, the name on the caller ID did not match the name of the person who called. Instead, it read, "Proud, Mary: 1-909-988-2003." *What did any of this mean?*

I felt an unexpected sense of warmth, my heart began to race, and I felt the hairs on the back of my neck stand up. A thought crossed my mind, *Proud, Mary… did I just receive some sort of sign?*

Sitting behind me, Nevar called out, "Hey Matt, what *is* a hat-proud anyway?"

I did not reply. I was too busy thinking about Nevar's earlier statement about 'making a Grandma's hat proud' and the fact that his proclamation came just moments before the words 'Proud, Mary' appeared on the display box of my caller ID.

I sat down and thought to myself, *Nevar's here spouting out the word 'proud' and the caller ID has 'proud' written across the display. There is no one at work named Mary Proud. Who could have called? What could the name Mary have to do with anything? Could it be a reference to Marianna? I'm over-thinking this way too much!*

I remained a Doubting Thomas, laughed at myself, and continued my thought, *It's just another one of those funny coincidences.*

****

Six months later, I received an update from Elo. He was in Colorado assigned to the National Guard. He wrote that forest fires were sweeping the countryside and his regiment had dug trenches to stop the spreading destruction.

Nevar's coincidental message from God had turned out to be more accurate than I thought possible. The next time he was preaching in the family room I asked him, "How did you know that Elo was going to help prevent the spread of forest fires?"

"I did?"

"Yes, you did."

I then asked him, "How long am I going to live?"

Nevar replied, "Matt, you're going to live forever. Don't you know that?"

"Good answer Nevar, good answer."

Part V – A Bold Finish

Chapter 30

Dental Dilemmas And Adult Care Audacity

One Sunday in March, a twelve-year-old Maryland child died from an infection that began as an abscessed tooth. The birth mother had access to the state health and dental plan but the boy's coverage had lapsed. The young man was not a foster child but he participated under the Medical Assistance program. Part of the reason the tooth infection went unchecked was because the child had not received regular dental care.

In the best interest of the children, DSS went on alert, requesting that foster agencies and all foster parents submit up-to-date dental records for every child in foster care. The foster care license auditors went to town and reviewed all dental records of foster children. The foster agencies sent a notification to foster parents emphasizing the need for a prompt response. If foster parents did not already possess complete dental records, they needed to obtain new documentation and fast. There was a mad rush to make dental appointments across the state of Maryland and this was a problem. The fact is, less than ten percent of Maryland dental offices accept Medical Assistance.

My wife and I had experienced our own foster care problems concerning dental care. The first problem pertained to acquiring an appointment. We did manage to find a dental office within thirty miles of our home that accepted foster children and their corresponding dental coverage, but mere availability was not the only problem. The dental offices that did accept Medical Assistance also refused to see patients within six months of the last patient visit. If they did, they would not receive payment from Medical Assistance. On the other hand, foster care agencies were under pressure to ensure that all foster children had complete dental care within the six-month benchmark. These two factors conflicted with one another.

Then there was a third problem associated with scheduling: In order to secure a dental appointment exactly six months from the last visit, you need to schedule an appointment three to six months in advance. This all becomes very difficult and confusing, and you had better not miss your scheduled appointment because they are not going to have an available appointment in the following next week. These dental offices are so booked up and busy that they do not send out reminder calls.

To appease the government beast of regulators, the foster care agencies use punishments to deter procrastination or documentation delinquencies. Punishments, penalties, and fees motivate foster parents, reminding them to stay on top of dental appointments and any other associated documentation. To make a bad situation worse, the foster care agencies feel compelled to penalize foster parents for being late with paperwork. If foster parents are excessively late with, or do not complete all requirements, the agencies are forced to revoke foster parent licenses. Unfortunately, the kids in those homes may transition to an institution or to an available foster home if lucky… and it is all in the best interest of the children. As a foster parent, you *really* have to stay on top of your licensing requirements.

The agencies, pressured by the state, keep the foster homes in strict compliance. They repeatedly remind foster parents that everyone is 'under the gun.' Unfortunately, foster parents often end up being the 'helping hand' that is 'left holding the gun.' In other words, the party with the least amount of lawyers, resources, and personal insurance – a foster parent – is most susceptible to blame in cases of dental or medical neglect. This is one more reason why Step 1 and Step 2 foster parents are less taxing on a state budget than the much more expensive Step 3 institutions; liability insurance inflates cost.

****

After I received an email from our licensing specialist pertaining to a missing physical requirement on Marianna's physical form, I called Krista to inform her. Krista was handling the doctor, therapy, and dental appointments.

"Hey Krista, I got an email from Nancy. It says that Marianna did not complete the tuberculosis test on her physical. What's up?"

"I'll tell you what's up. The doctor said she was too young for a TB test."

"I don't care what the doctor says. The foster care agency says that she has to have it."

"Matt, who should I listen to pertaining to medical advice… the doctor, the foster care agency, or the lawyers writing the requirements? I don't want Marianna injected with TB in order to fulfill an overcautious requirement. It's not like she just returned from a mission in the Congo."

"I agree, but then you'll have to figure something out! Call the foster agency. Call the doctor's office. See what they say. Find out if the doctor can write an exception letter. Just do something or they might revoke our license and pull the kids out of here!"

"Why don't *you* do something?"

Frustration had set in. Krista was tired of running back and forth to doctors and dentists when nothing was ever wrong with anybody. In the end, she followed through and took care of the issue… *in the best interest of the child*. In this case, the best interest of the child was not in the best interest of Marianna. But at age three, Marianna was officially 'TB free'; now the lawyers and insurance companies could rest easy.

To sum it up, foster care regulations and requirements are a balancing act, especially the dental care requirements. On one hand, you have the state demanding a six-month dental appointment, and on the other hand, you have Medical Assistance demanding a waiting period no shorter than six months. Then, on one foot, you have limited dental offices, and on the other foot, you have auditors pressuring the private foster care agencies for documentation. Balancing on your head is a stack of documentation and a tank of laughing gas. Who ever thought that taking foster kids to the dentist would be this big of a pain in the mouth? It is no wonder parents of disadvantaged youths do not go to the dentist; nobody wants you there in the first place.

If you actually get an appointment and make it to an accepting dental office, look out! I can only speak from my own experience, but the quality of service at the two random dental offices we tried was horrible! Sometimes the dentists did not even perform a cleaning. I thought that was the main point of the six-month dental visit. The dentist simply came in, looked in my son's mouth (perhaps checking for abscessed teeth), and then disappeared.

One time our Medical Assistance dental card vanished from the front reception desk. We went back to the desk to retrieve our card and it had magically poofed into thin air. I surmised that medical fraud might occur right at the front reception desk. The Medical Assistance dental offices we visited were so poorly run that I would rather perform my own root canal before returning for my kid's free lollipop.

Fortunately, a wonderful dentist agreed to handle the dental needs of our foster children. Wendy Brown was performing my six-month checkup in her office.

Krista inquired, "Do you accept Medical Assistance?"

Like ninety percent of dentists in Maryland, the answer was "No."

Krista informed Dr. Brown of our dental dilemma and she graciously volunteered to see our foster kids free of charge. My wife had performed countless hours of pro bono psychological therapy and karma had come full circle. We scheduled the appointments for our boys and Dr. Brown took care of the rest. She even sent us off with the dental paperwork we required for the State of Maryland. Unfortunately, I do not think the dental experiences of many other foster families were anywhere near as pleasant.

****

Spring arrived and it was time to transition Nevar into adult care. At the age of twenty-one, he could not legally reside within our home. My wife and I were licensed foster parents and not licensed to care for adults with disabilities. In order to perform adult care duties you have to complete another set of requirements for an entirely difference license. It requires additional training, additional inspections, and additional headaches. We were already doing our part to help as many kids as we could, and spending the rest of our lives caring for the needs of an adult with mental disabilities was not a part of that plan.

Numerous facilities in our area performed adult care services, even one in our own neighborhood. We hoped to transition Nevar to a place close to home. The transitional process to adult care began in the fall when I met Nevar's newly designated 'transition worker.' DSS uses these types of contract employees to complete the tedious process of transitioning children into adulthood as well as for other functions within the wild world of foster care. We met our transition worker, Penny, at a school fair designed to showcase local companies that provide specialized support. Penny, employed by a private contractor for the City of Baltimore, assisted.

The Adult Care Fair was crowded and loud with families of special need students. They were investigating the different companies that provide various types of adult care services. The companies and vendors had set up tables in the Oakland Mills High School cafeteria to display their products. Many different companies specialized in numerous job programs and assisted-living environments for young people such as Nevar. As we entered the cafeteria, I could still smell the Sloppy Joes from earlier in the day. We walked around the lunchroom, checking out the companies and the services that each one provided. People working the tables were handing out candy, pencils, pens, and other items branded with the company logos. There is a lot of federal and state funding available for adult care services and these companies were out to get as much of the funding as possible.

Nevar spoke up, "Maaaaaan, why do we need all of these pencils and stuff? This is like the junk people give out at Halloween if they're too cheap to give out candy."

I replied, "It's just a way to help us remember the name of each company from the tables. You see each pencil has the company name on it."

I held up a pencil for Nevar to investigate.

Nevar looked over the pencil, "Why do I need to remember a company named, *Number 2*? I ain't gonna forget that."

I laughed at Nevar's unintentional joke, then took the pencil, turned it around, and pointed to the inscription, "Here Nevar. The name of this company is, '"Patience."'"

"Man, I don't need no pencil to remember the name *Patience!*"

I held the pencil in my hand, spinning it between my fingers, and then replied, "Well, apparently I do." I looked up at the fluorescent lighting and softly uttered to the foam ceiling tiles, "Dad, I hear you loud and clear... *and I'm done with doubting!*"

Nevar looked confused. "Matt... why are you talking to the ceiling? I'm right here."

"I know you are buddy. I know you are."

****

The first thing I learned about the transition of a special needs child to adult care is that you had better start transitioning early and that we had not started transitioning early enough. The Developmental Disabilities Administration or DDA is the main agency inside of the government that funds adults with disabilities. In other words, it's Nevar's new sugar momma, and we needed to start shaking his moneymaker.

The waiting line for DDA funding is longer than the waiting line for Medical Assistance dental appointments. I would rather spend a week waiting at the MVA and end up with a revoked license than wind up on the waiting list for DDA funding. Evidently, you should not hold your breath waiting for funding. There is even a web site solely dedicated to the topic of waiting in line for DDA funding: http://www.endthewaitnow.com/faq.cfm.

The DDA application itself was a mini booklet... a mini booklet that I was not legally eligible to sign. I would need the help, or at least the signature, of my friendly neighborhood Baltimore City DSS worker; the signature of any assigned transition worker would not be legally acceptable. I cringed at the very thought of requesting any help from a city worker. Even though Nevar's DSS worker had been far better than Elo's, it was not by much.

After several attempts, faxes, and personally hounding the Baltimore City DSS worker, we succeeded in getting the form processed to the DDA and Nevar was on the waiting list. We hoped funding would be available to him by 2010... *2010!* It was currently 2007. Nevar would be ageing out of his current funding provider in less than two months, and the DSS funding under the Maryland Human Resources department would no longer be available. What were we supposed to do, drop him off in the city with some warm clothes and a shopping cart? Unfortunately, something like that can happen to a person in Nevar's situation who does not have a caring advocate. So what do *we* do?

Legally, Nevar could not live under our roof once he reached the age of twenty-one, so he was in for one heck of a birthday surprise. The law literally does not permit him to stay under the care of a non-related unlicensed provider. We needed to find Nevar funding and get him under the care of an experienced company that would provide his needed services.

Seeking help I called the Baltimore City Department of Social Services, I called our non-profit foster agency, and I called DDA. Guess what. At first, nobody had a good answer for me and it seemed as though everyone, except Krista and I, was comfortable with the current situation. As long as no one broke the law on the government's watch, nobody appeared to care what Krista and I did with Nevar.

Nevar's new transition worker, Penny, sent me an email stating her intention to assist me with expediting his case. I had recently met Penny in the fall when Nevar landed on her caseload. She was a kindhearted young woman who immigrated to the Baltimore region from one of the Virgin Islands. Initially, I did not understand the importance of her role with transitioning Nevar into adulthood or the importance of her role in transitioning him to DDA funding, but she informed me that our first goal was to inform DDA that Nevar was a special case.

Nevar was not like most of the cases waiting on the DDA funding list. Unlike Nevar, many of the others sought funding while living under the care of their legal birth family. DDA funding, designed for all persons with disabilities, is available to any approved person, not just foster kids moving to adult care. It is somewhat like funding supplied through the Social Services Administration, or SSA, and foster children do not exactly stand out in a crowd. Without pressure, DDA would not expedite Nevar's funding. Penny worked for a couple of weeks and was eventually successful. Thanks to her, Nevar became an emergency priority case who should receive funding by his twenty-first birthday.

It was spring and Nevar's birthday was just around the corner. We had not received another license to care for special need adults. Penny assisted us with the DDA paperwork and selection of Nevar's future service providers. The residential housing company, H.O.M.E., had a facility nearby in Howard County. It was located near bike paths and a recreational lake. The location was not perfect, but it was still within ten minutes of our house. I had hoped that Nevar would be placed somewhere in our neighborhood, but none of the nearby residential group homes had availability for him. To look on the bright side, being ten minutes away was far closer than any place in Baltimore City or D.C.

Nevar's new home was a small rancher that housed several other clients who had either physical or mental disabilities. He would have a nice little bedroom in a homey environment. The hired staff might not cook as well as Grammy, but at least Nevar would be living in an actual house, and it might feel like home. I did not want him to live in a hospital-type residential facility ever again. The facilities of H.O.M.E. were actually located in 'homes.' On a side note, for obvious reasons we decided against any company named *Patience.*

The job services corporation we selected called Energy was only a few minutes away from his new residential living facility. Here, Nevar could perform a job duty and earn a paycheck along with his fellow co-workers that shared a similar diagnosis. Some special needs classmates from Oakland Mills High School also had plans to work at this particular job program and Nevar could spend his days surrounded by familiar friends in a friendly working environment.

The job site offered shipping and packaging work. The team members packaged products along with padding to prepare them for shipment. Sometimes other work included tagging clothes or other products with a tagging machine. The best part of Energy was that it was located close to his future home. Nevar had spent enough time being transported back and forth on buses for his education. H.O.M.E. would handle his transportation needs and would bus him just ten minutes to and from Energy each day.

All we had to do was secure Nevar's DDA funding. H.O.M.E. and Energy's main concern was the status of his funding. Penny contacted DDA and received a continuous runaround. We called our foster agency placement coordinator as well as our assigned worker but they could not suggest a solution. When Nevar turned twenty-one, the foster agency would no longer receive funding from DSS and the stipend we received for Nevar would end as well.

Fortunately, the non-profit agency assured us that they would help support the costs of supporting Nevar after his birthday. Nevar's birthday came, and since he was still living with us, we were technically in breach of a regulation. But since the non-profit agency filed an extension, we got a pass. At least for the time being, we were no longer in violation of the law.

Still, outlaw or not, Nevar was now twenty-one and required transition. We were not his legal biological parents and we did not have a right to house him even if we were willing to do so temporarily. Frankly, we needed to transition Nevar for his own good. He needed to experience autonomy and the responsibility of having a job that young people his age endure. It is all a healthy part of growing up. Nevar was ready to live as an adult.

****

It seemed like many of the complications of dealing with a special need foster child did not stem from our special need foster child – but from everybody else! My wife and I were feeling a bit overwhelmed and frustrated. We continually ran into roadblocks and incompetence throughout our dealings with the government agencies. After Nevar turned twenty-one, DSS no longer funded him, while DDA was not yet ready to fund him, and neither was the MWH.

We had done everything required for transitioning our foster son into adult care but we had run into a stone blockade. Every form had been completed and every required signature obtained. We reminded and pressured the needed social workers to sign forms and get the job done. We worked with the transition worker to select service providers and confirmed that the service companies were ready to welcome Nevar. After all this, the last thing we needed was problems from Nevar's biological family and our nutty neighbors. But we got them.

As the time ticked by, Nevar's birth mom somehow caught wind of his successful life in our home and a light bulb (or "$") must have lit up in her mind. Someone was paying attention, (perhaps Wallace, Diynah or Carlyn), because Nevar's mother, Shirley, called our home with custody concerns exactly two days after Nevar's birthday. *In the best interest of the child*, I ignored this last minute effort to reunite with Nevar and I did not return her call.

In the final hours of Nevar's transition, our neighbors, on the other hand, were simply tired of our foster kids. Sick of kids cutting through neighborhood yards, a neighbor complained to Jared, and he in turn brought the message home. Neighbors never complained when it was just harmless Little J cutting through the yard, but I am sure the rules changed when a six-foot tall, African-American man was traipsing behind. One spring afternoon, the diesel fuel of Nevar's birth mom and the fertilizer of a disgruntled neighbor combined to create an unavoidable explosion.

Chapter 31

The Shin Hits The Fat

A slight breeze was blowing on a relaxing spring afternoon. The azaleas were in full bloom and the early season honeybees were drifting flower to flower. Everything else… went to *Hell!*

Just the night before, Nevar, Harper, Bryan, and Jared had enjoyed a fun-filled sleepover that included pizza, cake, and a full-blown video game tournament. Nevar had celebrated his twenty-first birthday with his friends in style. Now he was spending the day walking around the house talking on the telephone. It was a part of his regular routine. The world needed to know about his inside information pertaining to superheros and WWE wrestlers. Krista stayed home with the boys, cleaning up around the house, and going through some bins of summer clothing. I was up the street enjoying the warm spring afternoon while entertaining my four-year-old daughter.

To keep Marianna occupied, I often walked across the way to visit with a neighbor, Joe, who watched over his two sons. Joe was a single dad who shared a residence with his aunt, the actual owner of the home. Marianna liked playing with Joe's children and I enjoyed the company of Joe… as well as the company of Joe's cooler of Coronas. As the kids created mud pies, Joe and I would enjoy a late afternoon beer. The only problem was that Joe's aunt was less than thrilled about my visitation: It interfered with her ability to shout yard work duties to her nephew. However, she tolerated my presence for the sake of the children's play date. I had my suspicion that Joe's aunt was the person in the neighborhood who did not appreciate my kids cutting through her yard.

My boys liked to take shortcuts around the neighborhood and this particular home sat directly between my house and the local candy shop. The woman of this house seemingly had a problem with my boys using the timesaving route. She never directly expressed any concern to me, but managed to send subliminal messages to my wife.

Over the years, I have discovered that people tend to avoid conflict with me. I am not sure why. Perhaps it is the crazy look in my eye, my forked tongue, or the 6-6-6 birthmark located below my left shoulder. I have also discovered that people sometimes make their opinions known to my wife, simply to avoid conflict with me.

My wife had been very forthcoming when sharing her disheartening interactions. She experienced several rude incidents with a number of neighbors and recently felt the wrath of this one particular woman. The woman used her preferred method of punishment, displaying various gestures of ignorance while throwing societal norms into the wind. Unfortunately, my wife was the one standing downwind, slapped in the face by rude behavior.

The woman, only ten years older than her nephew, acted like a hag from a western film, the character that blatantly ignores any friendly gestures from the bubbly townsfolk. The woman and her pinkish orange hairdo simply wanted nothing to do with the rest of society. In passing, she would turn her head like a stuck-up poodle with PMS and she had mastered the art of being a 'binch.' Her greeting and disingenuous smile reminded me of a crocodile with an unsuspecting bird perched upon her snout.

As the sun prepared to set, Krista arrived on the scene. I was standing with Joe watching the children play when Krista called out to me, "Matt! I *need* you at home. There's a problem with Nevar."

I was a few sheets to the wind and my mind was not prepared for any disruption to my current state of relaxation.

"What are you talking about?" It appeared as though the mud pie festival and my good time with a bottle of Corona was about to end. I just hoped that anything pertaining to a broken appliance or teenage drama could wait.

"Somehow Nevar got his birth mom's phone number and then he called her. Now she has him all worked up and he's flipping out!"

"Birth mom… you mean he called an old foster mom?"

"*No!* I mean he called his birth mom!"

My mind was searching to explain this happenstance. "How did he come up with his birth mom's phone number?"

Shirley had called my cell phone the prior week and left a bizarre message about taking custody of Nevar. She had not seen or visited him since the day he became a ward of the state and I suspected her intentions lacked virtue. I had ignored the message, deleted it from my phone, and moved forward with the plan for Nevar. There was a good, solid, safe plan for his adulthood in place, and it did not include the influence of his mentally ill biological mom. But somehow he had managed to reach her and this phone call had ignited a fire in him that Krista and I had never before seen.

"You mean... Shirley?"

"*Yes*... Shirley! Now do you understand why I ran down here to get you?"

"Well why didn't you say so?" Krista rolled her eyes.

Just then, the pink-haired crocodile slithered down from her muddy abyss. She stood watching and listening to our dilemma.

Krista turned to her and cautiously said, "Hello."

"Hell ... O," the woman sneered. My wife was not in any mood for unfriendly or rude behavior.

Krista turned to me and replied with sarcastic optimism, "At least she said *hello.*" My wife had chosen to be sarcastic no more than ten times in her entire life and I am not sure that now was the best time.

The crocodile snapped. She was coming to attack. It was on. But before the bouncer from Jerry Springer could step in, I grabbed my family and we headed home. There were issues far more important than dealing with the neighborhood binch.

We arrived back at our house and found Nevar in a full rage. His voice was loud and repetitive. He was ranting and raving while pacing back and forth between the kitchen and his bedroom. Everything else was silent. Jared had hid in the basement and Krista immediately took Marianna upstairs. Now it was my job as alpha male to de-escalate this explosive situation.

I moved into Nevar's personal space, feeling his hot breath pressing towards me. He instantly shoved my upper chest pushing me backwards across the kitchen. Hopped up on adrenaline, he displayed extraordinary strength. His wild eyes were wider than the stuffed raccoon at Cunningham Falls and my eyes were almost as wide. My adrenaline kicked into overdrive fueled by the physical contact as well as several Coronas previously consumed. The fact that Nevar might require physical restraint was on the forefront of my mind.

I raised my voice. "Nevar, *you had better chill the heck out!*"

"*Or what?* I ain't afraid of you. I'll kick your ass!"

In his adrenaline-filled, enraged state, I considered the fact that he might just be able to do so. I flashed back to an episode of the TV show *Cops* and thought about the strength of those skinny persons whacked out on PCP. Unlike the fine officers of *Cops,* I was not equipped with a team of police officers to handle this situation. My only help was Jared and he was currently downstairs hiding in the playroom. In a slightly calmer voice I responded, "You *don't* want to try that."

He turned and faced the closet, then threw a right hook that landed against the door. The punch hit so hard it split open the wood with a loud 'crack!' Then he stood back, ready to throw another punch. Actually, it seemed as though he *did* want to try that.

My adrenaline was pumping hard but I focused on the problem in front of me, an oversized, whacked-out, heavily medicated, bi-polar young man in serious need of some direction. *How did I end up with this job?* I needed to redirect his adrenaline and de-escalate his anger as well as my own.

He was pacing back and forth across the living room floor blurting out all sorts of nonsense. I imagined this behavior had landed him in a rubber room on more than one occasion. The closest thing I had to a rubber room was our trampoline and I do not think that he was ready to jump away his frustrations.

I continued, trying to transfer my own anger into some form of humor, "Oh no! You are not going to start busting up my house! Remember... this place is *tight!*" Nevar did not laugh.

Nonsense poured from his lips. "Man, this *is* what would happen... trying to mess things up... they're *all* after nothing... I'm leaving." Then he stormed out of the front door and started walking down the street.

Powerless, I called out effortlessly, "You had better get back here."

Nevar disappeared around the corner and then out of sight. I sat down contemplating the problem before me. I imagined Jared was somewhere under a bed hiding next to Sadie. Minutes went by in the silent house until Krista reappeared from the upstairs bedroom.

"We can't have him running around the neighborhood in his kind of state."

I thought to myself, *Perhaps he'll run into the crocodile with the PMS problem. Maybe the two will cancel each other out.*

"I know. I'll go look for him." Before I stepped out the door, I saw him in the distance walking back towards our home. It was a beautiful day, but not a neighbor was in sight. I sat down on the front porch and waited for him to arrive. My adrenaline had decreased and I was ready for a new approach. He was still emotionally charged, but visibly more stable after his walk around the neighborhood. I patiently waited for him to speak as he paced back and forth in front of me.

"They're crazy. She ain't my real mom. They say I'm retarded. I'm not retarded. They held me under water. That's why I'm all messed up. She said they stuck me in a closet and fed me spoonfuls of cocaine. That's why I'm all messed up. I wasn't born retarded. My brain's not working right because they dropped me on my head when I was a baby. That's why I'm all messed up."

He wanted to cry, but anger overcame his sadness. His rant was a mixture of false stories that others had told him over the years. As I listened, I could hear the cruel words of former group home workers, an old foster brother, and perhaps the twisted theories of his own mentally ill birth mom.

I softly replied, "Nevar. It is not you. It is everybody else. They are the crazy ones. I am not sure what caused your brain to be different, but it is not something that simply 'happened' to you. Maybe everybody else fell on their head, maybe everybody else took spoonfuls of cocaine, or maybe everybody else was under water. No matter what people tell you about your brain, what they say does not matter. These people are telling you these things because they're the ones with real problems and you're... not... crazy."

I sincerely meant every word I said – even if Nevar *was* crazy – but more so, my words were meant to deflect his anger and blame. At that moment he felt mad at me, he felt mad at everyone, and he felt mad at himself. In reality, he was only upset because a mentally ill woman just told him all sorts of outrageous claims on a phone call, igniting a state of overdriven confused anxiety.

Then he exclaimed, "*Yea!* They are crazy. That crazy-ass woman was just telling me all that crazy stuff. She don't know what she's talkin' about! She's the crazy one!"

"That's right!"

"*Yea!*" Like the flip of a light switch I was no longer the enemy, we were now on the same team. Nevar was deescalating. I had redirected his anger and then supported his emotions.

Eventually I redirected those emotions toward a less volatile topic. "And Jared's a liar!"

"*Yea!* Jared's a liar and he's not going to heaven!" It was working. Nevar had transferred the anger from his birth mom towards a meaningless subject, the fibs of a twelve-year-old boy. Feeling supported, his emotional state of anger had defused. Finally, I helped him transfer the remaining emotional angst towards a topic of little consequence.

"That's right, but we're going to get Jared baptized!"

"*Yea!* And then he's going to go to Heaven... *and...* he'll stop lying!" Now his negative emotions had turned into positive suggestion. Jared went from being a liar to heaven-bound while Nevar had gone from devastated to euphoric.

"Hold on Nevar. Let us not get ahead of ourselves. We might get Jared into heaven, but I'm not sure if God can stop him from lying."

Nevar let out a boisterous laugh. "*Yea*, you're right!" He stood in front of me as I sat encouraging him to continue with his theories on the front steps of our home. In the meantime, his pacing had ceased. Jared appeared at the front door standing behind the glass window of the entrance. Now that Nevar was smiling and the atmosphere had lightened, he came to investigate the mysterious laughter.

"What's so funny?"

"Why...you're going to heaven Jared!"

Nevar confirmed, "Yea Jared! You're going to heaven!" Jared stood smiling with a confused expression. He was probably wondering how a hole in the closet door somehow related to his upcoming trip to heaven.

Jared stood with his head tilted, like a dog watching other dogs on television. "What?"

"Don't worry about it Little J." I was quite sure he was not going to heaven anytime soon and Nevar was now on track.

Our problem had been resolved. The mentally disabled, emotionally disturbed tirade was over. That was not so hard. Now… what were we going to do with the pink-haired '*binch*' living up the street?

Chapter 32

Take It To The Top

Marianna's birthday was at the end of April. To celebrate we had a kiddie extravaganza with 30 kids, pizza, cupcakes, and a new swing set. It was like a mad kiddie party that you would only see in a Hollywood film. Now that the attendees had reached the age of four some parents took advantage of the option to drop off their child. Like every busy family, the parents had to run Saturday afternoon errands. Once the kiddies finished eating and playing in the yard, I had a long afternoon including multiple restroom assists. I felt like I received a taste of my future servitude in hell. Never again will I throw a kiddie party with optional child drop-off.

Fast-forward two months. Now I had an even messier problem to overcome than the wiping duties for multiple four-year-olds. Since we were not in possession of a license to care for adults with special needs, my wife and I needed to get Nevar moving. He needed his DDA funding and he needed his residential placement within H.O.M.E. I called and spoke to the director of the H.O.M.E. housing facility. The man told me that Nevar's apartment and bedroom were ready to go, but we could not move him in until they received the funding from the DDA.

I called the DDA and talked with caseworkers, staff members, and anyone who answered the phone. The workers that did answer the phone did not have answers for me. Krista attempted to speak with someone at DDA as well. We figured that two guns aimed at one lame duck might make chicken soup for Nevar's soul. We were wrong.

A couple more weeks passed and so had our patience. Krista and I went on the offensive. I did some research on the internet and found that the main DDA office was right down I-695 from our old Violetville home. I got the address and I printed it out. Our plan was to go directly to the top. We were going to march in there, state the legality of our situation, and demand satisfaction… and my wife did just that.

On a sunny weekday afternoon, Krista and I drove to the DDA office located on the campus of the Sandstone Center in Green Spring, Maryland. I pulled into the circular campus and looked around for a sign that read DDA. There was no sign. The buildings were nondescript and only displayed old signs for a neighboring drug and alcohol treatment center. Nothing said DDA or anything remotely similar.

I checked the address and pulled up in front of an unmarked building that fit the location according to the addresses of the surrounding buildings. It was the only building around with a large number of parked cars and without a sign. The surrounding parking lots were abandoned and silent.

"This looks like it," I stated.

Krista replied, "How can you tell? There aren't any signs!"

"I can't tell. I'm just guessing. This is the only building with a bunch of cars around it. Unless the DDA is hiding in the back of the automotive facilities building, this *has* to be it. The only way to find out is to go inside and check it out. I'll wait here. If you don't come back immediately then I'll know this is the right place."

I parked the van on the outskirts of the parking lot. We decided that it made more sense for one of us to wait in the car with Marianna. There was no need for us to go traipsing around a building together with a four-year-old in tow. I suggested that she, being a woman, would probably yield better results. My wife hesitantly agreed. Neither of us wanted to perform this job of *advocating*. We felt like we were here against our will, doing someone else's job.

Krista tends to be a bit more assertive when it comes to achieving a desired result and she agreed to tackle this challenge. Krista, motivated by the ongoing DDA runaround, exited the van and disappeared into the main building while I sat quietly in the parking lot waiting with Marianna.

The campus of the Sandstone Center was a beautiful collection of old architecture mixed with several newer brick buildings. The old buildings surrounding the campus were fenced off and boarded up. It looked like Fraternity Row at the University of Maryland after a nuclear holocaust. Each building built along a green sloping hillside had tall concrete pillars that resembled ancient Roman architecture. I am sure these buildings looked beautiful when they were first constructed, but now they sat dilapidated and worn. I imagine the insides contained a variety of carcinogens like asbestos and lead paint.

Looking around at the nearby signs it was apparent that the Sandstone Center had been used as a rehabilitation center for alcohol and drug treatment. Many a former foster child had probably found his or her way onto these grounds. As I watched a person in the distance aimlessly walking around the hillside, I reached over and hit the lock button on the minivan door.

While examining the grounds of the Sandstone Center, I flashed back to a rehabilitated member of my own family. My sister Valerie did a few stints in rehab and would often tell stories related to her experience. My siblings and I used humor to transcend the tragedy of our lives. Humor transference was a trait that ran deep within my kin.

My eldest sister, Val, was an interesting character to say the least. She spent her teenage years incognito as a vampire. Oddly, the vampire lifestyle is even more common today. In her day, she was an innovator and was one of the first vampires on the scene. If someone were to slay her, I wondered if all other vampires would revert to humans: Probably not. My sister once stayed in a facility similar to the Sandstone Center. I believe her treatment location was more modern with less asbestos, but I could not say for sure. I had never joined my mother on any of the weekend trips to visit my sister while she was in treatment.

Once while on a vacation at the beach, Valerie told me about her rehab experience. My sister informed me of the group meetings, the time spent with roommates, as well as her time spent alone in solitary confinement. As we sat on the beach overlooking the Atlantic Ocean, Val summed up her rehabilitation experience with one comedic punch line.

She said, "The staff told me I tried to kill my roommate in my sleep… and I thought she changed rooms because I snore so loud."

In the words of my niece Ashley, "This *is* my family."

After thirty-some years living with the members of my own family, you would think I would not have been concerned about the person I saw stumbling across the rehab grounds. As I waited for Krista, I re-checked to make sure the doors remained locked. Who knows? It may have been one of my own relatives rolling down the green hills of the Sandstone Center on that pleasant midday afternoon.

****

It had been an hour since my wife first entered the building. She exited the front door of the unmarked brick structure wearing a huge smile. It was an expression drenched in success. As she walked towards the minivan, she raised her thumb up into the air. Good news was on the way. She climbed into the passenger seat and buckled up.

"So, it went well?"

"Very well!" and then she began to tell her story. "I walked in, spoke to the receptionist, and informed her of our situation. The place stunk like urine. It smelled so bad I felt like I had entered a nursing home. I told the receptionist about the legality issues pertaining to our situation. The woman was very curt. It was obvious that I was interrupting a complicated game of solitaire. She sent me around to several different offices in search of help. The assigned person that would have normally helped me was out for the day. I kept walking around and then I went back to the main receptionist, once again she directed me. I repeated this routine several times. Each time I returned, her level of rudeness increased. Eventually the receptionist simply shrugged at me and did not offer any more suggestions. I informed her that I was not leaving without a solution, and if I did, I planned to come back with my foster son's lawyer. Better yet, perhaps we will bring Nevar and his luggage. Suddenly her tone changed. She told me to hold on and made a couple of calls. I sat waiting. Finally, someone useful came to my aid. A man led me upstairs and then asked, 'How did you find us?' I told him that you found them on the internet. Jokingly I said, 'Guess you had better get that problem fixed.' He didn't find my joke that funny. He led me upstairs to the office of the director. She was a 'no nonsense' kind of person who was sympathetic to our situation. The director immediately put several people to work on Nevar's case. The first problem her staff ran into was that they could not find Nevar anywhere in their records. Just think... we filled out all of those forms over the past six months, and they still had no record of Nevar. I started filling out more forms and they started creating a new record. It only took fifteen minutes before the process was complete. The director said that she would take over for the rest of the case!"

In less than twenty-four hours, we received a call from H.O.M.E. They had received notification of Nevar's funding from the office of the DDA. It was that simple. We moved him into his apartment later that day. I packed up the minivan with all of his video games, suitcases (not trash bags of clothing), and personal effects. Then I crammed them into the back of our vehicle and we were on our way.

As we drove to Nevar's new home, everyone quietly looked out the windows.

Eventually Nevar turned to me and spoke with a solemn voice, "Can we drive by my high school. You know... one last time."

"Sorry Nevar, not today. We already passed the exit for your school. Besides, this is not the last chance for you to see it.

"You mean I get to go back next year?" He looked hopeful.

"No. Sorry, but you already graduated. There is no going back once you've graduated."

"Oh man, I'm going to miss that place." Nevar looked back out through the window.

Leaving home had reminded Nevar that not only would he miss living with our family... he missed Oakland Mills High School as well. His time spent at OMHS was perhaps the best time of his life. He had made friends, fit in, and even received straight A's. There, no one had called him names, left him in solitary, or dosed him with Thorazine.

"Well, when you come home for visits we'll drive by the school, maybe we'll even stop in for a visit."

"Really?"

"Sure."

Then Nevar sat up straight. I could see a smile on his face. He looked outward towards the road ahead of him.

****

We arrived to unload and investigate Nevar's new crib. Through H.O.M.E., he had received placement in a basement apartment of a large rancher on Montgomery Road. It was spacious and clean. The rooms were fully furnished and ready for Nevar to move in. An entertainment bar and recreational furniture were spread around a large living room area. Marianna and Jared ran about the apartment, "*Wow!* You've got your own refrigerator… and a microwave!"

Nevar smiled and boldly replied, "*Yep.* I'm an adult now."

Krista commented, "Nevar, this is so nice. You are going to do so well here."

I jumped into the conversation. "But don't worry Nevar, we're right down the road and I'll be checking in on you. Also, have your secretary pencil you in for the Fourth of July next month."

"Okay!" he replied.

We entered the bedroom and Krista began to unpack Nevar's clothes and put them into the bedroom dresser. My wife specialized in clothing organization. It is too bad all of her hard work invariably ends up in a pile on the floor. Marianna and Jared were busy running around the living room area of the apartment and I stood behind Nevar giving him an encouraging pat on the back. He was a little happy, a little nervous, and a little pensive.

"Can I still live with you?"

"Nevar, you know how it goes. You are a man now, and you will come over and visit like a man."

"I know… and it's okay. God told me it was going to be okay… and he told me about the little boy too."

"Little boy? Whatchu talkin' 'bout Willis? We don't have no little boy." My wife and I were a long way from considering any new kids.

"God told me that you needed room for a little boy named Miles."

"Well, we'll see about that." I laughed at his odd remark. Here he goes again with another prophecy from God. Soon Nevar would be telling me the next president would be of African descent. I walked over and stood behind the bar. "So when's the house warming party?"

"I... I... don't know."

"Well, I had better be invited... and don't forget... No girls allowed!" Krista rolled her eyes.

Nevar laughed. "I'm staying away from those girls!"

"That's right! You're too clever for them. You'll be making that money and they'll want to get their pretty hands on your paycheck. You can either buy games for yourself or give all your benjamins to them."

"*Noooooooo!*"

"Nevar, I think you're living on top of the world."

Nevar replied with nothing more than a huge grin. For the first time in his life, Nevar was speechless.

Chapter 33

Something Stinky This Way Comes

We had a pleasant summer in 2007. Life was simpler without the stress of transition. Having some additional free time was nice as well. Much work went into caring for a mentally disabled person and for the first time in over a year, we were living our lives free of those demands. Nevar came home on various weekends as we eased him into independent living, reassuring him that he still had a place in our family. On one car ride he apologized for the hole he once made in the closet door.

The staff at Nevar's home quickly found out how much he enjoyed talking, and adjusted to life with their new vocal client. Many of the current clients at the Montgomery home were considerably impaired. They were in wheelchairs and some were inaudible. Nevar was the missing piece of the puzzle. He kept the clients entertained, courtesy of his nonstop ramblings about God and life. Nevar did not care if the other clients did not respond. He often was not listening to the person on the other end of the conversation anyhow.

Nevar's new arrangement was working out well for everyone. The only problem was that he no longer had a playmate. Before he moved to H.O.M.E., Jared would keep him company, sitting next to him while holding the second video game controller, and Harper would come over to go on long walks or ride bikes with Nevar. Now Nevar was playing only one-player games. To resolve this issue H.O.M.E. recommended a roommate.

A month later Nevar had his new roommate, Tarone. He was around the same age as Nevar, also a former foster child, with a similar story. The young man was another one of Baltimore's children left to the care of the state. He was in a wheelchair, resulting from a birth defect, but the young man was upbeat about his mere existence. He was thankful that a nice doctor named Ben Carson had operated on him. Otherwise, he might not be here today.

Tarone was an excellent complement to Nevar. The two kept each other company and enjoyed watching comedy films together. Of course, they played two-player video games as well. It would not be long before our family would get to know Tarone too. He became the ying to Nevar's yang and after several months, my foster son would eventually invite his roommate to come to our home for the holidays. It was a little more work to transport Tarone, but it was well worth the additional effort. He was kind and humble, a young man that always made sure Krista and I felt appreciated. At each visit, he continually thanked us for our contribution that improved the quality of his life.

****

School was only one week away and we were busy purchasing the ridiculous amount of items required for students of the public school system. Marianna's preschool had requested more items than we could fit into a stagecoach trunk. They even asked for a hundred dollar contribution towards snacks. What did the teachers plan to buy? Were the goldfish crackers literally made of gold? I did the math. With twenty kids in one class, that would add up to $2,000 for pretzels. Those pretzels were making me thirsty.

We arrived home from our shopping spree and there was a message on our home answering service. While Krista divided thirty-nine glue sticks evenly between three book bags, I listened to the message. It was a call from our non-profit foster agency and they had another prospect for our home. The placement coordinator left a message about a new three-year-old male with a severe speech delay. His current foster placement could not maintain the rigorous requirements of foster licensing and therefore the boy was transitioning.

I informed my wife. She dropped the backpacks and we discussed the new proposition before us. We agreed that a three-year-old boy might fit in well with our family. Who knows? He might be a nice little playmate for Marianna. Krista picked up the phone and returned the call. What was next in store for us?

A little boy was born on the east side of Baltimore City. His parents were deaf and already struggling with an older male sibling. The parents of the little boys loved their children and wanted the best for them but were faltering financially. Life was not easy for a deaf couple living in the lower income housing projects of Baltimore City and their firstborn son entered foster care due to negligence – not abuse or abandonment. A failure to provide appropriate food, shelter, and healthcare had forced the Department of Social Services to intervene.

Social services kept watch over the family as the deaf couple moved from place to place. DSS performed checkups on the younger sibling after the older sibling's removal. Eventually, the living situation was determined to be unsuitable when workers discovered the younger sibling sleeping in bed with a raging fever. The bed sheets were covered in cat feces and the boy's diaper was putrid and soiled from days of overuse. He was nearly septic and severely ill. Social services called emergency services. The child recovered in a local hospital and awaited placement in foster care.

The boy spent the first ten months of his life in squalid surroundings and then the next two years in a city foster home. In foster care, an elderly woman cared for the boy in her downtown apartment. As he grew in size, he grew out of his foster mom's control. He spent his days in a city daycare center making his own rules, learning to fight while defending himself from other institutionalized Baltimore City children. The toddler adopted a fighting survivalist lifestyle before his second birthday.

The boy had also learned how to take a licking. His speech, on the other hand, had not progressed as quickly as his self-taught boxing skills. For the first ten months of life he had lived in the silent environment of his deaf birth parents. With his speech not challenged and his mind not trained, the muscles of his tongue did not develop properly.

Two years after entering foster care, the time came for the little boy to transition. His elderly foster parent was having difficulty keeping up with the requirements of foster care. Eventually her foster care license expired due to a variety of reasons including the stringent demands of training. Foster care training had risen from 19 to 29 hours in the previous year and many foster parents had become disenfranchised by the entire process. Auditors badgered the non-profit foster agencies and inspectors badgered the foster parents. Dental requirements had become increasingly difficult to fulfill, as did regular training requirements. Maintaining a foster parent license had become too much of a burden for the elderly foster mother to bear.

The boy's social worker gathered his information and contacted the agency's child placement coordinator. The coordinator reviewed a list of homes to search for an available location. She found a home that matched the young man. The spot in this family's home had opened up just two months prior. She picked up the phone and made a call to investigate the possibility. The answering machine kicked on, and she left a message...

We had just received a message from our placement coordinator and my wife quickly called her back. The placement coordinator described a young man named Miles who had a severe speech impediment and was showing signs of ADHD and ODD. We believed that we could handle his Attention Deficit Hyperactivity Disorder combined with Oppositional Defiant Disorder. The speech impediment offered an interesting twist.

Marianna could handle anything a three-year-old boy could dish out, and we hoped Jared could help us transition the young man. Maybe a three-year-old boy would fit in nicely.

After spending a year and a half working with Nevar, Miles sounded like a piece of cake, and our first visitation with Miles was set for the following Saturday. Krista and I would meet the little boy and his current foster mom at a Baltimore City McDonalds restaurant. 'Mickey D's' is such a popular spot for this type of foster visitation. I bet Ronald never knew that he would play a vital role in foster care. The restaurant play places are perfect for this sort of introduction. Krista confirmed the plans with the placement coordinator and I concurred. The meeting with the little boy and his foster mom, Ms. Greene, was set.

****

The following Saturday arrived and it was time for the initial meet and greet with Miles. My wife and I packed up Marianna and drove to a McDonalds located in the northeast section of Baltimore City. We parked and entered the restaurant and found the little boy sitting next to his current foster mom in a booth just outside of the play area. Across from them sat a younger woman. She was assisting the foster mom as the little boy shoved French fries into his mouth.

We walked over to the trio and I spoke up. "Ms. Greene?"

"Yeeeees."

The two women looked up at me while the little boy feverishly inhaled his lunch.

Using hand gestures to identify my party I made introductions, "Hi, I'm Matt Hoffman, this is my wife Krista, and this is my daughter Marianna."

Krista threw a wave, "Hello."

Marianna had hidden her face in my wife's side. She was playing shy.

Ms. Greene answered, "Hellllloooo."

She had a long drawn out way of speaking and responded in the one-word replies of an old, retired grandmother. The woman looked to be in her late sixties, an older version of a typical Baltimore City foster mom. The creases around her kind smile showed years of wear from decades of raising abandoned children of Baltimore City.

Then the younger woman spoke, "Hello, I'm Jasmine Greene. I came along with my mother to give her a hand. I'm a foster parent as well. My mother and I often work together as a team to handle our kids."

Jasmine, a second-generation foster parent, followed her mother into foster parenting. I took a moment to think about that. *Jared is a third generation foster child. Generations of foster care families are caring for generations of foster children. The intertwined families are inadvertently bound to one another over decades.*

"And this must be Miles," Krista interjected.

The boy looked up briefly from his meal. He was a sturdy looking little fellow with an oversized head and big eyes. I thought to myself, *Why do all these foster kids start off with bug eyes? It must be something in the city water supply.* I could not help but notice the little boy had a potbelly that protruded from the bottom of his shirt.

"Yes, this is Miles. My mother has been caring for him for about eighteen months and she can no longer handle his needs. Miles is a little sweetheart. I would adopt him myself if I was not already in the process of adopting two others. So we think it's best to transition him while he's still young, and… here we are today."

I asked, "So what kind of stuff does Miles like?"

"He likes the usual, Thomas the Train, trucks and cars, Handy Mandy… and French fries."

The boy was continuing to stuff the remnants of McDonalds fries into his mouth.

"Really?" I sarcastically replied. Then I continued, "We're into Angelina Ballerina right now, but I'm sure we can adjust. I've seen enough of that dancing mouse to last me a lifetime."

Jasmine let out a laugh as Ms. Greene sat quietly smiling. She was cleaning up after the lunchtime mess that Miles had left strewn across the table, ketchup smeared in one spot and fries scattered across the seat of the booth. It looked like the Tasmanian devil had just spun through the booth as Miles sat there sucking down what remained of his soda. Ms. Greene finished picking up the fries and then walked over to the nearby trashcan to dispose of the waste.

She turned to Miles and asked, "Miiiiiiiiiiillllles, are you ready for the playroom?" He shook his head yes and nearly climbed over the booth before Jasmine moved out of his way. He jumped from the booth and made a beeline directly for the playroom entrance. Ms. Greene was about ten feet behind as she followed him out towards the playroom door. As he pulled on the door, I could hear her saying, "Hoooold on now Miiiiiles." She caught up to him as he attempted to pry the door open. She opened the door for Miles and the little boy disappeared from sight. Jasmine picked up the remaining wrappers of trash left behind by the little boy.

Krista turned to Jasmine, "We're going to get Marianna a few chicken nuggets to eat and then we'll come join you in the playroom."

Jasmine replied, "Okay," and then hurried off to catch up with Miles and Ms. Greene.

Krista took Marianna over to a clean booth while I got in line to order the corner stable of Marianna's diet, chicken nuggets. It was her favorite meal before she eventually graduated to the double cheeseburger. She ate chicken nuggets so often that she referred to 'a number two' as, 'chicken nuggets in my hiney.' McDonalds has affected my parenting in so many interesting ways.

Marianna ate her nuggets with honey as Krista and I talked.

She started the conversation. "I think he's cute, but what's up with that head?"

"I don't know. His nose is unusually flat. There is no nose bridge, no neck, and he has that huge forehead. The kid looked like a living, breathing… bobble head. Did the placement coordinator say he was retarded or something?"

"I don't think so, but I'm not sure if you can always tell at such a young age. He may just need to grow into his features. He is only three years old and retardation is not listed anywhere on his rap sheet. Perhaps he just needs to catch up with his head. He's got beautiful hair."

My wife has a bizarre fascination with hair. A kid could be a Cyclops but if he has nice hair then he might be the next Brad Pitt.

"Yea… great… hair." I rolled my eyes. In the meantime, Marianna had finished her nuggets. I continued, "Well, let's hit the playroom and see how he and Marianna interact together." We stood up and headed towards the play equipment for the main event.

The room was your typical McDonald-land playroom filled with tall climbing tubes that eventually led around to a spiral slide. A shoe holder sat underneath the climbing apparatus and tables were located near the window of the room. Ms. Greene and her daughter were sitting at one of the tables and we walked over to join them.

I turned to Marianna, "Hey Boo-Bear. Take off your shoes and go play. Mommy and Daddy are going to talk with our new friends."

She removed her shoes and headed for the entrance to the climbing maze.

Jasmine spoke up, "Boo-Bear eh? That is funny. We call Miles Buddha-Bear because he has a little round tummy. What a coincidence."

"That *is* funny," Krista replied. "Matt has a little round tummy too." She looked at me with a smile.

I sarcastically commented, "*Coincidence…* hmmm."

Jasmine and Ms. Greene filled us in concerning Miles, his diagnosis, and his birth family. The mother and daughter appeared happy to meet us and they expressed a desire to find a good home for their little boy. Krista and I watched as Miles and Marianna played together in the overhead tubes. They did not interact with each other very much, but crawled past one another at several different occasions. After a bit of playtime it was time to say goodbye. I called Marianna down from the tubes and she slid out through the slide exit. She followed her instructions and put her shoes onto her feet.

"Is that right?" referring to which shoe she should place onto which foot.

"Yep."

I looked up and saw Miles sitting in a plastic model of a space shuttle. He was looking down at us through the window of the shuttle.

Ms. Greene called out, "*Mmmiiiiiiiiiiiiiiiiiiiiilz*, let's go! Get down here."

He looked out of the window with a mischievous smile and then went back to playing inside of the shuttle. She called to him several more times, but he did not budge.

"*Come on Miles!* Come say goodbye."

He sat there smiling, looking down at Ms. Greene. His expression gave the impression that he was trying to say, '*Screw you lady. I'll come down when I'm good and ready... and what will you do about it?*'

Jasmine turned to us, "I guess we'll have to say goodbye for him. It might be a while before he decides to come out of the shuttle. He values his playtime at McDonalds."

Krista responded, "Oh, no problem. We'll see him soon enough."

I waved goodbye and followed Krista and Marianna as we walked out of the playroom. As we crossed the McDonald's parking lot, I could hear the muffled voice of Ms. Greene calling out to Miles, '*Mmmmmmiiiiiiiiiiiiiiiiilllllllllzzz! Get dooooooown here!*'

Chapter 34

You Never Get A Second Chance To Make A Good First Impression

It was August and our new foster son would be transitioning to us in less than a week. We had plenty of time to get him registered for preschool. Once again, we would have two foster sons living under our roof and the front bedroom was set up and ready for his arrival. The playroom had plenty of Jared's old toys and we even had a nice collection of hand-me-down clothing that would fit Miles. We were prepared.

There was an upcoming foster parent training session on Tuesday. It incorporated a movie pertaining to foster care. This was the one training per year where foster children participated with foster parents. At this training, I had the chance to visit with Miles one last time before his transition to our home. I brought Jared along with me so that he would have the opportunity to meet Miles before his transition.

At this training, the foster agency usually showed a G-rated movie to educate or entertain the audience of parents and children. Sometimes an inspirational movie like *Radio* was featured on the agency's big screen, but this year the agency showed *Finding Nemo*. Perhaps the intent was to inspire parents caring for an orphaned fish. I imagined the following year they would show the movie, *The Blind Side*. The agency training room was set up like a theatre with a small food buffet located at the back of the room. Parents and their children sat together in the long rows of training tables to enjoy the dinner and the show. I had never before seen this many foster parents in the front row.

For Jared, the real show was meeting Miles. As we arrived and took our seats, I noticed Miles standing across the room. He was easy to spot and I pointed him out to Jared.

"Over there. He's the little kid with the big head and no neck."

"Is he the one standing on the table?"

I replied, "Yep."

Unlike every other child in the room, Miles was standing on top of the long row of tables. Ms. Greene urged him to get down from the table but he was not being very cooperative. Jared and I walked over to say a short hello as Miles appeared unconcerned with our visit.

"Hi Ms. Greene, remember me from last weekend?"

"Ummmm hmmmmm," Ms. Greene replied. She was preoccupied with holding onto Miles' arm as he attempted to start a food fight with a handful of macaroni. After a moment of awkward silence standing next to Ms. Greene, we returned to our initial location on the other side of the room. The next time I looked back, Ms. Greene and the little boy were gone.

Saturday arrived and so did Miles. It was a beautiful day with crisp, cool, fall weather and Miles had arrived just in time for a birthday party at Elliott Oak's Farm in nearby Ellicott City. The rambunctious three-year-old probably thought the party was all for him but it was actually for a neighbor's child.

The neighbor had rented a pavilion at the local amusement farm that had a collection of old attractions from a closed park once known as The Enchanted Forest. As a child, my mother would take me to The Enchanted Forest and I relished the thought of reliving my youth as I watched the kids climbing upon the various attractions. I had my camera in hand and ready as Marianna and Miles enjoyed pony rides. Then everyone, but me, partook of a hayride. I performed my duty as father and photographer of Miles' glorious arrival. In just one day, he made new friends, ate cake, climbed on amusements, and rode around on various farm rides. He seemed very comfortable with the situation.

On day two, we began sorting through Miles' black plastic trash bags of clothing and toys. Every toy in the bag was broken. There appeared to be an obvious pattern. I could only imagine how many things in my home this kid was going to snap into multiple pieces. I immediately hid my cell phone. Later that day, he pulled apart my bike pump, leaving it in several broken pieces.

My wife and I took notice of the clumsy habits that Miles displayed. He could not walk twenty feet without falling flat on his face.

Krista commented, "He sure is clumsy."

"I see that. He's like a Weeble Wobble that still falls down."

As Miles moved around the house, he bumped and banged into just about every table, chair, and appliance. He even tripped in the middle of an open room and one time he fell inside of the dishwasher. I am not sure how someone does that… but he did. This kid was the proverbial bull in a china shop.

Miles reminded me of a big dopey Labrador retriever in need of training. Many times I just wanted to call out to him, *'Down Boy, down!'* Thank goodness, he did not have a tail. As he knocked over furniture and decorations, he smiled and laughed at the hilarity of it all.

One of his favorite hobbies was wrestling. He even liked to greet people as if he were the 1980's wrestler Jimmy Superfly Snuka. If anyone entered the room, he would greet them by sprinting headfirst across the divide and diving into their crotch. If you were not very quick, you were going to be hurting.

He felt comfortable running into just about everyone or anyone even if he was not familiar with the person. This tendency was courtesy of his Reactive Attachment Disorder or RAD diagnosis. RAD is a condition that either hinders a child's ability to develop an attachment with others or it does just the opposite. Sometimes children diagnosed with RAD instantaneously become your best friend. His RAD could be good or bad. People would meet Miles and comment, "He sure is friendly."

"Sorry, it's a symptom of his RAD diagnosis… Come on Miles… *let go* of Ms. Arbuckle's leg."

There is nothing quite like having a strange kid fully wrapping himself around your thigh.

Jared's RAD was exactly the opposite of Miles' RAD. That was a good thing because Jared was nine years older than Miles and an over-friendly hug from Jared might border on assault.

Miles, never embarrassed by any behavior, liked to exhibit his ability to produce gaseous fumes. My friend Mike had trademarked a phrase, 'Silent but deadly' but Miles was every bit the little stinker. The bellows from the bowels of this kid could have been mistaken for a trumpet player in a jazz orchestra. He enjoyed nothing more than playing his tune and then laughing at his audience.

Miles was an interesting influence on my daughter Marianna and it was not long before my daughter got in on the flatulent fun as well. She had her own gastro-intestinal issues and Miles had truly made his mark on my home. I just hoped that that mark would eventually come out with carpet cleaner. Henceforth, I nicknamed him 'Stink.'

He was every bit of a Stink, not just digestively speaking. His attitude and behavior fulfilled every requirement of a little stinker. At school he had already taken out a couple of teachers, and yes, he 'fro'd' chairs. He was defiant in every way that would supply him with entertainment. Breaking, smashing, and throwing all fell under that description, defiance entertainment.

In school Miles punched, kicked, threw, and he did it all with a stink and a smile. He specialized in manhandling anyone with a gentle personality. Those who were not assertive with Miles felt his wrath. He would seek and destroy any 'weak sheep in the herd.' This kid was not a challenge to his teachers; the teachers were a challenge to him. Kneel before the Great and Powerful Stink! It was a good thing that everyone at school found his antics manageable or else he might have ended up in a Level 5 school.

****

My wife and I could not help but notice the distinct similarities Miles had with my friend, Mike. Physically they were both stocky and possessed large round heads. Both were boisterous, clumsy, and comedic. They also had very similar mannerisms. If I did not know better, I would have thought of Miles and Mike as biologically related.

One afternoon I called Mike and asked him to stop by our home to meet Miles. I joked with Mike over the phone, "You've got to come over and meet your long lost son." I was curious to see how Mike would get along with Miles.

"*Oh my!*" Mike belted out. "You know that I have no children of my own… of which to speak!"

Mike had his own language, his own way of speaking. It was some sort of "Pigtown" Latin, learned from his parents. Mike held a guarded attitude when it came to kids and his interactions with children were always comical and often unpredictable. The introduction of Mike to Stink and vice-versa was bound to render a hilarious windfall.

I was sitting on the couch when Mike knocked on the sliding glass door of our family room. He opened the door and stuck his head into the room with a big, "*Hello!*"

I waved to Mike and returned the greeting, "Hey."

"Where is this young man that I have heard *so much* about?"

A part of Mike's Pigtown Latin included speaking in a boisterous, inflated tone.

I called across the house, "*Miles!*" Then I heard the sound of Marianna and Miles rounding the corner of the dining room table.

Marianna's head appeared first and she responded by singing as if she was in an operetta. "Wha-a-a-a-aaaaaaa-t?"

"Hi Marianna, lovely singing, but I called for Miles." Stink's head popped up from behind Marianna. The two had no trouble matching up as playmates. Miles played the little brother role well. It would not be long before Marianna would have Miles dressed up in high heels and a tiara.

"Wah?" Miles' speech impediment left just about every word cut short.

"I want you to meet my friend, Mr. Mike. He stopped by to say hello."

The rest of Mike's body had eventually followed his head completely into the family room and Mike was now standing in the center of the room.

Stink trotted down the steps and stared at Mike inquisitively from across the room.

Mike acknowledged Miles. *"Oooooh... hello young man."*

Stink walked closer to Mike. Mike put his hand out as if to shake Stink's tiny hand, but before Mike could react, the tiny hand had already bypassed his own and landed a right hook onto Mike's testicular punching bag. Stink ran away laughing as Mike dropped to the floor in agony.

"Miles! Get back here!" I called out. He was long gone, hiding downstairs in the playroom. Marianna ran after him.

I directed Marianna, "Tell Miles to get up here," but the chance of Miles coming upstairs was about the same as Mike rising from the floor ready to perform jumping jacks.

My first instinct was to go downstairs and grab Miles so that I could send him off for a routine time out, but Mike's groan of agony was too amusing to ignore. I decided to check on Mike. He had worked his way up onto his knees and was attempting to speak.

He muttered the words, "What the hell is wrong with that kid?"

"I don't know. He's diagnosed with RAD. Sometimes he hugs strangers. Apparently, sometimes he does not. Today it looks like his fist randomly attached itself to your groin." Stink was as unpredictable as Mike.

****

Fall came and we had a birthday extravaganza for Miles. Most of the guests were girls from Marianna's collection of school friends. He must have felt like the belle of the ball. It did not take long for Miles to appear upstairs in full Cinderella apparel. Ordering around a small male came naturally to my daughter and I already felt bad for any future husband. Even Miles' communication issues were no match for Marianna's persistent requests and demands. Around Marianna, it was sink or swim, and verbally Miles swam. His speech and language skills were improving at an exponential rate.

Miles easily adapted to our family during the fourth year of his life. He had earned a special place in our home and eventually earned his expanded title, 'The Stink.' His personality was far too intricate to be simply nicknamed Stink. He required a full title sort of like Jerry Mathers as 'The Beaver.' Therefore, in his noble moments I referred to him as 'Stinkerton.'

Nicknames were a tradition in my family; I have a nephew that goes by the name Beaver, and another that goes by Pickle. Even our dogs were no longer Sadie and Sassi; their given names had transformed into Clause and Frass. During my childhood, my father had nicknamed me Wolfgang and just about every one of his company coworkers knew me as such. I do not believe they ever knew my actual name, Matthew. They even addressed me as Wolfgang at my father's funeral. My father went by Jules, a shortened version of his middle name Julius. It takes a special personality to earn a good nickname, and The Stink had done just that.

Another reason Miles went by The Stink was his tendency to forgo toilet paper. For some reason, that product was often a center of controversy in my home. We were always running out of the stuff. It is as if somebody was eating it. The kids went through a roll a day, yet there was evidence to show that nobody ever wiped their butt. When Jared had arrived seven years earlier, he quickly earned the nickname, Skids.

My seventy-year-old mother heard the title and asked, "Oh... is that nickname because he comes from a rough part of town? That is so cute!"

"Yes," I replied. "The nickname definitely has to do with a rough part of town." There was not a pair of tighty-whiteys that could escape Jared's wrath. Fortunately, he switched to a new line of dark colored boxers and I jumped on any pack of brown camouflage boxers I could find. Miles' handiwork was not much better than Jared's but at least he was only four and there was still hope for what remained of his Spiderman underoos.

With two four-year-olds in the house, our butt wiping duties literally doubled. The first thing I discovered about my new foster son is that the kid appeared to have two arseholes! Upon his first pediatric physical, his doctor reassured us that in time he would outgrow what the physician called his "upper rear dimple." Maybe his upper rear dimple was the spot where his tail used to grow. Until the joke wore off, I referred to Miles as 'the new kid with two buttholes.' The best part of it was that The Stink had a sense of humor. At age four, he understood complex humor and liked to joke with his new friends at school about his second 'bo'hole.' I can only imagine what the teachers thought of his unusual comments.

It took Miles a while to adjust to a school without physical violence as part of the daily curriculum, but no one ended up hurt and he continued to adjust. The staff at Appleton Elementary had done an excellent job with Jared. Now they were doing an exceptional job with Miles. Miles' original behavior was overly aggressive but a full day of structured preschool helped get him in line. Initially placed in a half-day program, the program did not have enough structure for The Stink. In fact, we felt it was only doing half of what a full day program could accomplish.

Krista and I recognized his overwhelming need for structure and made a request to the school. Extended speech and behavioral therapy would greatly benefit Miles. In order to receive additional services, we 'advocated' for our child. We hoped we would receive some additional services for Miles. I do not enjoy being the 'squeaky wheel', but in this case, we were desperate.

We loved having Miles in our home but we struggled with several issues. I composed a letter to the Howard County Public School system to reach out for additional assistance and effectively advocate for our child. I kindly begged, then justified our case, and finally described the aspects of our daily routine with Miles.

Request for a meeting concerning Miles Hoffman. 9/24/07. Miles turns four on 11/16.

Introduction: We are Matt and Krista Hoffman, foster parents of a Howard County Preschool student named, Miles, as well as the birth parents of MINC student peer Marianna Hoffman. We have also raised three other foster children with various diagnoses ranging from ADHD, PTSD, PDD, ODD, RAD and Mental Retardation. Krista is a licensed psychological counselor, behavioral specialist, former teacher and former employee of University of Maryland Hospital Child Day Program. Matt is a graduate of Sociological and Information Sciences at UMBC as well as a graduate of HCPS going from Oakland Mills High back to Appleton Elementary itself. He also works within HCPS as a substitute teacher and has subbed for MINC. We are very pleased with Howard County special need services and consider our three older children to be great success stories. We are proud of them and very thankful for the Howard County School System for its contributions to them. Our natural daughter Marianna has been a peer for MINC since age two and we are very pleased with this program as well.

Opening Points:
-The 10 hours of services with 1 hour of speech therapy is not enough services for Miles.
-The IEP written in Baltimore City is not on target to help Miles relate with his peers.
-He needs the peer services available in Howard County in order to curb his previously learned social behaviors. These behaviors are not acceptable in Howard County schools or area day care.

*GOAL - age appropriateness in 3 categories: Language, Behavior and Motor Skills.

Examples of Miles' Current Behavior

1) Language or Speech
-Miles currently speaks as a two-year-old. He uses one or two word sentences relying heavily upon facial and hand gestures to communicate and make requests
-Miles cannot answer questions clearly if at all. His pronunciation of words, sounds, and letters are unintelligible. He cannot pronounce his own name. His name comes out as Iyles or Iiis
-When Miles attempts to initiate questions or statements, they are completely unintelligible. This leads to questioning in order to understand him, which eventually fails. He becomes extremely frustrated and upset or sad

-His language deficits are evident when asking him any question that is not a Y/N answer. The word "Yes" is difficult for Miles
-He regularly screams to express a range of emotion. He cannot articulate words

We hope to have daily Speech Therapy services rather than 1 hour per week. Ideally, an extended day specifically targeting Speech Therapy is desirable.

2) Behavior currently resembles that of a young two-year-old such as:
-Use of the word "No" for everything
-Touching a hot stove even after warned
-Eating sand and throwing it into his eyes and hair.
-Toy sharing issues, everything is "mine"
-Peeing in his bedroom trashcan
-Wetting self regularly, even though he is potty trained
-Standing one foot from the TV, blocking others and staring
-Unable to maintain attention in a show or activity for more than five minutes
-Repeat behaviors such as repetitive rule breaking
-Hitting, biting, kicking, pinching, and spitting
-Self play preferred over social play, and much more

We hope to have Miles involved more with peers to learn age appropriate behaviors such as higher levels of speech, sharing, safety and problem resolution. Ideally, we would like to have Miles in an extended or full day program that gives him more time with peers and peer-socialization to receive the benefits of peer modeling.

3) Motor Coordination
-Miles falls during normal walking at least ten to twenty times per day
-Miles does not have fine motor development of his right or left hand
-Miles walks into danger, such as walking into a moving swing
-Gross motor skills are a problem while some fine motor skills are excellent
-In his first month Miles has had a black eye, swollen lip, bruises and scrapes

We hope to have motor coordination therapy time increased to help Miles improve.

Thanks again for everything you do to help Miles.

The letter, received with sympathetic concern, effectively advocated for Miles. He started a full day program immediately after winter break and everything was uphill from there. The Stink's behavior, speech, and overall communication skills greatly improved with his new program of services. His numerous requests for refills of 'monk,' eventually translated to 'mulk.' Perhaps one day he would ask for a glass of 'milk.' I guess it is tough when you never learned to imitate natural speech as an infant.

The tongue is one of the first muscles you learn to develop. Each human language develops the human tongue in a specific way. Ask any native German speaker to say, 'Darth Vader.' Even coming from the mouth of the best English speaking German it will sound comedic. It rolls off the German tongue as *Darf Waiter*. Just like the German *Star Wars* fans, Miles will forever sound comedic as well. Fortunately, he has a great sense of humor.

****

Spring passed and Elo had relocated to his first tour of duty overseas. Luckily, he landed in Europe and not anywhere near the combat zone. His toughest challenge would be teaching a German girl to pronounce the words *Darth Vader*.

Nevar's life was also going well. He adjusted to life with a household composed mainly of caretakers from Nigeria. I found that there was a large workforce of immigrants working in human and health services. Some of the staff even had friends and family that worked in the home where my grandmother was cared for in the last few months of her life. The staff was helpful with coordinating Nevar's home visits. He came home at each major holiday and on other random weekends as well.

Miles was improving at school each week while Marianna and my wife were busy with theatre. My daughter landed her first professional theatre gig filling the role of 'Gretle' in a dinner theatre production of the musical, *The Sound of Music*.

Jared was busy with middle school classes and introductory relationships with girls in the neighborhood, but the video game console was still his first true love. Sexual education was always a challenge when it came to working with special needs children. Elo had learned everything before I met him. Nevar received repetitive instruction concerning relationships and my conversations with Jared were always interesting. One day Jared dropped the video game controller to ask me a few questions pertaining to health class.

"Matt, when can I start to date?"

"When you get a job, dating is not cheap. Why do you ask?"

"The school health teacher gave me a list of questions to discuss for homework."

I turned around and noticed that Jared was holding a sheet of questions. "Okay, shoot."

"Shoot what?"

"Nothing Jared, just read the questions."

Nervously he asked, "When is someone ready to have a sexual relationship?"

"You'll know when your period arrives."

"What do you mean? Health class is third period every Tuesday and Thursday." Once again, another one of my jokes flew over Jared's head.

"Jared, I was joking. You know, *a* period.   Like blood from menstruation."

"Men's tray shun! I'm going to bleed?"

"No Jared. What's the next question?"

He looked down and continued reading, "Does everyone have sexual intercourse?"

"Well, not if they're married."

"What?"

"I'm just kidding Jared. Not everybody has sex. Some decide to remain abstinent."

"What's that?"

"Something you may become very familiar with. Get the dictionary and look it up." Jared trotted off to complete his homework assignment with his number one study partner, the dictionary. I am sure he would discover more about puberty and abstinence over the next ten to twenty years.

Chapter 35

Stink Or Swim

I started the summer by changing jobs and moving into a daytime position as a government contractor. It was a new support position but I was comfortable in my new role. As a psychological therapist, Krista saw patients in the evenings and spent her afternoons entertaining the kids. The local pool served as a wonderful distraction.

Jared was a foster child with exceptional middle school grades and even better classroom behavior. A local organization called the Columbia Association rewarded students like Jared. Rewards like these are one more benefit to foster parenting.

The Howard County Public School system had a behavior-based program designed to motivate children labeled as "at risk." Jared was technically "at risk" but otherwise "risk free." Jared would not even risk sunburn while inside Luray Caverns, yet he fits the category "at risk." Fortunately, he was too much of a chicken to ever get into a fight or challenge a teacher so he received exemplary scores on his behavior chart. The reward each child received was a membership to the Columbia Association's fitness program. Among other benefits, this program included access to three gyms and about thirty pools.

Miles was treading water in his school environment but had not yet mastered the art of swimming in a pool. One day Krista arrived at the local swimming hole wearing shorts and a t-shirt. The kids were already suited up and ready to go. Miles was still a novice swimmer and my wife chose a Columbia pool with the safety of a beach entrance. She instructed Miles to proceed with caution onto the gently sloping entrance of the pool that was equipped with a sprinkling umbrella, waterfall, and watchful teenage lifeguards.

Krista set up camp under the nearby cabana and Miles walked over to retrieve his goggles from her pool bag. After she assisted him with his goggles, he walked towards the deep end of the pool, looking for Jared and the older kids.

Krista watched and warned Miles, "Be careful near the edge!"

He looked back without a word... wearing a devilish grin. As Krista cautiously rose from her chair, Miles took off at a full sprint.

Krista shouted, "Miles get back here!" Then she called out to Marianna who was watching from the other side of the pool, "Marianna, grab Miles!"

The chase was on.

Miles circled around the diving area and headed for the far corner of the pool. Krista and Marianna herded him onto the sidewalk, adjacent to the diving well. As Krista and Marianna worked in tandem like Border Collies rounding up a rouge sheep, Miles searched for an escape route. Krista approached carefully, as if ready to tackle a suicidal jumper from the ledge of a skyscraper. Meanwhile Marianna blocked Miles's only other route of escape.

Marianna closed in and exclaimed, "Gotcha!"

Miles looked at Marianna with a playful smile as Krista moved closer and softly called out, "Come here Miles. Let's go over to the kiddie pool and play with some of your toys."

Miles looked back towards Krista, grinned with his baby teeth, jumped over the edge, and dropped to the bottom of the pool. As he sank like a rock to the pool floor, my wife jumped in, glasses and all. If only she had worn a bathing suit that day. It was going to be a long foster care summer with The Stink.

****

Fall arrived and so did Jared's fourteenth birthday. The DSS reactivated his adoption status and his former adoption worker Kathryn was back on the job. Jared's adoption was ready to go but we were also dealing with other adoption issues. Since transitioning Miles into our family, his birth parents had not yet made a request for a bio-visit. The foster family of his biological sibling, Samuel, was currently preparing for adoption and needed the birth parents to relinquish parental rights. Now DSS was pressuring the biological parents to sink or swim.

Krista and I were both very nervous concerning Miles' biological parents. We did not want to lose Miles as he integrated into our family and he had developed a strong bond with all of us. Miles did not even remember the parents that he would soon visit. He could only recall a woman he referred to as 'Black Mom', or Ms. Greene. We were already considering adopting Miles, but we would first have to meet his biological family.

Once again, we determined that it was best for me to handle the bio-visits. I prepared myself for the mission by packing up numerous photo albums that contained pictures of Miles. There were shots of Miles playing on the beach, enjoying amusement park rides, and riding the pony at the Elliot Oaks Farm. I had pictures of him at school, pictures of his classmates, and pictures of the Halloween school parade. When I met his deaf parents, I wanted to be able to communicate how much we loved him and that we provided him with a good life.

I made sure to have the pictures of him hugging Marianna and pictures where he was wrestling with Jared. I purposely left out pictures of Krista or myself. In my experience, bio families enjoyed seeing their children with friends and siblings, but were not always excited to see pictures of any new parent figures. Besides, nobody would want to look at my ugly mug anyhow.

The visitation location was set for a psychiatrist's office in downtown Baltimore. This particular psychiatrist specialized in family bonding studies. DSS was running this session to study the attachment between Miles, his biological brother Samuel, and their biological parents. Miles and I said goodbye to Krista and traveled to the appointment in Baltimore City. I found the downtown professional building and carried Miles in through the doors of the office.

We signed in and took a seat in a small playroom. Miles immediately began to play with nearby toys while I fumbled through some magazines. I watched another child that was playing by himself over in the corner of the play area. The boy looked very much like Jared at age ten. He had the same physique and pale skin. I wondered to myself, '*Could that be Miles' brother Samuel?*'

Miles walked over to the boy and spoke to him, "Hi. Ma name Iyles." Unlike Jared, Miles never had a problem with being assertive and was very confident for a five-year-old. The boy in the corner shook his head no and looked away. I watched as an older couple sitting nearby glanced in my direction and I delivered a small wave. After they returned the wave, I stood up and walked over to the two sitting near the older boy.

"Hi, I'm Matt Hoffman and this is my foster son Miles."

"I thought so. I'm Janice and this is my friend, Bill... and this is Samuel." She gestured towards the boy as she said his name.

"I thought that that might be Miles' big brother, but he looks nothing like him." Miles was stocky with a very different physique.

"I know. Miles has never looked much like his brother. He looks more like his birth father while Samuel looks like his birth mother. Sometimes that's the way genes go."

I agreed. My sister Cindy once claimed to be unrelated to the rest of us. She had blond hair and unHoffman-like facial features. But Cindy was out of luck. She managed to grow into the Hoffman genes as she gained weight and her hair turned dark.

I turned to the boy playing in the corner, "Nice to meet you Samuel." I was anxious to interact with Miles' biological brother. He looked and acted so much like Jared it was eerie. Samuel did not reply.

Janice spoke up, "He is kind of introverted. We believe he may have Asperger's Syndrome." Asperger's is a condition sometimes referred to as a mild form of autism. I knew about Asperger's Syndrome; people with this diagnosis often have trouble in social situations. I had long assumed that Jared had a mild case of Asperger's Syndrome; my own brother as well. Either that or my brother had partied too much back in the 70's.

Miles cut in, "Hi Samue. Ma name Iyles."

Samuel produced a fleeting wave. Miles was as different from his brother as I was from my own. Just then, the psychiatrist appeared in the lobby and called out to Miles and Samuel. He escorted the two boys into a back meeting room. The biological parents were running late so the psychiatrist decided to begin the bonding study with the boys until the parents arrived. Janice, Bill, and I waited in the lobby.

While the boys met with the psychiatrist, Janice filled me in on the history of the family. The biological parents were having a hard time keeping themselves afloat, monetarily and socially. They had not worked to complete any of the DSS requirements and she believed that they had reached the final step before relinquishing parental rights. This bonding study was a final examination to offer some sort of data that would evaluate the connections between the immediate family members. Janice informed me of her plans to adopt Samuel once the biological parents terminated parental rights. We had the same plans for Miles.

A half an hour later, a couple strolled into the lobby and headed to the front desk. They were Miles' birth parents. I was hoping for a chance to communicate with them. The receptionist took down their names and immediately directed them down the hallway. They disappeared in the direction of the meeting room without even looking towards the waiting area. I was eager to share my photo album and let Miles' birth parents know that their little boy was safe and loved. Janice and her boyfriend sat down next to me, and we waited as the meeting continued. She informed me of the mother's reluctance pertaining to parental rights termination but stated that the biological father was prepared to relinquish rights.

Another twenty minutes passed before the psychiatrist reappeared from the hallway. The birth parents, Samuel, and Miles were following behind. Samuel straggled over to Janice, and Miles made a bull run towards me. He had no idea what had just happened or that the people in the meeting were his biological family. The birth father was obviously perturbed and threw waves of disapproval at the birth mother as she walked alongside of him communicating in sign language.

They looked in our direction and the mother moved towards me. The father grabbed her arm and she pulled back as I stood and motioned to both of them. The birth mom was obviously distraught and looked back to her partner for approval. I waved to her. The man looked on with disdain but eventually let the woman's arm go, allowing her to join me. As she approached, I sat down and she sat next to me. I reached under the chair and pulled out my book of photos.

The birth mother smiled as tears began to roll down her face. The awkwardness of the situation kept my emotional disposition in line. I did not want to waste any of our time as the biological father stood across the lobby, waiting, choosing not to participate. Birth mom exerted the sounds of guarded laughter as she flipped through the album filled with Miles' numerous expressions.

When she had finished, she looked up at me and signed, "Thank you."

As she stood to return to her companion, I touched her arm. She looked back and I handed her a package of duplicate photos. Her face lit with joy, she wiped tears from her cheeks, took the photos, and walked away. Then I sat back down and composed myself for the drive home while Miles continued to play. My family and his were tied to the bright, funny, little boy nicknamed Stink. I thought to myself, *A hundred years ago, Miles' parents might have been deemed defective. Miles might never have existed. I'm sure glad he does.*

A few weeks later, we received word that the biological parents terminated parental rights. The parents requested the ability to contact Miles if needed, as well as some yearly photos. That was fine with us.

Jared was well on his way to adoption and now Miles would be too. I just wanted to ensure that Jared's adoption would process first. After all, he had been waiting for seven years. He already displayed a few signs of jealousy concerning Miles and I did not want to pour gasoline on a smoldering fire.

The winter holidays were just around the corner and Elo had plans to return home. Little did we know that many friends were coming for the holidays as well.

****

A week before Thanksgiving, the phone rang. It was Elo calling from Europe. His plan was to travel home and spend three weeks of military leave in Columbia. He informed me that he was bringing a friend and that he would arrive… tomorrow. Providing advanced notice was not one of Elo's strengths. He also delivered one other piece of important information.

The conversation revealed a surprise. "No problem Elo, you can bring a friend home for the holidays."

"Cool. Hey Matt, I also want to let you know that my friend Megan is also my fiancée."

"*What?*"

"Megan is my fiancée." Had Elo not learned anything from the years of bickering provided by my wife and me... specifically for his instruction? I guess he had not, but before I could hang up the phone and talk with Krista, Nevar beeped in. He too was calling to make reservations for his holiday plans. He requested two spots at our best table and once again, I received another 'friend request'. Thankfully, Nevar did not inform me of an engagement. He simply had plans to bring home his roommate Tarone.

The next day, Elo and his new fiancée Megan arrived to join us for the holidays. The two kept themselves busy snuggling on the family room couch watching television over the days leading up to Thanksgiving. I eventually pried the two apart to have Elo help me with the transportation of Nevar and Tarone. Tarone was unable to walk and needed assistance to and from the minivan. Moving his wheelchair around could be somewhat cumbersome.

We drove to the nearby H.O.M.E. residential facility and retrieved Nevar and Tarone. As Elo and I lifted Tarone into the van, we experienced the scent of an unwashed post-pubescent male.

"Tarone, when was the last time the staff put you in the rolling shower?"

He sheepishly answered, "Ahhhhh, ah last week."

"I smelt so."

One problem with rotating staff members of adult homecare is that no one likes to perform the bathing on their shift. I cannot say I blame them. It is a lot of work to bathe a full-grown adult. Fortunately, Nevar did not compound the smell growing inside the minivan. He was fully mobile and it only took a little peer pressure to send him to the showers. Once motivated Nevar could shower independently, but Tarone required assistance.

Elo interjected, "Damn Tarone. You smell funky!"

Nevar let out his high-pitched laugh.

"Don't worry Tarone. I will throw you in the tub when we get back to the house. We wouldn't want the Thanksgiving turkey to catch a whiff of you and run off."

Tarone laughed.

Then he quietly uttered the words, "Thanks, thanks Matt. I ain't had a bath since I was a kid. Every place I ever been has a roll-in shower and the plastic waterproof chair. Is the bathtub deep?"

"Don't worry about it Tarone. I'll make sure your head stays above water and we'll have you smelling like a rose in no time."

Elo joked, "Maaan… sink or swim."

Tarone gave Elo a nervous glance. We arrived home and hauled Tarone into the tub. I filled the tub with 103-degree water and dumped in some Avon bubble bath, left abandoned under the bathroom sink by my mother.

It was the first bubble bath he had experienced in almost twenty years. His state of pure enjoyment put things into perspective. Tarone was in bathtub heaven and would now look forward to a yearly holiday bath… me, not so much. Dragging a wet naked man out of a bathtub was not exactly my idea of eggnog and Christmas cookies, but hopefully the 6-6-6 on my shoulder would fade over the next few years.

Overall Thanksgiving went off without a hitch. Marianna and Miles used Elo's fiancé as a human jungle gym and Jared, Nevar, and Tarone enjoyed a weekend of video game competitions. Elo and Megan returned to their military placement but eventually parted ways. After a week with my family, they must have decided to reconsider a military wedding. I guess Elo did learn something after all.

Chapter 36

The Year Of The Bean And The Stone

Adoption paperwork was in process for both Jared and Miles. I hoped that Jared would stand in front of a judge before Miles' adoption. Jared had already developed a bit of jealousy concerning The Stink. Stinkerton was the dominant personality and demanded a large amount of the family's attention in any situation.

In several family portraits, Jared was standing behind Miles seething in the background. After seven years of waiting, I did not want Jared to be seething on the day that Miles became a Hoffman. It turns out I had nothing to worry about. The Baltimore City DSS adoption process would have plenty of delays and did a great job of dragging out Miles' adoption process. The stalled adoption process itself paved the way for Jared to go first.

My wife and I started the adoption processes for both Miles and Jared at the same time, but each adoption would progress differently. Jared's case, handled by the Baltimore County DSS would be in a race with Miles' case, processed through the Baltimore City DSS. Jared's original adoption paperwork, completed years before, was reusable. DSS only needed to obtain current data including an updated home study, updated physicals, updated paystubs, and a recent tax return. Once again, I would have to turn and cough. The city on the other hand needed everything imaginable in order to process Miles' adoption.

We were stepping up into the adoption phase of our life. It was something we had never intended to do but now it was our reality. I would rush home from work in order to meet the adoption worker and fill out the required paperwork. Our home was studied, our bodies examined, and our dogs again violated; it was the same process we undertook when we initially applied for our foster care license.

I found that requests tended to be redundant in any government agency but the worst part was submitting many requirements twice. In the process, I even inspired one city contract worker to learn about email. Not every person working with foster children was onboard with the latest communication tools. I began to receive voicemails from a contract worker named Martin Cartwright. He continued to leave messages stating that I had not turned in any of my adoption paperwork. It seemed as though every step of the adoption process was a challenge for everyone.

The voice on my answering machine sounded broken and tired like an old man from a Country Time lemonade commercial. Mr. Cartwright genuinely sounded confused. I emailed the required paperwork to him numerous times. After verifying the successful status of my delivered emails, I called Mr. Cartwright to investigate.

"Hello, I'm calling for a Mr. Cartwright."

"Yes, this is he."

"Hi Mr. Cartwright, I'm Matt Hoffman, the adoptive parent of Miles. I've received the voice messages you left on my machine stating that Miles' adoption has been put on hold due to missing paperwork."

"Yes, that is correct. If you do not send in the forms, the physicals, and the license information, I will have to postpone the adoption of Mark."

"You mean Miles."

"No, my name is Martin."

"Not you Mr. Cartwright, my soon-to-be adopted son, his name is Miles."

"Yes. Well you will not be able to adopt Max if I don't receive the paperwork."

I replied, "It says on the form that I can mail, fax, or email the paperwork. I do not have a fax and I do not completely trust the regular mail, so I emailed you the documents. I have emailed them several times and I have made sure they are going to your email account. They have not come back to me rejected."

"How could they have been rejected? I haven't even reviewed them yet."

"Forget it... Have you checked your email account?"

"The email here doesn't work."

"Sure it does. I emailed a city social worker earlier today. I copied the emails and sent them to the licensing specialist, Nancy, at our non-profit foster agency. Perhaps I can send the information by telegraph?"

"Well mine doesn't work. I mean my email doesn't work."

"Ahhhh, okay. I will ask the agency licensing specialist to get you the information. I have received confirmation that they have received everything. Thanks Mr. Cartwright. I'll be in touch."

Then I emailed our non-profit foster agency worker, Nancy.

Hi Nancy, The adoption for Miles is on hold because the contract worker, Mr. Cartwright, is unable to receive the document attachments I have sent him. He says his email does not work. Could you send copies to him? Thanks – Matt

...Ten minutes later, I received a response from Nancy.

Hi Matt, I have run into this problem before with Mr. Cartwright. I have contacted him and the problem is resolved. Once I informed him that I was driving downtown to help him use his email, he found a coworker to help him with his account. Now he has the attached documents in his hand. Good Luck with the adoption – Nancy

In other good news, we were able to kill two birds with one stone by submitting duplicate physicals to both Baltimore County and Baltimore City. Unfortunately, we were still required to have our fingerprinting performed twice as well as submit two separate home studies. Each DSS agency performs its own method of adoption processing and will not accept copies of paperwork from any another jurisdiction. I heard numerous times, "It's *got* to be on *our* form." Why? Why? Why?

****

Of course, the daily problems of life also added to our usual level of household stress. Stink was the real life version of the Judy Blume character, *Superfudge*. His latest drama included a bean that he had shoved into his ear. This kid had enough problems with ear tubes and oversized tonsils and now he had pushed a bean in the direction of his brain. I wondered how many other beans were already sprouting in there.

Kids like Miles should not perform arts and crafts or anything that requires beans, beads, stones, or glitter. At five-years-old, he was performing more taste tests than Emeril Lagasse. Now this kid decided to consume a bean using his ear hole instead of his mouth. At least he had not shoved anything else into any other holes that would be difficult to explain to a pediatrician.

The school nurse could not retrieve the bean, the nighttime pediatric office could not retrieve the bean, and the Ear-Nose-and-Throat specialist could not retrieve the bean. Surgery was required to remove the bean. I called Miles' social worker to inform her of the good news. As I dragged him from appointment to appointment, she called me back. Excitedly she said, "We received the adoption date for Miles and it is only one month after Jared's adoption date. Isn't that great?"

"Yippee." I am going to be the proud father of Jack and his beanstalk;

only the beanstalk will be growing out of the side of this kid's head.

"Isn't that wonderful?"

I answered back with as little sarcasm as possible, "Definitely."

****

It turns out that removing the bean would require rendering Miles unconscious. That was the first bit of good news I had received in days. Since this was the case, the doctor recommended performing a 'two for one' as Miles would eventually need his tonsils removed. If he was going to go under anesthesia, now was the best time to have his tonsils removed. We agreed with the pediatrician and the surgery went well. When all was completed, he was tonsil *and* bean free.

Miles experienced so much pain upon waking that he never again shoved a bean into his ear. Unfortunately, that did not stop him from shoving a rock up his nose. Six weeks later, we were back at the Ear-Nose-and-Throat doctor. Miles and the ENT doctor were now on a first name basis. Thankfully, the doctor's eight-inch tweezers were long enough to dislodge the latest problem. As the adoption dates approached, I wondered if I was putting myself between a rock and a bean place.

Jared's worker Kathryn called to give us the date for Jared's adoption. On a weekday morning we drove to the Baltimore County courthouse, met with a judge, and completed the adoption process. In March, Jared officially became a Hoffman.

I joked with him, "I just purchased a license to spank. After the last seven years, I have to make up for lost time."

In the upcoming week, Jared would enjoy his second adoption party and life would continue as it had for the last seven years.

The evening after the adoption, I received a call on my personal cell phone from our former social worker, Gail Witherspoon.

"Hello"

"Hi Matt, this is Gail Witherspoon."

"Ahhh... h... hi Gail." Her unexpected call had taken me off guard. We had completed our business with the Baltimore County Department of Social Services and here I was talking with the unofficial czar. I had not heard from Gail in months and had not expected to hear from her ever again.

"Hey. I was just calling to say congratulations. I was so glad to hear that Jared's adoption went through. I know he is going to have a great life." I could hear the unfamiliar sound of emotion escaping her usual business-like tone.

"Well... thanks Gail. He's looking forward to his party this Friday."

"Um... I'm sure he is... well again... congrats..." There was an awkward silence, almost as if she did not want to say goodbye or let go. Never before had I glimpsed the love and care that Gail, the devoted advocate for 'Place Matters,' had for Jared. Her professionalism and thick skin had kept her emotions hidden over the years, while 'Stepping Down' reflected her duty to professionalism.

"Thanks for calling Gail."

She cleared her throat and then replied with regained professionalism, "My pleasure."

"Goodbye Gail."

"Goodbye Mr. Hoffman." With that, our conversation ended.

****

Miles' adoption occurred three months later after we managed to keep him from shoving anything else into any other orifice. Everything was working out for Miles. The city adoption ceremony was similar to Jared's county adoption ceremony except that Miles was a part of a courtroom-wide ceremony. Jared had a ceremony individually held in the private office of a judge. Each child's ceremony coincidentally fit the personality of the child.

Nevar visited over the holidays. He and Tarone were building a collection of video games and popular music while enjoying 'the good life' of a Howard County residential treatment facility. Thanks to a song written by the *Black Eyed Peas* called *Let's Get Retarded*, he no longer felt self-conscious about having a mental handicap. Coincidentally, Maryland Democratic Senator, Barbara Mikulski, sponsored a bill that became law; the law called 'Rosa's Law' changed the phrase, 'mentally retarded' to 'an individual with an intellectual disability.'

Elo managed to come home once again for the month of April and stayed for a long visit before going back to Europe. He had acquired a set of braces compliments of the Army and his life was moving in a positive direction. His next transition would be to Afghanistan. The military had helped Elo mature and perhaps one day it might do the same for Jared.

Jared was searching for maturity but still had a long way to go to find puberty. He watched Miles complete the city adoption ceremony and smiled in the background of the family photograph. He also managed to develop an understanding of humor over the years. When I referred to him as Gollum, he would stoop over and say, 'Our precious. We wants our precious.' About to enter high school, Jared was beginning a new chapter in his life. In 2009, he finally got his wish; it finally snowed for Christmas.

Jared looked out the window and joked, "Hey Matt, snow means Christmas... right?"

Marianna and Krista were keeping busy in the world of Broadway musicals when Marianna landed a role in the musical *Annie* as well as an upcoming role in a new musical with Broadway potential. First, she would perform at a local dinner theater then it was off to who knows where. What a coincidence. She began with a role as Gretl in *The Sound of Music* and now was playing Molly in a group of orphans. That was similar to the role she played at home.

Interestingly, the character 'Annie' ends up assisting President Franklin D. Roosevelt. Coincidentally, her paternal great grandfather actually did work as an assistant to Franklin D. Roosevelt. I showed Marianna a picture of my grandfather, William F. Hoffman, and a picture of his old boss. My daughter was perplexed. Marianna wondered, "How am I related to the man from *Annie*?" Sometimes these coincidences in life give me a mysterious sense of purpose. Could everything just be a series of random coincidence?

Either way my wife was busy running around on cloud nine. Her theater-mom dreams were coming to fruition. Everyone has some kind of drug. Perhaps one day my daughter would make it big in Hollywood or New York. I kept myself busy with my favorite pastime, travelling. Traveling was my dream and I planned to have some fun on an upcoming reunion vacation to Europe. It was now time for my search for immaturity. Perhaps I would run into Elo before he deployed to the Middle East, or catch up with some other traveling friends. If not this year, then perhaps Elo and I would reunite for a future trip planned to Africa.

Nothing was for sure except that Krista and I were approaching our tenth anniversary and our firstborn dogs were now in the later years of their lives. We weighed the option of allowing our foster license to expire, but decided to renew. I guess my wife and I were both gluttons for punishment. To add to the mix, Krista went out and found a new Border collie, Kit Kat. My wife wanted a new "dog sister" for Sadie and Sassi.

****

Now we were operating as full time parents without a foster child in our home, but the job had not gotten any easier. One day I was working away when the phone rang. The caller ID indicated a call from an overseas military base. I hastily answered the phone in the expectation of a call from Elo but was surprised by the voice of a military sergeant.

"This is Sergeant Olengarthy. I'm calling for Mr. Hoffman who is listed as the primary contact for Private First Class Eloiro Winford."

My heart began to race as I imagined a number of worst-case scenarios. Had something happened to Elo?

Cautiously I replied, "Yes… this is he."

"I am calling to inquire about the funeral arrangements for his brother. We are attempting to determine the urgency for Private Winford's return to Baltimore."

My mind was racing. I did not know what to think. Elo was okay, but was Nevar? I had just talked to him yesterday. Had something gone wrong with his meds? Was there some sort of accident?

I could feel my level of anxiety spike, "What? Who? When? What are you talking about?"

"We have been notified that his younger brother Wallace has died and we are weighing the possibility of sending Private Winford home for the funeral. Do you feel it would be appropriate or necessary?"

I was sad for the Winford family, but my anxiety was relieved just the same. Thankfully, my boys were okay.

"Eloiro and his brother Wallace are not very close and I have not heard anything from my end. I am not even sure if I could locate the family much less find information for a funeral. Besides, are you positive that your information is correct? It wouldn't surprise me if the death report was false."

"I understand. Most likely Private Winford will not be returning home for any arrangements, but we wanted confirmation from his family before making a decision. Thank you very much Mr. Hoffman."

The man finalized the conversation with an abrupt, organized, military fashioned goodbye... and the phone call had ended. It appeared as if foster care had once again proved the better option for my Winford boys and I hoped that I never received another call from military personnel again, unless of course it was from Elo.

I searched the local news and never found anything about the death of a man named Wallace Winford. The only thing I discovered about the Winford family was a rumor that the little sister Carlyn had given birth to a son. That rumor, perpetuated by Nevar, came from an unknown source. Perhaps it was another message from God. I have learned not to doubt Nevar's source. Whatever their fate, I hoped the best for the Winford family. I continued to advocate for my sons, now incorporated into this group we call *The Hoffmans*.

Later I received correspondence from Elo. "A lot has been happening over here. The war is about to kick into hyper-drive. That is all I can say. People are going to die, but I will try my best to stay alive. I am hoping to come home in October and I am just trying to have patience. I sent my address for Afghanistan and I want to know how the whole family is doing. Love you all. Later." We were all praying that luck, fate, good fortune, and the grace of God would bring him home.

****

In the remaining months of 2009, we answered the foster care hotline several times. The new candidates did not fit into our family as well as the new dog my wife had rescued and we had to decline all requests from our placement coordinator. In the current economic conditions, the state was once again *'Stepping Down.'* The children identified as a match for our home were not in any way a match for our home. One child they suggested had put a cat in the microwave. Other cases included severe impairment, physical, mental, and medical issues. We declined them all, not being able to provide for extensive needs with two six-year-olds at home.

Maryland foster care was back on a mission to *Step Down* using *Place Matters* and every other tool necessary to do so. The latest foster children we met were ultimately sent back to live in unsuitable environments with unsuitable relatives. This usually does not happen in a better financial economy, but the kids are stepping down to Step Zero. Had *Place Matters* taken the place of *Placing Out?* Were foster children, particularly therapeutic foster children, on the brink of extinction?

We met a pair of foster kids in 2009 that were brother and sister. The little girl, sent back to Step Zero, lives with an aunt in the city. It did not matter that the aunt's job title is exotic dancer because *Place Matters.* It didn't matter that the medically fragile little brother was sent back to Step Zero to live with a relative with HIV in an erratic home environment because *Place Matters.* When the economy goes bad, *the best interest of the child* no longer seems to matter.

The foster care hotline rang again. In the faltering economy, foster care would like to reduce the number of children on its caseload. Sometimes this means convincing unprepared foster parents to adopt. The foster parents advised to adopt their foster children should do so, or risk losing their foster children. The state knew that Krista and I had recently babysat two particular kids and that we might be willing to adopt them. We told the workers that we would take the children and perhaps one day adopt them, but we would need time to determine *the best interests of the children.* I imagine our proclamation of possible adoption got back to the current foster parents. After the threat of transition, the current foster parents were suddenly ready to adopt.

At the beginning of 2010, we received a letter from our foster care agency. It was a reminder notice concerning the state's financial problems. It reported that the Maryland State budget shrunk three times over the last twelve months and that changes were on the way. The budget, cut over one billion dollars since July, expected another $290 million in cuts before the end of the year. The state had already cut funding to our foster care agency and more was to be expected. What changes were on the way?

The non-profit agency itself was doing its best to reduce costs. They eliminated a supervisory position and were no longer replacing the social workers that planned to leave. The workers themselves endured increased individual workloads despite experiencing reduced benefits and required furlough days. As long as they can manage, the agency will continue to function with as little resources as possible. Who knows what will happen if they cannot? I guess if they cannot, I will never win foster parent of the month.

****

My wife and I sat mulling over the events of the last ten years. We were ready for bed but took a moment to reflect. Life had been diverse, humorous, difficult, and sometimes extraordinary. So many coincidences fell into place and so much of our lives revolved around foster care. Many orphans fall victim to their predicament but my grandmother Hattie had beaten the odds. She survived, married, and the composition of her genes carried on to my father. Now they rest somewhere within my own chemical framework. Coincidentally, I was now associated with the business of orphans and each of our abandoned children had beaten the odds as well.

I turned over in my bed and said to my wife, "It all seems so... *usual* to me... being our life and all. There really have been some amazing *coincidences* as well as *good timing* along the way."

Krista set down a book that she was reading. "Don't you mean good times?"

I paused and then replied, "Well... those too, but no, I meant good timing."

"What do you mean?"

"Like the time Elo decided to leave foster care just months before turning twenty-one and then Nevar needed to be relocated at that exact same time."

"Do you think that was planned?"

I laughed, "If it was planned, it certainly wasn't planned by Elo, Nevar, or any social worker."

"That is sort of odd... and how about Nevar's predictions? That was some weird stuff. I remember the day you told me about Nevar's reference to a little boy named Miles. That was right on the money."

"I said *what?*"

"You told me that Nevar told you about a little boy named Miles... you know... it was another one of his messages from God."

"When did I tell you that?"

"Years ago, not long before we got Miles."

"I'd completely forgotten about that one. That is somewhat creepy. I knew that one of Nevar's predictions really hit home but I could not remember which one. That *must* have been it."

My wife and I fell silent. I rolled over and thought more about our life in foster care as I tried to fall asleep. I was tired and like every weekday, I had to work in the morning. Tomorrow the kids had to get on the school bus and Krista had to be in court. As Krista turned the pages of her book, I eventually fell off to sleep.

****

I hope life turns out better for every child caught up in foster care, but especially if the *Place Matters*. In 2010, my wife and I remained in the business of our daily lives. We answered the phone when it rang; we returned the messages when they appeared. Some child must have been in need of a foster parent. I read it in the paper. I heard it on the radio. I saw it on commercials… and still we waited. I guess I just needed to have patience.

Perhaps in this economy, kids will *step down* to biological homes until one of those placements goes terribly wrong. The needless tragedy of a child's death, media exposure, and lawsuits may be what pushes the pendulum back towards appropriate foster care placements. I hope not, and I hope that the children of foster care do not have to wait until then.

Over the years, I sometimes felt like crumbling to my knees and crying over the sad stories of child abuse, child neglect, and child abandonment. Instead, I do my best to stand strong and use humor to combat the sad realities of foster care. I did not plan to write this book, and I did not plan to be a foster parent. Perhaps it is all just a matter of coincidence.

Just as I was ready to give up on foster care, the phone rang. I picked up the phone.

A man on the line said, "Hello, Matthew?"

"Yes, this is he."

"Hi this is Bob from the NPFCA. We have a potential placement for you…"

The social worker on the other end of the phone was an older man whom I'd spoken to a number of times over the last ten years. Normally, Bob only supervised the agency placement workers, but today he was calling me directly. He read off an introductory rap sheet that sounded vaguely familiar:

"Placement needed for a seventeen-year-old high school student. He has no negative medical history and has a limited psychological history, including ADHD diagnosed when he was younger. Already through several placements, he has transitioned due to abuse, neglect, and/or abandonment issues. He has been in foster care for somewhere over twelve years."

Responding to the man on the phone I inquired, "So how'd he end up in foster care?"

"As the story goes, his mother died of an illness, siblings too, and the father didn't take responsibility. Eventually the kid ended up at St. Xavier's."

Without hesitation I replied, "What is his name, and how long is his transitional plan?"

Bob laughed. I guess he could hear my eyes rolling in the back of my head.

"Patience Matthew… patience, we would like to have him placed in about ten days and his name is Daniel."

"What did you just say?"

"I said that we would like to have him placed in about ten days and his name is Daniel."

"No, no… before that… what did you say just before that?"

"Ah, I don't know."

"Did you say… *patience?*"

"Oh yes, I believe I did."

"Huh, that's funny. Patience was always my dad's advice."

"Well Matthew, the funny thing about patience is the power it wields. Patience requires enduring love for and faith in… something or someone. Your father must have understood this. I bet foster parenting has taught you a little about patience as well."

The lessons of patience rushed about my mind. I remembered the time that my father first uttered the word 'patience' and the times when I had uttered the word myself. I remembered each child's arrival at our home, biological family visitation sessions, waiting for social worker appointments. I remembered taking Jared to respite care, watching him catch sunfish, and waiting with him at the emergency room. I remembered coaxing Nevar into a waterfall, bringing him to fruitless therapy sessions, fighting to get him funding for adult care. I remembered taking Marianna to music lessons, supervising play dates, and holding her for hours while she slept in my arms. I remembered Miles's expulsion from daycare, the rock pulled from his nose, and apologizing to the neighbors when he pooped in their front yard. And I remembered helping Eloiro swim, teaching him to drive, and hearing the words, 'Later Matt' the day I dropped him off at the Army recruiting station.

I paused and considered my response. The repetitious exercises that construct the fragile layers of patience include love, faith, responsibility, trust, and time. After a moment, I replied. "Thanks Bob. You just helped me realize that I never had the patience to understand patience. It is not something you learn from a parent, it is something you gain from life experiences… such as parenting."

"Yes. That sounds about right. So Matthew, are you ready for your next session of foster parenting?"

"Sure… why not."

Extras

Better Than Europe: A Brief History Pertaining To American Foster Care

Today's American foster care system is rooted in the regulatory commissions of the U.S. federal government. Dating back to the Colonial era, foster care grew from the seeds of a common practice called 'binding out' which was formally known as 'indentured servitude.' Children in the early 1900's experienced several aspects of what would later become part of the modern day foster care system. Many living in European orphanages immigrated to America to become indentured servants. Oftentimes children resided with nonrelatives in what was essentially a monetary transaction, while others, like my grandmother, lived with and worked for a blood relative. This in itself is another aspect of today's foster care system, known as 'kinship care.'

The U.S. abolished traditional slavery in 1865, but a different variant of slavery, child labor, was still popular in the early 1900's. In fact, the Federal government did not even attempt to regulate child labor before 1924. The practice of child labor began with the old English tradition of selecting a child to learn a particular trade by assigning them to a trade master. I imagine that those kids without advocating parents literally ended up with the 'crap jobs.' If a family was unable to provide care for a child then indentured servitude might be the next best option.

There was still hope for the children of the nineteenth century when the Society for the Prevention of Cruelty to Children or SPCC established itself in 1875. Notice the similarity to the name, Society for the Prevention of Cruelty to Animals, or SPCA. The SPCA founded decades before in 1824 provided similar protection for animals. It is hard to imagine that in those days kids were relatively equal to farm oxen and received similar protection. To put it all into perspective there was no official organization advocating for children until approximately a hundred and thirty-five years ago. In comparison, man had invented movie cameras, roller coasters, and the dishwasher. Heck, before the founding of the SPCC we had aspirin, Jell-O, and even the ability to use wireless telegraph. Like jumbo shrimp and government worker, *man-kind* is another oxymoron.

Early on, a man named Charles Loring Brace decided that sending orphans to work on farms might be better for children than any lifestyle resulting from an auction. At least in the country children could get some fresh air while in servitude. Brace was the individual who got the ball rolling for child welfare in the United States. Until he came up with the idea of shipping kids to "better" homes and families, most orphans were stuck in orphan asylums or almshouses. Almshouses were like early incarnations of nursing homes.

Instead of having kids sold off to care for the elderly, Brace founded The Children's Aid Society in 1853. He and his organization did wonders for abandoned children, starting with the orphans of New York City. The Big Apple was a good place to start as orphans shipped there, literally, by the boatload. Many children like my grandmother slipped through the city and managed to make a connection elsewhere in America, but for many other kids, the afternoon dockside carpool never arrived.

Brace had taken a private citizen's approach to resolving abandoned children issues and it was not long before various public concerns came into play. For example, apparently placing Catholic orphans on Protestant farms or vice-versa was a big no-no in the 1800's and no good deed should go unpunished. Soon, the government stepped in to monitor private foster organizations and would eventually come to regulate the whole enchilada. Of course, when the government takes over, that is when things tend to get interesting.

Around the same time, other visionaries such as Alexander Graham Bell were testing theories that would significantly affect the lives of the homeless and foster children. As it turned out Bell was interested in more than just telephones. He performed studies on the congenitally deaf and their offspring. His theory was that congenitally deaf parents were more likely to produce deaf children. Then take this theory and apply it to any group considered, 'defective.' Folks in the late 1800's were not as sensitive to 'special needs' as we are today.

Even before the Great Depression, the Federal and state governments were working on other forms of foster control. In 1907, Woodrow Wilson, a member of the Progressive Movement, helped make Indiana the first state to pass involuntary sterilization laws. Social Darwinism had become popular and an ideology rooted in 'survival of the fittest' evolved into something called eugenics. Eugenics is the theory and practice of selective breeding within the human population.

If deemed 'in need of an intervention,' consider yourself 'unfit' for general society. Guess what happens next. You receive a first class ticket to the front lines of sterilization. Oddly, there seemed to be a large number of poor, homosexual, blind, sexually active women, mentally ill, and minority people considered unfit. I would like to say, 'We've come a long way,' but I am not so sure just how far we have come. The 2010 'science czar,' John Holdren co-authored a book in 1977 that recommended compulsory sterilization to carry out a government-regulated population control program.

By the time federally funded sterilization programs ended in 1979, over 62,000 Americans had received sterilization. The federal brainchild, partially aimed to reduce the number of orphaned children, did not change a thing in this regard. In 1900, around 500,000 children remained orphaned in America, and that is roughly the same amount as we have today. It took the unpopularity of Nazi Germany's methods to remove eugenics from the Federal government's "things to do" list. Since a Nazi government had sterilized over 450,000 people in less than a decade, governmental proscribed sterilization no longer remained politically correct.

Government involvement was not *all* bad. Even though President Theodore Roosevelt was a big supporter of eugenics, twenty-five years later, his fifth cousin and fellow member of the Progressive Movement, President Franklin D. Roosevelt, took a different approach to people management. FDR signed the Social Security Act of 1935 as part of the New Deal. Government incorporated various social policies for women, children, and families into formalized programs such the Aid to Dependent Children Program. The creation of this program would help define the government's role in foster care and lead, eventually, to its growth. In 1938, FDR signed the Fair Labor Standards Act, which created the first federal limits on child labor. That same year someone invented Teflon and somebody else invented a little something called nuclear fission. At least we had our priorities straight.

By the 1940's the government was moving away from the old practices of institutionalized childcare and heading towards the catch phrase of the day, 'placing out.' This was the early incarnation of today's foster care system. As orphanages overflowed, the government coordinated efforts to move children into homes with extended biological relatives. Persons looking to adopt or even strangers willing to help were the next option. Soon the modern day social worker was born and the phrase "in the best interest of the child" became a motto.

By 1950, more kids were living in foster homes than in traditional institutions for the first time in American history. Ten years later the number of children in foster care had doubled and by 1970, foster care had become a common function performed by government agencies. Eventually other practices such as 'child client confidentiality' incorporated into foster care as well as 'matching' or 'planned child placements.'

Foster care and adoption had become part of mainstream America. In 1960, the musical *Oliver* premiered in London's West End. The musical *Annie* hit Broadway in 1977. Suddenly, living the orphan life was chic. Being an orphan could lead to so many other possibilities. Disney came out with one of my all time favorite films, a story about an orphan named Pete who received help from a friendly dragon. In 1983, a little orphan named Webster was living the good life with former professional football player George Papadopoulos. Then Arnold and Willis landed a spot with Mr. Drummond in 1984 and even Punky Brewster made it onto the scene.

My favorite Hollywood orphan was Junior from the movie *Problem Child*. He was probably the most accurate depiction of a foster child of today. His rambunctious behavior was frustrating, yet hilarious... much like the real deal. Eddie Murphy got into the act as the soft-spoken character *Norbit*. Heck, even Batman was an orphan. I have enjoyed each one of these orphan tales over the years and perhaps that is why I ended up volunteering as a foster parent. In 2009, Hollywood came out with a horror film simply called *Orphan*. It is about a foster kid who comes in and slashes up an adoptive family. I think I had better skip out on that one.

Hollywood celebrities became advocates for adoption. Most people know of Brad and Angelina's contributions to the cause. Madonna and Oprah have done their part as well. Do you know that the list of adoptive celebrity parents is much longer than the front page of *The Inquirer*? There are easily over a hundred and fifty well-known Hollywoodites and other notables who have adopted children. Here is a list just to name a few past and present adoptive parents: Alexander the Great, Billy Bob Thornton, Charles Bronson, Dan Marino, Ed McMahon, George Burns, Harpo Marx, Julie Andrews, Kirstie Alley, Loni Anderson, Magic Johnson, Nell Carter, Ozzy Osbourne, Paula Poundstone, Rosie O'Donnell, Sandra Bullock, Tom Cruise, and Walt Disney. That is not such a bad crowd. It seems as though most are tough as nails or at least have one hell of a sense of humor.

On the other side, here are some adopted folks: Aristotle, Bo Diddley, Crazy Horse, D.M.C, Edgar Allan Poe, Faith Hill, Gerald Ford, John Lennon, Leo Tolstoy, Moses, Ray Liotta, Steve Jobs, and Tim McGraw. I cannot forget to mention Michael Oher, *The Blind Side* tackle of the Baltimore Ravens. It is amazing what a set of parents can accomplish. What would be our history without foster and adoptive parents?

Today, foster care operates under the regulation of Federal and state governments. Adoption and foster care programs receive government funding since the implementation of the Adoption Assistance and Child Welfare Act of 1980. This act designed to motivate would-be adoptive parents offers stipends even after the adoption of a child. The next year forcible sterilization was finally acknowledged as unconstitutional... just a few years after a U.S. Supreme Court decision called *Smith v. Offer* determined that foster parents were no longer entitled to normal constitutional rights. With licenses and paid by the government, foster parents must meet accountability requirements and must adhere to the standards and regulations set forth by an appropriate governing agency... and this is foster care today. Along with the Adoption and Safe Families Act of 1997, the government and regulating agencies work to ensure the safety and success of every abandoned child designated as "a ward of the state."

Foster Care – Instructional Outline

Part 1: Historical Timeline

- Modern foster care originated in the colonial era (1500-1754) out of a common practice called binding out
- Charles Loring Brace founded The Children's Aid Society in 1853 in New York City
- The Society for the Prevention of Cruelty to Children was founded in 1875 in New York City
- The U.S. federal government began to monitor child advocacy organizations in the late 1800's
- Child labor was still popular in the early 1900's and views on Social Darwinism were on the rise
- The U.S. federal government attempted to regulate child labor in 1924 when Congress passed a constitutional amendment to give government the authority to regulate child labor but failed as it required additional states to ratify the amendment
- Franklin D. Roosevelt signed the Social Security Act of 1935 as part of the New Deal and initiatives like the Aid to Dependent Children were born
- Franklin D. Roosevelt signed the Fair Labor Standards Act which created the first federal limits on child labor
- In the 1940's the government was moving away from institutionalized childcare, the term "Placing Out" was used to refer to early forms of foster care, and a new job position called "Social Worker" was created
- By 1950 more kids were living in foster homes than traditional institutions in America
- By 1960 the number of children in foster care had doubled in just ten years
- By 1970 foster care had become a common responsibility of government
- Stories pertaining to child neglect/abandonment found notoriety in mainstream American in the 1960's, 1970's, and 1980's
- In 1977 a case called Smith v. Offer limited the constitutional rights of foster parents
- In 1980 the Adoptions Assistance and Child Welfare Act of 1980

allowed adoption and foster care to be subsidized
- The Adoption and Safe Families Act of 1997 defined and clarified laws aimed to protect the best interest of the child

Part II: Example of the Lifecycle of a Foster Child

- CPS or DSS are alerted or become aware of a child in distress
- Child and/or family are monitored or child is removed when necessary
- Possible biological adoptive resources are investigated
- If none available, child may be placed into permanent or temporary institution dependent upon the needs of the child
- Foster care placement is determined when a child's need matches an available foster home
- DSS determines a long term plan for the child including the following possibilities:
  Return to biological family
  Adoption by a biological relative
  Adoption through foster care or adoptive services
  Children remaining in foster care are moved to an appropriate resource or adopted
  Children remaining in foster care age out per state requirements and are then no longer "a ward of the state"; additionally older children may elect to leave foster care early

Part III: Goals and Progression of Foster Care

Goal 1 – Return foster child to placement with parent or biological relative
Goal 2/Progression 1 – Find an adoptive placement for the child, first with the current placement/foster placement of the child
Goal 3/Progression 2 – If the current placement is unwilling to adopt, find another adoptive resource other than the current placement
Goal 4/Progression 3 – Long term foster care with current foster placement
Goal 5/Progression 4 – Stable institutionalized care leading to adult care
Goal 6/Final Progression – Successful placement into adult care at age 21
Overall Goal – To return children to biological resources or find other permanency; to advocate in the best interest of the child

Part IV: Types of Government Childcare & Associated Child Category

- Institutions, orphanages, residential group homes: Step 3
- Therapeutic foster homes: Step 2
- Standard foster homes: Step 1
- Return to birth or adoptive family: Step 0
- Independent living for foster children/ Supervised Home Care: Step ½

Part V: Examples of Common Issues Affecting Children in Foster Care

EMOTIONAL
- Reactive Attachment Disorder
- Separation Anxiety Disorder
- Conduct Disorder
- Oppositional Defiant Disorder

PSYCHOLOGICAL
- Attention Deficit Disorder
- Attention Deficit Hyperactivity Disorder
- Obsessive Compulsive Disorder
- Borderline Personality Disorder
- Dissociative Identity Disorder
- Pervasive Developmental Disorders including:
  Asperger's Syndrome
  Autism
  Rett Syndrome
  Childhood Disintegrative Disorder

PHYSICAL
- Blind
- Deaf
- Amputee
- Paraplegic
- Physical Deformity
- Multiple Sclerosis

MEDICALLY FRAGILE
- HIV, A.I.D.S.
- Tuberculosis
- Hepatitis
- Organ Deformity

Part VI: Examples of Foster Care Training, Standard Rules & Regulations

TRAINING
- Application completion and submission
- Signature to relinquish various rights in order to comply with foster care regulations; includes weapon restriction, information privacy authorization
- Complete fingerprint and background check
- Physical exams for all members of the household
- Submission of pet health records including up-to-date shots
- Complete home inspection including fire and safety
- Completion of Adult, Child & Infant CPR certification
- Completion of First Aid certification
- 40 hour training session
- State determined annual continued training hours

STANDARD RULES & REGULATIONS
- No more than the state allowed number of foster children per home
- Male and female foster children must reside in separate bedrooms
- No bunk beds of any kind allowed in foster child rooms
- Smoke detectors must be placed throughout the home including each designated foster bedroom; fire escape routes must be posted in home
- Child health and personal information must be protected; locked storage required in some states
- Cleaners, chemicals, and medicines should be out of the reach of children; locked storage required in some states

Part VII: Glossary of Terms
Adoption and Foster Care Analysis and Reporting System (AFCARS) - a national system that reports statistical data pertaining to foster children

Advocate – a supporter or defender often on another's behalf, someone who argues for a cause

Best Interest of the Child – a statement of rationale to justify a decision pertaining to a child; can be positively or negatively used

Binding Out – the early practice of assigning a child to a trade master

Bonding Study – a study performed by a specialist to examine the emotional bond between members of a family unit

Child Protective Services (CPS) – government agencies that work to identify and rescue children from abusive or dangerous situations

Children's Aid Society – a society that advocates for children, founded by Charles Loring Brace in 1853

Department of Social Services (DSS) – government agencies that provide a wide range of social service programs and financial assistance to vulnerable children and adults within their particular jurisdiction

Developmental Disabilities Administration (DDA) – government agencies that provide service and funding for adult individuals with disabilities

Dual Diagnosis – having two or more separate special needs, for example being born with a heart condition and also being diagnosed with Autism

Eugenics – selective breeding when applied to humans with a goal of improving the species

Foster Care – providing care for a neglected child or children in a substitute home

Indentured Servant – an early American worker bound to contracted labor over a period of time

Independent Living – a living arrangement for older children in foster care, usually set up like half-way houses in area apartments; here teens live independently but monitored

Kinship Care – foster care provided by a biological relative of a child

Level 5 – a term used in special education referring to students who require substantial intervention

Matching – a practice of placing foster children into homes using factors such as culture, religion, and ethnicity

Non-Profit Foster Care Agency – a private company managing and performing the aspects of foster care and/or therapeutic foster care

Performance Based Funding – awarding funds based upon the results of statistics related to some type of defined performance categories

Place Matters – a term used by government and foster agencies referring to an effort to return or place children back into homes associated with their past and/or culture

Placement Coordinator – a person who works for a foster care agency and matches the placements between foster children and foster families

Placing Out – an early 20th century term referring to placing an orphaned child into a home outside of standard institutions such as orphanages

Poor Placement – a term to describe a mismatched family/foster child arrangement

Psychiatrist – a medical doctor who performs medication management and sometimes therapy for individuals and groups

Psychologist – a licensed professional who performs psychological therapy for individuals and groups, also known as a therapist or psychotherapist

Rap Sheet – a slang term used in foster care for the history of a child

Respite Care – using licensed foster care parents that perform babysitting for other licensed foster parents, some only perform the service of respite care

Social Darwinism – a theory that society should make attempts to advance "survival of the fittest." Survival of the fittest is then used to perpetuate the concept that those considered best adapted or already in the upper rungs of society have been elevated through natural conflict and are now in a position to enhance society

Social Worker – a mental health professional trained to assist groups, families, or individuals

Society for the Prevention of Cruelty to Children (SPCC) – organization founded in 1875 to advocate for children

Special Needs – a determined condition or conditions which may require services, for example mental, physical, or medical conditions

Stepping Down – a term used by government and foster agencies referring to a method or effort to move children out of institutions and into foster homes, or moving children from foster homes into birth or adoptive homes

Stipend – monetary compensation for childcare, issued by the state or governing agency

Therapeutic Foster Care – providing care for a foster child with disabilities in a substitute home

Transitioning – moving a child from one placement to another

Survival of the fittest – the struggle for survival or life in reference to natural selection, the life that adapts is able to reproduce and carry on genetic traits

Ward of the State – a term used to identify a child or adult whose guardianship is determined by the court system and is under the care of a government agency

Part VIII: Questions for Thought

What does "birth mom" represent? Why do you think the narrator never mentions "birth mom" by name? Why is Aunt Pat able to use "birth mom's" first name?

The narrator gives the names of three sisters, Jenny, Cindy, and Valerie, but never identifies the name of his brother. What is the significance? What other characters from the book have similarities to Jenny, Cindy, or Valerie? What relationship does each male character experience with his biological brother? Evaluate the relationships between Eloiro and Wallace, Jared and Troy, Miles and Samuel, Matthew and his brother.

What is the significance of Hattie *"catching up with a wry"* sailor? What character does it pertain to and why? What is the literal meaning of this phrase similar to the title of a classic literary work?

What is the significance of the character named Daniel? What does he represent? What does the narrator mean by the following statement? "… for the first time, *I* could see Daniel waving goodbye."

The narrator expressed that fostering children could help him relate to his own immature tendencies. Why did he say this? What underlying reason led the narrator to volunteer as a foster parent?

How did the narrator's story about a neighbor's accusation of sexual deviance factor into the storyline?
What other characters found themselves in similar situations?

The narrator describes three types of transitional methods in foster care: Monthly, weekly, and the ten-minute transition. Which type does each foster child in the story experience?

Does the narrator appear to be confused about welfare and the government's role in foster care? What evidence can you find to support your answer?

What does the book infer about immigrants? Whom does the character Tietha represent? Does the author imply that Tietha will receive something, if so, what? Are other characters in the book similar to Tietha, in what way?

What evidence shows that "those cared for" can become "caretakers"? Which characters transform into caretakers? Which characters will need to be cared for in the future? What is the narrator referring to when he uses the term "caretaker" negatively?

What do the news articles found in Hattie's safety deposit box suggest?

What is the purpose of the wishbone story? What does it symbolize or represent?

The narrator states, "My job was to fill in for the bus driver." What or who does the story about the bus driver parallel? Who do the neighbors in the corresponding story parallel?

What is the significance of the man named Jax who purchases lobsters to trade for crack cocaine? How does he relate to others in the book, who? How do the characters connect through Jax?

What does the character Gail Witherspoon represent?

What does the character Arlene Fitzpatrick represent?

The characters Nevar and Jared each represent a different group of kids in foster care. Which group does each character represent? How does Nevar intellectually compare to Jared? Why is this significant?

What do characters like Harper, Sammie, and Bernard represent? What do characters like Cooter and The Binch represent? Which group would be more likely to advocate for government regulated foster care over privately regulated foster care?

What is the significance of the narrator's experience with a bully? How does it relate to Jared's relationship with his birth mom?
Did you notice anything about the names of the three characters, Wallace, Diynah, and Carlyn? Did you notice anything about the names of the two characters, Eloiro and Nevar? What do the names represent and what does this representation imply?

The narrator states that everyone has a drug. What appears to be the narrator's drug? What is the drug for each main character in the book?

How do Nevar's homeschooled therapy sessions relate to reconnecting with his biological family? What solution does the narrator suggest? Why would the narrator suggest this?

How do families intertwine through the foster care system and in what ways? How many families connect with the narrator through his experience with the foster care system?

How do the underlying themes of fate, coincidence, karma, destiny, and subconscious action fit into the story? What example or examples can you find for each?

After Thought: A Recent Matter Of Coincidence

The day I completed the manuscript for *Hattie's Advocate* I also received several emails referring to my duty as a foster parent and community role model. It is surprising, yet flattering, that someone would refer to me as the latter. My first publication, *Life, Liberty, and the Pursuit of Immaturity* detailed a desire to escape the realities of life including involvement with the foster care system. The new manuscript just compiled, *Hattie's Advocate*, described the harsh reality of the Maryland foster care system. The two stories intentionally differ, like "Jekyll" and "Hyde."

At the same time, friends and family members were emailing me the same message with "You must see this movie" typed in the subject line. They were referring to a movie called *The Blind Side*. It was a Hollywood feel-good production about the success and rise of a foster child turned pro athlete, Michael Oher. Coincidentally, Mr. Oher played for the local NFL football team, the Baltimore Ravens. Baltimore also happened to be the setting of my own tale, which mentioned the Baltimore Ravens at several points.

Mr. Oher's personal story of abandonment and rise to greatness under the guidance and love of a caring family is an American dream come true. I applaud the Tuohy family for taking a chance on a young man, taking a risk, and walking the path of inconvenience in order to help someone less fortunate. In helping others, you ultimately help yourself.

The tale of Mr. Oher and the Tuohy family is a true Cinderella story reflecting our nation's desire to feel good in uncertain times. In reality, the average tale for foster children is far less magical or glamorous. Some neglected children are fortunate to find placement in foster care. Many other children find themselves shipped to group homes or residential treatment facilities for years of their lives. More often, abandoned children like Michael Oher fend for themselves on the streets of our U.S. cities. I imagine that every foster parent watching *The Blind Side* could design a wish list that might compare with the fortunes of Michael Oher and the Tuohy family. A high-end private school, a high-end private tutor, and a high-end private home would be on the top of my own wish list.

In the movie *The Blind Side*, the Tuohy family operated outside of the standard regulations of foster care while caring for a ward of the state. Normal foster homes are subject to guidelines and laws from a society that is overflowing with lawsuits and legal demands. The foster children of the state live under these legal guidelines and the foster care volunteers must abide by them to the letter of the law. *The Blind Side* touched on the legal issues pertaining to foster children but only from the vantage of the NCAA legal counsel. In reality, there are scores of Federal and state legal stipulations put in place to manage the foster care system.

After receiving the emails and watching the trailer on television, I delved into *The Blind Side* a little more. The lead actress of the film was no other than Sandra Bullock. My mother-in-law used to tell me how much Sandra Bullock reminded her of Krista. I felt that it was an odd twist of fate that this particular actress played the wife and mother in this foster child's tale. My mother-in-law must have been in charge of casting because I would have selected Sarah Jessica Parker instead. If the happenings of my slightly less than mundane life ever made it to a Hollywood production, I guess Bullock could play my wife. I would not kick her out of bed for eating crackers.

I put my kids to bed, said goodbye to my wife, and headed out to the local movie theater to see *The Blind Side* for myself. The movie began and my mind went into overdrive. I shook my head in recognition of every trial and tribulation associated with the foster care system. I have been to Baltimore's version of the Memphis' Hurt projects. I have waited in long social service processing lines and dealt with the inadequacies of the state system. I have met with birth moms, heard their stories, and felt their pain. I have fought through adoption complications tied down by system bureaucracy and I have faced individuals with underlying agendas.

I recommend seeing *The Blind Side*, taking in the Hollywood emotions, and doing something about them. There may not be many future NFL players waiting for a good foster family, but there are plenty of "Stinks" waiting for a new home!

Immigrant Manifest Information

Passenger Record

Name Listed at Time of Immigration: Weiss, Elisabeth
Initial Place of U.S. Residence:Cincinnati, Ohio
Date of Arrival:August 31, 1924
Age at Arrival:14 years
Year of Birth:1910
Gender:Female
Marital Status:Single
Ship of Travel:S.S. George Washington
Port of Departure:Bremen, Germany
City of Origination:Munich, Germany

Inspirations

My Real Family –The Inspiration for My Fictional Characters.

Top left: Darrien Hoffman 2001 and 2009;

Left: Darrien and Susanna Hoffman 2004;

Bottom from left: Krista Hoffman, Yelosis Dixon, and Matthew Hoffman 2001;

Bottom right: Yelosis Dixon 2006

Top-from left: Susanna Hoffman and Levi Dixon 2005, Levi Dixon 2007, with Sassi and Sadie; Middle – James Hoffman 2006 and 2008; Bottom-from left to right, bottom to top: Susanna Hoffman, Matthew Hoffman, James Hoffman, Darrien Hoffman, Ashley Hoffman, Krista Hoffman, Levi Dixon, and Yelosis Dixon 2008

More Inspiration

Top left: Robert J. Hoffman; Middle: Hedwig "Hattie" Hoffman; Right: William F. Hoffman.

Middle: Hedwig "Hattie" Hoffman. Bottom–Left: Hattie, Right: Susanna Hoffman (Both at age 5)